ORIENTALIA CHRISTIANA ANALECTA
N. 222

WOMEN'S MONASTERIES IN UKRAINE AND BELORUSSIA TO THE PERIOD OF SUPPRESSIONS

ORIENTALIA CHRISTIANA ANALECTA
222

SOPHIA SENYK

Women's Monasteries in Ukraine and Belorussia to the period of suppressions

PONT. INSTITUTUM STUDIORUM ORIENTALIUM
PIAZZA S. MARIA MAGGIORE, 7
00185 ROMA
1983

ORIENTALIA CHRISTIANA ANALECTA

Edited by

R. TAFT S. J.   T. ŠPIDLÍK S. J.

and

S. SWIERKOSZ S. J.

DE LICENTIA SUPERIORUM

TYPIS PONTIFICIAE UNIVERSITATIS GREGORIANAE — ROMAE

TABLE OF CONTENTS

LIST OF ABBREVIATIONS .... p.   5

INTRODUCTION   7

Chapter
  I. CATALOG OF MONASTERIES   11
Doubtful Monasteries   50

 II. THE FOUNDING OF MONASTERIES   55

      Founders   56
      The Gentry as Founders   58
      Cossack Founders   61
      Brotherhoods as Founders   63
      Hierarchs and the Foundation of Monasteries   63
      Procedure of Foundation   65
      Prerogatives of Founders   68

III. THE ECONOMICS OF MONASTERIES   71

      Belorussia   73
      Halyčyna   86
      Volyn'   88
      Podillja   89
      Kiev   91
      Hetmanate   93
      Slobidščyna   98

 IV. RELATIONS WITH HIERARCHS AND WITH OTHER MONASTERIES 101

      Dependence on Hierarchs 101
      Rules 105
      Visitations 110
      The Holy Synod and Monasteries 112
      Monastery Groupings 114

  V. THE COMMUNITY 123

      Novitiate and Profession 123

Age and Social Background of Nuns .... p. 126
Foreigners in Ruthenian Monasteries   135
Statistics   137
Laywomen in Monasteries   142

VI. INTERNAL ORGANIZATION   147

The Superior   147
Administration of Monasteries   154
Common Life   156

VII. THE LIFE OF THE NUNS   165

Literacy   165
Monastery Churches   169
Prayer   171
Chaplains   176
Occupations of the Nuns   181
Monastery Schools   184
Enclosure   187

VIII. SUPPRESSIONS   195

The Merging of Small Monasteries   195
State Suppressions   196
Suppression in Territories under Russia after the Partitions of Poland ...   200

IX. CONCLUSION   205

APPENDIX

I.   A Summary Table of Monasteries   211
II. Statistics of Individual Monasteries   214
III. Alternate Names for Monasteries   216
IV. List of Terms Defined in Text   218

BIBLIOGRAPHY   219

INDEX   229

LIST OF ABBREVIATIONS

AI	Akty istoričeskie.
Akty JuZR	Akty otnosjaščiesja k istorii južnoj i zapadnoj Rossii.
Akty ZR	Akty otnosjaščiesja k istorii zapadnoj Rossii.
AOSBM	Analecta Ordinis Sancti Basilii Magni.
APF	Archivio di Propaganda Fide.
Arxiv JuZR	Arxiv jugo-zapadnoj Rossii.
AS	Arxeografičeskij sbornik dokumentov, otnosjaščixsja k istorii severo-zapadnoj Rusi.
AV	Akty izdavaemye kommisieju vysočajše učreždennoju dlja razbora drevnix aktov v Vil'ne.
ČN	Čtenija v istoričeskom obščestve Nestora letopisca.
ČOIDR	Čtenija v imperatorskom obščestve istorii i drevnostej rossijskix pri Moskovskom universitete.
EM	Epistolae metropolitarum Kioviensium Catholicorum.
IJuM	Istoriko-juridičeskie materialy.
ISOXE	Istoriko-statističeskoe opisanie Xar'kovskoj eparxii.
LB	Litterae Basilianorum.
LE	Litterae episcoporum historiam Ucrainae illustrantes.
OASS	Opisanie dokumentov i del xranjaščixsja v arxive Svjatejšogo Pravitel'stvu-juščogo Sinoda.
OAZM	Opisanie dokumentov arxiva zapadnorusskix uniatskix mitropolitov.
PSPR	Polnoe sobranie postanovlenij i rasporjaženij po vedomstvu pravoslavnogo ispovedanija rossijskoj imperii.
PSRL	Polnoe sobranie russkix letopisej.
SPR	Synodus provincialis Ruthenorum.
TKDA	Trudy Kievskoj Duxovnoj Akademii.
UA	Ukrajins'kyj arxiv.
VZR	Vestnik jugo-zapadnoj i zapadnoj Rossii, later Vestnik zapadnoj Rossii.

INTRODUCTION

In the field of Ukrainian church history the topic of women's monasteries has been totally ignored in scholarly research and literature. Lists of monasteries have appeared, but there have been no studies of individual monasteries or particular aspects of the life of women's monasteries, much less any general survey.

The present work intends to be such a survey, with some qualifications. The area covered is Ukraine and Belorussia, the territory of the metropolitanate of Kiev, with the addition of certain regions of Ukraine on the Left Bank of the Dnieper river, colonized mainly in the second half of the seventeenth century and never forming part juridically of the Kievan metropolitan province, but sharing its traditions[1]. With regard to the span of time, although the present work covers the entire period from the first founding of monasteries in Kiev in the eleventh century to the large-scale suppressions at the turn of the eighteenth-nineteenth centuries, the two divisions of that period, that of the Kievan state before the Mongolian invasion in the mid-thirteenth century and that subsequent to the invasion, merit different treatment and introduction.

For the first division, there exists the study of pre-Mongolian monasticism in Rus' in E. Golubinskij's *History of the Russian Church*, which includes a critical list of all the monasteries that existed in that period[2]. The use of chronicles as sources permits some additions to that list to be made in this work, and these are noted in the catalog which forms Chapter one. For the rest, precluding possible archaeological finds in the future, it is unlikely that we shall ever know more about

---

[1] Before the creation of the Belgorod eparchy in 1667, and in some cases even after, the settlers in their church matters turned both to Kiev and Moscow (cf. *ISOXE*, 1: 9, for examples). Until the formation of the eparchy of Slobids'ka Ukraine in 1799 the Belgorod eparchy was treated as consisting of two parts—that with a Russian population and that with a Ukrainian one—which were dealt with separately. For an example, cf. *OASS*, 19: 98, where the Holy Synod, asking for statistics from the eparchies, required the Belgorod eparchy to provide them separately for Russian and Ukrainian clergy; the statistics are given on p. 727-730 (Russian) and 731-734 (Ukrainian).

[2] E. GOLUBINSKIJ, *Istorija russkoj cerkvi*; the monasteries are covered in 1, pt. 2 (Moskva, 1904): 512-752.

these monasteries than the few scanty lines the chronicles bestow on them. Everything else is sheer fantasy.

This work, then, will deal primarily with the post-Mongolian period, and, as sources relating to women's monasteries before the late sixteenth century are scarce in the extreme, primarily with the seventeenth and eighteenth centuries.

The chief sources available for this study are the many-volumed collections of documents published in the nineteenth century by archaeographic commissions in various centers of the Russian empire. In all these series one finds abundant materials on monasteries in general and women's monasteries in particular.

The first to be founded was the Archaeographic Commission of St Petersburg, which published the *Akty zapadnoj Rossii* and the *Akty južnoj i zapadnoj Rossii*, devoted to Ukrainian matters, as well as the *Akty istoričeskie* and their *Dopolnenija*. The latter two series, while not particularly concerned with Ukrainian history, nevertheless contain documents pertaining also to some women's monasteries in Ukraine. The Temporary Commission (Vremennaja Kommissija) of Kiev founded nine years later, in 1843, and which stayed in existence eighty years (until 1921), published the *Pamjatniki* and the *Arxiv jugo-zapadnoj Rossii*. Materials for western Belorussia are found in the *Akty* of the Vilna Archaeographic Commission, founded to publish documents from the Vilna Central Archives (though not limited to that), and in the series *Arxeografičeskij sbornik*, also published in Vilna. The collection *Istoriko-juridičeskie materialy* is the most abundant source for the study of eastern Belorussian monasteries. Church matters exclusively appear in the descriptive catalogs of the archives of the Holy Synod, the *Opisanie arxiva Svjatejšogo Sinoda* and the *Polnoe sobranie postanovlenij i rasporjaženij*; both series obviously are an important source on eighteenth century Orthodox monasteries.

Some material on Catholic monasteries is found in the *Opisanie arxiva zapadnorusskix mitropolitov*, which describes the part of the archives of the Catholic Kievan metropolitanate that was preserved in St Petersburg. The Polish collection *Akta grodzkie i ziemskie*, on the other hand, has disappointingly little on our topic.

In addition to these large series of published primary sources, there are also smaller collections, confined generally to a specific topic. Single documents on the history of monasteries are scattered in scholarly publications, alone or as appendices to monographs and articles.

As concerns other works, there have been no studies devoted to women's monasteries in Ukraine and Belorussia outside one, by S. C'orox, on the modern period. However, a wide range of works on the most varied aspects of the history of these lands provides information also on monasteries. These are all the more valuable when the primary sources on which they are based no longer exist or are no longer accessible. Although none suffices in itself to illustrate any one aspect of monastic history, in this totally unexplored field even small contributions may clarify fundamental points.

A word may be said about catalogs of monasteries and similar compilations. The first to appear was the *Hierarchy of the Russian Church* of Ambrose Ornackij (though not entirely his work). Throughout the nineteenth century other catalogs appeared at steady intervals, culminating in those of Zverinskij, the fullest, and of Denisov. In the entries on women's monasteries little advance was made from start to finish in this entire progression; in fact, once an entry appeared it was often copied literally in successive lists. Monasteries of western Ukraine, outside the sphere of the Russian empire, appear in the lists of Kossak, Krypjakevyč, and C'orox, again mostly without any new contributions of the successive compilers.

The aim of this work is to portray the life of women's monasteries as it actually was lived, not as it was perhaps envisioned. Sources of a legislative character, whether civil or ecclesiastic, have consequently been used only in conjunction with examples that illustrate how they were applied.

The present work does not claim to be a history of women's monasteries in Ukraine and Belorussia, even of a limited period. The information possessed is far too sketchy for that. As an example one can look at the monastery of Navahrudek: we know the date and some of the circumstances of its foundation in 1629, there follow two bare mentions of it in 1671 and 1703, and then from the 1750's there are materials on a property dispute in which it was involved. Even a monastery frequently mentioned in sources, such as the Holy Trinity in Vilna, is known mainly from its most external aspects.

An outline of such a history, however, can be presented, shedding more light on some features than on others, according to existing materials. As could be expected, it is the external aspects that emerge most clearly, especially the economic one, for the reason that records of one kind or another are always kept of it. This may, therefore, at times seem to be a dominating aspect; in reconstructing a way of life it is important to remember that written records do not necessarily reflect exactly the relative importance of various sides of that life. Much that was important and that we would like to know was self-evident to contemporaries and not recorded.

A catalog of all women's monasteries that existed in the territories and periods concerned is given in the first chapter, with documentation of essential data. Successive chapters deal first with external and then with internal aspects of monastic life. Two appendices are meant to give a general overview of the monasteries: the first presents the information of the catalog in tabular form for quick reference, while the second collects statistics on the number of nuns in individual monasteries. A third appendix gives divergent names of monasteries as found in sources and literature, and the name under which it appears in this study. Finally, a short list of unfamilar terms is given, with the page numbers on which they are explained.

CHAPTER I

CATALOG OF MONASTERIES

No complete list of women's monasteries in Ukraine and Belorussia has appeared before now, far less a documented one. Yet such a list is essential in providing basic information for a discussion of any other aspect of monastic life.

The present catalog is arranged alphabetically according to locality. If a monastery was referred to by several place names, it is listed under the one most often used in sources, while references from the others are found in Appendix III. Place names are given in their modern official form, but if a name in recent times has been changed to something quite different, the name current in the centuries concerned is used. Brief indications as to geographical position and administrative divisions, both those when the monastery existed and those at present, are given. As concerns the titles of the monasteries, where there is more than one, it generally indicates a number of churches at or a relocation of the monastery.

Neither histories nor even outlines of the histories of individual monasteries are given here. Rather, only essential information on the founding and duration of the monasteries is provided and when a monastery was Orthodox or Catholic. As this chapter is intended to have a reference character, the documentation given here is not repeated if the same facts need to be brought up again in the course of this work.

1. BARKALABAVA, on Dnieper r., 35 km from Mahilev; Mscislav voev.; Mahilev obl., Belorussia.
    Ascension / Birth of St John the Baptist.

Both Denisov[1] and Zverinskij[2] give 1623 as the date of foundation

[1] L.I. DENISOV, *Pravoslavnye monastyri rossijskoj imperii* (Moskva, 1908), p. 386.
[2] V.V. ZVERINSKIJ, *Material dlja istoriko-topografičeskogo issledovanija o pravoslavnyx monastyrjax v rossijskoj imperii* (S.-Peterburg, 1890-1897), 2: 82.

of this monastery, but the deed of Bohdan Stetkevyč of 1641 says definitely that the pious intention of founding a monastery in Barkalabava was not carried out during the lifetime of his wife, Helen Solomerecka, who died in 1633[3]. In fact, the 1641 document speaks of the monastery as still to be built, and nuns to start the foundation as still to be chosen at the monastery in Kutejno, an earlier foundation of the Stetkevyč family. At the end of the document, however, Stetkevyč names the superior of the Barkalabava monastery, Fotynja Kyrkor[4]. As the document published is only a contemporary copy, not the original, it may reproduce both the original deed and a codicil added when the deed was given to the superior of the newly founded monastery, as the wording of the final paragraph suggests. In any case, the date of foundation should be placed between 1633 and 1641. The Barkalabava monastery was large and prosperous in the seventeenth century. Later it began to decline, but continued to exist until the twentieth century.

2.   BATURYN, on Sejm r.; Starodub polk (1648), Nižyn polk (1654); Černihiv obl., Ukraine.
       Exaltation of the Holy Cross / Dormition.

The history of this monastery, although brief, is not easy to unravel. Zverinskij makes two monasteries out of one[5] and is thoroughly confusing: after naming a superior Eugenia in 1674 he goes on to state that the monastery was transferred to Novi Mlyny by hetman Xmel'nyc'kyj, a manifest contradiction. Xmel'nyc'kyj, in fact, issued a universal for the benefit of this monastery, although the universal is known only from references to it in other documents[6]. The date ascribed to Xmel'nyc'kyj's universal is 3 May 1650, so the monastery must have been founded at least some months previously. There is no mention of it, however, in the detailed census and register of Baturyn prepared by Muscovite officials in 1654[7]. In any case, a community of nuns did not

---

[3] "Ješče za žyvota prežrečenye nebožčycy pany malžonky moee majučy s neju spol'nu-ju radu, ...osoblyvo umyslyly jes'mo byly monastyr panenskij černyckij v maetnosty našoj Borkolabovskoj ufundovaty: kotoromu, odnak, pobožnomu umyslu pomĭnenoj malžonky moee smert' prudkaja zaperečyla". *Akty ZR*, 5: 68. For Solomerecka's dates, cf. the genealogical table of the Solomerecki family in Adam BONIECKI, *Poczęt rodów w Wielkiem Księstwie Litewskim w XV i XVI wieku* (Warszawa, 1887), p. 330.

[4] *Akty ZR*, 5: 72. The same deed from another copy is printed in *IJuM*, 14: 504-511, without any mention of Fotynja Kyrkor's name at the end.

[5] Cf. ZVERINSKIJ 2: 194-195, and 3: 84-85.

[6] The references are cited in A. LAZAREVSKIJ, *Opisanie staroj Malorossii* (Kiev, 1888-1892), 2: 295.

[7] *Akty JuZR*, 10: 817.

exist here more than a few decades. In 1657/1658 the superior, Eugenia Xlevyns'ka, received a deed to some property in Novi Mlyny[8]. It seems that some nuns from Baturyn went to Novi Mlyny immediately, but the larger part of the community stayed in Baturyn. Demetrius Tuptalo mentions this community in his diary and reports that on 12 October 1683 the church and the refectory burned down[9]. Perhaps after this disaster the nuns from Baturyn joined their sisters in Novi Mlyny, as after 1683 there are no further references to a women's monastery in Baturyn except in the title of the superior of Novi Mlyny[10].

3. BIAŁA PODLASKA (Bila), 26 km from Lublin; Brest voev.; Lublin voev., Poland.

This monastery is mentioned by C'orox with a reference to the diary of the bishop of Xolm (Chełm) and later of Peremyšl' (Przemysl) Maximilian Ryllo[11].

4. BIBRKA, on Boberka r., 42 km from Lviv; Rus' voev.; Lviv obl., Ukraine.

In 1698 a certain Paul Bodnar bought a book for pious reading for this monastery[12]; a Triod printed in Lviv in 1699 was bought by the superior Evpraksija and a sister Marianna[13]. Beyond this information provided by inscriptions in the books themselves nothing is known of the fate of this monastery. However, since the first book was taken to the St George monastery in Lviv by order of metropolitan Athanasius Šeptyc'kyj (1729-1746), it can be inferred that the monastery was probably closed during his time.

5. BIL'ČE, E of Drohobyč; Rus' voev.; Lviv obl., Ukraine. Birth of Mother of God.

---

[8] The deed is published in A. LAZAREVSKIJ, Akty po istorii monastyrskogo zemlevladenija v Malorossii (1630-1730 gg.), ČN, 5 (1891): 60-61.

[9] Drevnjaja rossijskaja vivliofika, 17 (2nd ed., Moskva, 1791): 17.

[10] As in a universal of Mazepa dated 17 December 1688: "Trofymija Konsevycovna, ihumenija monastyra dĭvyča Baturynskoho Novomlynskoho" (in Lazarevskij, Akty, p. 64); the communities and their properties were combined.

[11] Salomija C'OROX, Pohljad na istoriju ta vyxovnu dijal'nist' monaxyn' vasylijanok (L'viv, 1934), p. 58. Cf. A.S. PETRUŠEVIČ, Xolmskaja eparxija i svjatiteli eja po 1867 god (L'vov, 1867), p. 242.

[12] Ilarion SVJENCICKYJ, Kataloh knyh cerkovno-slovjanskoi pečaty (Žovkva, 1908), p. 10.

[13] Ibid., p. 30.

A women's monastery in this locality near Peremyšl' is mentioned in a legacy of 1608[14].

6.   BILYLIVKA, on Rostavycja and Sytnja r.; Kiev voev.; Žytomyr obl., Ukraine.

Petruševyč, citing metropolitan Leo Kyška, informs us that this monastery was founded by Anna Xodkevyč Korec'ka before 1626[15]. From the metropolitan's diary we learn that it was still in existence around 1710[16].

7.   BOREJKY, between Kričev and Klimavyčy; Mscislav voev.; Mahilev obl., Belorussia.
Dormition.

A deed of the Svadkovski family granting certain lands, dated 15 September 1728, mentions this monastery as already existing[17], but it seems that the foundation occurred only a short time previously. When the heirs of the founders sought to reclaim the property the nuns abandoned the monastery, fleeing from their violence to the Černihiv eparchy, where they settled at a skyt in 1751[18] (see the entry on Sosnycja below).

8.   BRAHIN (Brahyno-Sidlci), on Brahinka r.; Kiev voev.; Homel' obl., Belorussia.
Annunciation.

Prince Adam Korybut Vyšnevec'kyj and his wife Alexandra Xodkevyč founded this monastery on their property circa 1609[19], but for some reason it was soon deserted. In 1632 the founders' daughter

---

[14] In that year a certain Feska of Peremyšl' made a legacy "Monialibus aut vulgo Czernicam cum Priori alias Ihumeno ad Ecclesiam Beatissimae Virginis Mariae rit. gr. in villa Bilcze sitam", *Peremyšljanyn*, 1854, p. 13, 18, as quoted by M. Nykolaev Kossak, Korotkyj pohljad na monastyry i na monašestvo ruske, *Šematyzm provincii Sv. Spasytelja Čyna sv. Vasylija Velykoho v Haliciy* (L'viv, 1867), p. 204.

[15] A.S. Petruševič, *Svodnaja galicko-russkaja letopis' s 1600 po 1700 god (Literaturnyj sbornik izdavaemyj galicko-russkoju Maticeju, 1872 i 1873*; L'vov, 1874), p. 458.

[16] He mentions it in his diary, now in the Österreichische Nationalbibliothek, Codices latini, vol. 3845 (s.n.) Acta Kisciana, vol. VI, fol. 29r.

[17] *IJuM*, 17: 269-273.

[18] Cf. *OASS*, 31: 175-177, 547-548, where this typical example of szlachta lawlessness is presented as a premeditated persecution of "blagočestie".

[19] This is mentioned in a grant made to the monastery by the founders, *VZR*, 2 (1863), October, 4.

Christine Vyšnevec'ka Malyns'ka gave the monastery to nuns who had
come from the Ascension monastery of Kiev[20]. The Orthodox complained
in 1754 that in 1752 the monastery had been forcibly taken by the
Uniates[21]. It was closed along with other Uniate monasteries by the Russian authorities in 1844.

9.   BRASLAV, Vilna voev.; Vicebsk obl., Belorussia.

Zverinskij lists this monastery as existing in the fifteenth century[22].
Perhaps it is the same one for which Vasilissa Sapieha, superior of the
Holy Trinity monastery in Vilna, received a charter in 1609. In
Sapiehowie it is called a women's monastery[23], whereas the charter as
printed has no reference either to monks or to nuns, but names only an
ihumen, which does not necessarily contradict the statement of
Sapiehowie[24]. In studying the contents and wording of the document at-
tentively, however, one is drawn to the conclusion that there was no
monastic community at all here, the monastery lands having been ag-
gregated to those of other monasteries.

10.   BUČYNA, 13 km S of Brody; Volyn' voev.; Lviv obl., Ukraine.

This appears on several lists of women's monasteries, each of
which simply repeats the notice of its predecessors, without providing
sources or further information[25].

11.   BUS'K, 9 km NE of Lviv on Buh r.; Belz voev.; Lviv obl.,
     Ukraine.

This monastery is called newly founded in a grant of land dated 25
August 1602[26]. C'orox says it was closed in 1784, but according to
Petruševyč it had died out by 1776, and in 1780 the badly dilapidated
church was also taken apart[27].

---

[20] *Ibid.*, September, p. 55-57. This monastery and another neighboring one are called
in this deed of 1632 "na tot čas spustošalye".

[21] *Arxiv JuZR*, pt. I, 4: 512.

[22] *Zverinskij*, 3: 34.

[23] *Sapiehowie*, 1 (Petersburg, 1890): 246.

[24] *Akty JuZR*, vol. 2, no. 33; *VZR*, 5 (1867), no. 9, 83-85. An example of the
hieromonk charged with providing religious services for a women's monastery being called
ihumen of that monastery is given in footnote 14 above.

[25] Thus C'orox, p. 58, repeats Kossak, p. 204, who repeats *L'vovjanyn*, 1862, p. 90.

[26] Petruševič, *Svodnaja letopis' 1600-1700*, under 1601, p. 11.

[27] C'orox, p. 58. Petruševič, *Svodnaja letopis' 1600-1700*, p. 12.

12.   BYCEN' (Byten'), on Ščara r.; Navahrudek voev.; Brest obl.,
      Belorussia.

Well known as a men's monastery, it was originally founded in the
first decade of the seventeenth century by Gregory Tryzna and his wife
Regina Sapieha for their daughter Euphrosine[28]. After a few years,
however, Euphrosine and her companions transferred to the Pinsk
monastery, and in 1616 their place was taken by Basilian monks who
established their novitiate there[29].

13.   BYSTRYCJA (Vepryk), on Vepryk r., 13 km E of Hadjač; Hadjač
      polk; Poltava obl., Ukraine.
      Dormition / Ascension.

This was not a monastery of the traditional pattern, but a community of common life without profession (postryženie) founded in 1709
by Anna Borzanovs'ka, widow of a protopop of Hadjač. This
monastery survived until the period of suppressions at the end of the
einghteenth century[30].

14.   ČERČYCI, 1/2 km from Luc'k, on Styr r.; Volyn' voev.; Volyn'
      obl., Ukraine.

---

[28] Brief accounts of the foundation may be found in Ignacy Stebelski, *Dwa wielkie
światła na horyzoncie połockim*, 2 (2nd ed., Lwów, 1867): 154, and in Alphonse Guépin,
Un Apôtre de l'union des Églises au XVIIᵉ siècle, 1 (Paris, 1897); 138-140. The former has
Euphrosine entering after 1620; the latter has the monks replacing the nuns already in
1613, and the nuns going to Vilna. C'orox, p. 57-58, has the foundation occurring before
1607. It can also be added that Nikolaj [Truskovskij], *Istoriko-statističeskoe opisanie
Minskoj eparxii* (Sanktpeterburg, 1864), p. 143, has Euphrosine already superior in Pinsk
in 1595. This last notice can easily be discounted, as incompatible with the fact that she
died in about 1664 at (slightly) over eighty years of age as superior in Pinsk, cf. *LE*, 2:
324. The Basilian "Obiasnenie praw y konstytuciow zakonnych", printed in *AS*, 12, on p.
19 speaks briefly of the two foundations, of nuns and of monks, in Bycen' without providing dates, but reporting that the nuns moved to Pinsk. Myxajlo M. Vavryk, *Narys roz-
vytku i stanu Vasylijans'koho Čyna XVII-XX st.* (Rym, 1979), in his table on p. 191
merely gives the period 1607-1613 as the date for the foundation of the monks in Bycen'.
Though no foundation documents have been discovered, one date is certain. In 1610 there
were eleven nuns in the Bycen' monastery; their names were inscribed that year in the
pomjanyk (list of departed hierarchs, members, and benefactors, for whom special prayers
are offered) of the Suprasl' monastery, cf. *AS*, 9: 459. The first name is that of Helen
Boktevna, followed by Euphrosine Tryzna; very likely Helen was the superior.
[29] In a letter of 28 September 1617 to cardinal Scipio Cafferelli Borghese metropolitan
Rutskyj says that already the second group of monks is undergoing its one-year training
there, *EM*, 1: 31-32. On the nuns going to Pinsk, see Jacobus Susza, *Cursus vitae et certamen martyrii B. Josaphat Kuncevicii*, ed. Joannes Martinov (Parisiis, 1865), p. 25.
[30] Zverinskij, 2: 386.

Transfiguration / Birth of the Mother of God.

Because the Čerčyci monastery is often referred to as the Luc'k monastery and because it is titled after one or the other of its churches, it is not surprising that Čerčyci and Luc'k are sometimes taken for two distinct monasteries. The first mention of it is found in 1597, but it seems to have been well established by then[31]. This is borne out by the provisions of the last will and testament drawn up in April 1607 by the bishop of Luc'k Cyril Terlec'kyj for the construction of the monastery church, the timber for which, he says, has already been prepared[32]. This is to be understood not that the monastery had no church as yet, but that its existing wooden church needed to be replaced. According to the testimony of the Catholic metropolitan Felician Volodkovyč from 1774 the monastery, after being destroyed by (Tatar) incursions, was renovated by the Orthodox bishop of Luc'k Athanasius Puzyna in 1640 and was still flourishing in his, Volodkovyč's, times[33]. The monastery seemingly was closed about 1795, when Luc'k passed to Russia at the third partition of Poland.

15. CERKOVIŠČY (Carkavišča), 5 km from Klimavyčy; Mahilev obl., Belorussia.

A bare mention of this monastery is made in 1748[34]. Bantyš-Kamenskij has a notice that it became Uniate in 1730, but nothing else[35]:

---

[31] In *Pamjatniki*, 1 (2nd ed., Kiev, 1848): 21, note 1, it is stated that this monastery was originally inhabited by monks and that only in 1625 did it pass over to nuns. From documents published in another series of the Vremennaja Komissija, *Arxiv JuZR*, pt. I, 6: 200-201, 555-556, it is evident that either the monks were at a different monastery or that they left Čerčyci much earlier.

[32] *AS*, 1: 231.

[33] Cf. *EM*, 6: 420.

[34] All our knowledge about this monastery is based on one phrase in one solitary document, published twice, from two different copies. This already provided several variants, and authors commenting on it added others of their own. The Vremennaja Kommisija, from an original in its possession, published in *Arxiv JuZR*, pt. I, vol. 4, a list of churches and monasteries taken from the Orthodox by Uniates, in which, on p. 448, we have the following: "1734. Monaster panienski w Czerkowiszczach zaiechał na unią p. Iwanowski y zakonnice powypędzał". The Vilna Archeographical Commission printed later in vol. 27 of its *Akty* a copy of the same document from the registers of the Xolm tribunal. We read there on p. 344: "Roku tysiąc siedmsetnego trzydziestego czwartego monaster panienski w Czerwowiszczach zaiechał na unię p. Janowski". The place name should definitely be Czerkowiszcze; a Czerwowiszcze did not exist. In Zverinskij, 3: 209, this appears as a men's monastery, with a reference to *Arxiv JuZR* alone.

[35] Nikolaj Bantyš-Kamenskij, *Istoričeskoe izvestie o vozniksej v Pol'še Unii* (Vil'na, 1866), p. 374.

16.   ČERNIHIV, Černihiv obl., Ukraine.
      St Paraskeva.

Supposedly there is a mention of this monastery in the fifteenth century[36]. Efforts in mid-eighteenth century to determine its origins uncovered only that it was built after 1600[37]. That could mean either a totally new construction or new buildings in place of old, but the former seems to be understood. Reliable information about it begins only with 1659, in which year hetman George Xmel'nyc'kyj issued to the monastery a universal (a political or administrative decree of hetmans or occasionally of other officials) confirming some properties[38]. A little later the sister of bishop Lazar Baranovyč Martha was superior here[39]. The monastery was suppressed in 1786.

17.   ČETVERTNJA, on Styr r., 45 km N of Luc'k; Volyn' voev.;
      Volyn' obl., Ukraine.

Although it is generally stated that the monastery here was founded by Maria Hulevyč Balaban, the aunt of prince Gregory Četvertyns'kyj, in 1618, and in fact the deed of the prince, dated 30 September 1618, also speaks of a new foundation[40], there is evidence that a women's monastery existed here much earlier[41]. Apparently it did not survive to the seventeenth century. The monastery became Catholic when the village passed from the Orthodox Četvertyns'kyj to the Catholic Horain family[42]. It was suppressed after 1793[43].

18.   ČYHYRYN, on Tjas'myn r.; Čerkasy obl., Ukraine.
      Holy Trinity.

Ivan Vyhovs'kyj founded the Holy Trinity monastery outside Čyhyryn in the 1650's for monks[44]. It became a women's monastery at

---

[36] ZVERINSKIJ, 2:288.

[37] *OASS*, 19: 507-508.

[38] Mentioned in the universal of hetman Apostol, in N.P. VASILENKO, ed. *Materialy dlja istorii ekonomičeskogo, juridičeskogo i obščestvennogo byta staroj Malorossii* (Černigov, 1901-1909), 3: 465.

[39] Cf. Vitalij ĖJNGORN, O snošenijax malorossijskogo duxovenstva s moskovskim pravitel'stvom v carštvovanie Alekseja Mixajloviča, *ČOIDR*, 1899, 1: 897-898.

[40] *Arxiv JuZR*, pt. I, 6: 471-473.

[41] There is a mention of a women's monastery in Četvertnja in the fifteenth century, see *AV*, 13: 87.

[42] The transition was marked by violence from both sides, see *Arxiv JuZR*, pt. I, 6 197-199, 221-222.

[43] C'OROX, p. 67-68.

[44] Cf. the mention of his request for books, vessels and vestments for its church and

some point between 1708 and 1735. The monastery was always Orthodox and continued to exist until the twentieth century[45].

19. DOBROTVIR (now Staryj Dobrotvir), on Buh r., 17 km N of Kaminka Buz'ka; Belz voev.; Lviv obl., Ukraine.

Kossak reports this monastery, also called Jazvyn from the section of Dobrotvir where it stood[46]. It is supposed to have become Catholic in 1682[47]. The monastery was in existence at least until 1759, when some of its nuns went to Slovita[48].

20. DROHYČYN (Drahičyn), on Buh r.; Brest voev.; Brest obl., Belorussia.
Holy Trinity.

Metropolitan Dionisius Balaban authorized the foundation of this Orthodox monastery, and king John Casimir confirmed it with a charter dated 9 June 1659[49]. Of its fortunes nothing is known, but the monastery was still in existence in 1780[50].

21. DUBNO, on Ikva r.; Volyn' voev.; Rovno obl., Ukraine.
Holy Trinity / Ascension.

This monastery, situated outside the town of Dubno on an island near the village of Pidbirče, is referred to sometimes under the one and sometimes under the other name. It was founded by prince Constantine Ostroz'kyj in 1592[51]. Zverinskij has it as Catholic only from about 1719[52], but actually it accepted the Union about a century earlier, at the same time as the other two monasteries of Dubno, Transfiguration and Holy Cross, since it was associated with them[53]. In 1804 it was recom-

---

patriarch Nikon's reply in documents relating to the embassy of Burlij and Mužylovs'kyj from hetman Xmel'nyc'kyj to Moscow in 1653, *Akty JuZR*, 8: 368, 369.

[45] AMVROSIJ [ORNACKIJ], *Istorija rossijskoj ierarxii*, 6 (Moskva, 1815): 707-709; ZVERINSKIJ, 2: 378-379.

[46] KOSSAK, p. 210.

[47] Cf. *AV*, vol. 23, Introduction, p. lxvii.

[48] Cf. C'OROX, p. 233, 234 (a list of nuns in Slovita reports those that had come from Jazvyn).

[49] *AV*, 33: 399-400.

[50] Cf. *Materialy dlja statistiki rossijskoj imperii* (S.-Peterburg, 1841), p. 202.

[51] His act of foundation is printed in *Arxiv JuZR*, pt. I, 6: 90.

[52] ZVERINSKIJ, 3: 45.

[53] For the Dubno monasteries, cf. VAVRYK, p. 5, 192. Cassian Sakovyč mentions explicitly the women's monastery in 1639, referring to his office as archimandrite of the

mended that the monastery be closed[54], but there is still mention of it in 1833[55].

22. FOROŠČA, by village Luka between Dniester and Bystrycja r.; Rus' voev.; Lviv obl., Ukraine.

Kossak alone reports the existence, and only that, of this monastery[56].

23. FYRLIJIV (now Lypivka), on Hnyla Lypa r., 15 km N of Rohatyn; Rus' voev.; Ivano-Frankivs'k obl., Ukraine.

The Krexiv pomjanyk is the only authority for the existence of this monastery[57].

24. HAMALIJIVKA, 32 km from Hluxiv; Nižyn polk; Černihiv obl., Ukraine.
St Charlampius.

The monastery had its origins as a skyt that arose near the church of St Charlampius, which had been founded by Anton Hamalija, a Cossack officer. After 1709 the skyt was endowed with lands by Nastasja Markovna, the wife of hetman Ivan Skoropads'kyj, and transformed into a regular monastery of common life. Other endowments followed, and the monastery acquired great wealth[58]. In 1729 Markovna decided to have monks there instead and made out a will to that effect. As a consequence, after her death an exchange of monasteries took place in 1733 between the nuns of Hamalijivka and the monks of Mutyno[59].

25. HLUXIV, on Esman' r.; Nižyn polk; Sumy obl., Ukraine.
Transfiguration / Assumption.

Not many years after its foundation in 1670 by Agatha Kymbar,

---

Transfiguration monastery: "Maiąc wzgląd na podeszłe lata moie y oslabienie zdrowia mego, które nadwątlałe iest pracami koło iedności swiętey y reformaciey monasterow Dubienskich, to iest S-go Spasa y Czesnego Kresta y monastyra panienskiego...", S.T. GOLUBEV, Materialy dlja istorii zapadno-russkoj cerkvi, ČN, 5 (1891): 225.

[54] Cf. AV, 16: 74.
[55] In a report to metropolitan Bulhak described in OAZM, 2: 951.
[56] KOSSAK, p. 210.
[57] Ibid.
[58] Cf. LAZAREVSKIJ, Opisanie, 2: 351-354.
[59] Cf. OASS, 10: 140-141.
[60] Cf. VASILENKO, 1: 360-361.

widow of a Cossack official[60], this monastery was affiliated with the Ascension monastery in Kiev. When hetman Mazepa's mother, Maria Magdalene, was superior of the two monasteries, she transferred the one in Hluxiv from its original location by the marketplace to a quieter spot by the church of the Assumption built by the hetman[61]. A fire in 1784 put an end to the monastery[62].

26. HOLOSKIV, 30 km from Kolomyja; Ivano-Frankivs'k obl., Ukraine.

The only record of this monastery dates from 1774, when it had three nuns[63].

27. HORODYŠČE, near Buh r.; Belz voev.; Lviv obl., Ukraine.

This is one of the monasteries mentioned in the Krexiv pomjanyk[64]. In addition, there is an early mention of it on the occasion of metropolitan Rutskyj's visit in the Xolm-Belz eparchy in 1628[65], and a later one in the first decades of the eighteenth century[66].

28. HRODNA, on Nemen r.; Troki voev.; Hrodna obl., Belorussia. Birth of the Mother of God.

In 1635 metropolitan Rutskyj is supposed to have called nuns from the Holy Trinity monastery in Vilna to start this foundation[67]. They were certainly well established there by 1650. The monastery remained Catholic until 1843, when it was taken over by Russian authorities who sent there a group of Orthodox nuns. It then continued to the twentieth century[68].

---

[61] Cf. *Arxiv JuZR*, pt. I, 5: 347-348, where in a letter to her patriarch Adrian of Moscow repeats a report that the monastery stood "na meste mjatežnom, sredi toržišča, i dvorami obselen korčemnymi".

[62] LAZAREVSKIJ, *Opisanie*, 2: 437.

[63] Władysław CHOTKOWSKI, *Historya polityczna dawnych klasztorów panieńskich w Galicyi* (Kraków, 1905), p. 136.

[64] KOSSAK, p. 205. C'OROX, p. 60, has the wrong district: materials on that Horodyšče in the Peremyšl' eparchy do not indicate any monastery there.

[65] *AV*, 23: 62.

[66] It is reported in 1763 that a nun of the Slovita monastery, Pamfilija, received profession in Horodyšče "lat temu więcey, jak 50" (C'OROX, p. 234).

[67] WOŁYNIAK [Jan Marek GOZDAWA GIŻYCKI], Z przeszłości Zakonu Bazyliańskiego na Litwie i Rusi, *Przewodnik naukowy i literacki*, 32: (1904), 67. DENISOV, p. 212, puts the foundation at around 1633. A document regarding them is described in *OAZM*, 1: 291-293.

[68] DENISOV, p. 212.

29. JASENIV (Jaseniv-Pil'nyj), near Horodenky; Ivano-Frankivs'k obl., Ukraine.

A monastery in Jaseniv existed at least in the first half of the eighteenth century[69].

30. JASNOHOROD, 53 km W of Žytomyr on Synjavka r.; Žytomyr obl., Ukraine.
Holy Trinity.

The monastery was founded in the sixteenth century about 2 km from Jasnohorod, at a spot later called on that account Monastyrok, but we have no particulars about it until the eighteenth. At that time it was Catholic. After the third partition of Poland the Russian authorities turned it into an Orthodox monastery, but already in 1796 most nuns were transferred elsewhere[70]. Nevertheless, the monastery was still struggling on in 1804[71].

31. JAVORIV, 48 km NW of Lviv on Šklo r.; Rus' voev.; Lviv obl., Ukraine.
Pokrov / Dormition.

In 1621 some nuns came and settled near a church in Javoriv. Fifteen years later, in 1636, a local woman, Margaret Dyškevyč, gave the nuns a grant of land. Soon afterwards she joined them and left all her possessions to the monastery. After 1680 the monastery began to decline; in the period of suppressions it barely escaped being closed. In the nineteenth century it revived and continued to flourish until the 1940's[72].

32. KAMENS'KYJ XUTOR (present name unknown), on Snov r.; Brjansk obl., Russia.
Dormition.

This monastery, originally for monks, was begun under hetman Samojlovyč, but owed its development and prosperity to Mazepa. Only

---

[69] A visitation of the Mykulynci monastery in 1773 notes that one of its nuns had spent some years in the Jaseniv monastery, E. SECINSKIJ, Materialy dlja istorii pravoslavnyx monastyrej Podol'skoj eparxii, *Trudy Podol'skogo eparxial'nogo istoriko-statističeskogo komiteta*, 5 (1890-1891): 346.
[70] ZVERINSKIJ, 2: 30.
[71] *AV*, 16: 74.
[72] C'OROX, p. 73-75. Margaret Dyškevyč's grants are printed on p. 241-246.

in 1786 did it become a women's monastery, when the nuns from Pečenyky were moved there[73].

33. KAMINKA STRUMYLOVA (Kamjanka Buz'ka), 40 km NE of Lviv; Rus' voev.; Lviv obl., Ukraine.
Annunciation.

In a land grant of 24 July 1669 this monastery is referred to as of old standing[74], but the earliest notice about it dates from 1666[75]. It is mentioned in 1782, but it did not survive much longer[76].

34. KASCJUKOVIČY, Mscislav voev.; Mahilev obl., Belorussia.

This monastery is named only in official lists; of its internal life nothing is known. According to Petruševyč it was founded in 1665[77]. In 1720 a charter issued by king Augustus II which confirmed the rights of Orthodox monasteries, among which Kascjukoviču is listed, attests to its existence[78].

35. KIEV, capital of Ukrainian SSR.
St Irene.

Jaroslav the Wise founded this monastery and named it after the patron saint of his wife Ingegard-Irene[79].

36. KIEV.
St Nicholas.

The Patericon of the Monastery of the Caves relates that the mother of St Theodosius made her monastic profession here—the only mention of this monastery in the sources[80].

---

[73] LAZAREVSKIJ, *Opisanie*, 1: 430-432.

[74] "Zdawna zfundowanych", as quoted by PETRUŠEVIČ, *Svodnaja letopis' 1600-1700*, p. 161.

[75] A. PETRUŠEVIČ, *Dopolnenija ko Svodnoj galicko-russkoj letopisi s 1600 po 1700 god (Literaturnyj sbornik izdavaemyj Galicko-russkoju Maticeju, 1889-1890*; L'vov, 1891), p. 446.

[76] CHOTKOWSKI, p. 136

[77] *Ibid.*, p. 879.

[78] It has been printed several times, with variant readings: *Arxiv JuZR*, pt. I, 4: 403-405; *IJuM*, 12: 362-365; 29: 30-34; *AS*, 4: 199-201.

[79] The chronicle notice appears under 6645 (1037), cf. D.S. LIXAČEV, ed., *Povest' vremennyx let* (Moskva, 1950), 1: 102.

[80] Cf. D. ABRAMOVYČ, ed., *Kyjevo-pečers'kyj pateryk* (Kyjiv, 1930), p. 31. ZVERIN-

37. KIEV.
St Andrew.

Great prince Vsevolod founded this monastery in 1086 for his daughter Janka[81], and it is often called Jančyn. While it is mentioned a numer of times in the chronicle—its church served as a burial place for many members of Vsevolod's family—, nothing is known about the monastery itself.

38. KIEV.
St Lazarus.

The Hypatian chronicle notes the death of an ihumenja of this monastery under the year 6621 (1113)[82]—the only reference to its existence in the sources.

39. KIEV.
Sts Florus and Laurus / Ascension.

The church and monastery were founded in 1566 by the Hul'kevyč family, which retained possession of it to 1632, when Ivan Bohuš Hul'kevyč, a monk at Sluck, ceded it to the ihumenja of the monastery[83]. From that time it has always been one of the largest and most important monasteries of Kiev. When early in the eighteenth century the nuns from the demolished Ascension monastery were also sent here, the Florovs'kyj monastery acquired the additional title of "Ascension monastery". It was still open as late as 1979[84].

40. KIEV.
Ascension.

This monastery stood opposite one of the entrances to the Kiev Lavra and is itself often called "Pečers'kyj monastyr" in the sources. Nothing is known of its origins. The first mention of it comes from 1586: monks of the Lavra who had been to Moscow received alms also for this women's monastery[85]. Evidently in the first quarter of the seven-

skij, 3: 141, connects this monastery with a much later one of St. Nicholas, but there was no continuity between them and no tie other than the same name.

[81] Hypatian chronicle, *PSRL*, 2, 3rd ed., 194-195.

[82] *Ibid.*, p. 273.

[83] *Akty JuZR*, vol. 2: no. 52, the legal document of 1632, relates also the founding of the monastery.

[84] Cf. *Pravoslavnyj visnyk*, 1979, no. 2, 14.

[85] K.V. Xarlampovič, *Malorossijskoe vlijanie na velikorusskuju cerkovnuju žizn'* (Kazan', 1914), p. 13.

teenth century the monastery was renovated both in its physical aspects and in the monastic life proper with some kind of assistance from the archimandrite of the Kiev Lavra Jelysej Pletenec'kyj (1599-1624), as a panegyric written after his death testifies[86]. In the late seventeenth century hetman Mazepa's mother, Maria Magdalene, was superior here[87]. About 1707 the nuns were transferred to the monastery of Sts Florus and Laurus in Kiev, and this monastery was razed to make room for a fortress[88].

41. KIEV.
Jordan / St Nicholas.

A church of St Nicholas, called also Jordans'ka, near the monastery of St Cyril in the Podil section of Kiev is mentioned already early in the seventeenth century. Accordingly, some authors date the founding of this monastery soon after 1600[89]. However, there is no mention of a monastery in the sources of this period. Another account has it that it was founded by three sisters of Demetrius Tuptalo, which could have occurred towards the middle of the seventeenth century[90]. The first documentary evidence of its existence comes from 1653, when it is mentioned as a beneficiary in a will[91]. The monastery was closed in 1808[92].

42. KIEV.
St Michael / St John the Evangelist.

---

[86] The panegyric "Vizerunok cnot" by Alexander MYTURA has been printed many times. One of the most recent editions is *Ukrajins'ka poezija. Kinec' XVI-počatok XVII st.* Ed. V.P. KOLOSOVA, V.I. KREKOTEN' (Kyjiv, 1978), p 223-227. The section on "The Founding of Monasteries and Churches" says: "Svidčyt' Panjan monastyr, prez tebe zrjaženyj, / v monastyru Pečarskom; pienkne sporjaženyj".

[87] On Maria Magdalene Mazepa, see S. SENYK, Two Maria Magdalenes, *Mitteilungen*, 18 (1981): 146-154.

[88] According to the chronicler (*Sbornik letopisej, otnosjaščixsja k istorii južnoj i zapadnoj Rusi* [Kiev, 1888], p. 45-46), although other authors give other dates, between 1707 and 1712. Its location with respect to the Kiev Lavra may be seen on the plan of 1745, between p. 24-25 in Ivan FUNDUKLEJ, *Obozrenie Kieva v otnošenii k drevnostjam* (Kiev, 1847).

[89] As ZVERINSKIJ, 2: 226-227.

[90] Cf. K portretu Savvy Grigorieviča Tuptalo, *KS*, 3 (1882, 3): 196; also A. LAZAREVSKIJ, Dokumental'nyja svedenija o Savve Tuptale i ego rode, *ibid.*, p. 383-384, where the will of the youngest of the three sisters, Paraskeva, is printed. The will is dated 1710, and in it Paraskeva calls herself ihumenja.

[91] In the will of Adam Markevyč dated 16 January 1653, among other Kievan monasteries there is an entry "na monastyr czernicki Lordonski złotych piędziesiąt" (*AV*, 12: 560). The "Lordonski" is obviously a misreading of "Iordanski".

[92] P. L-V, Istoričeskie zametki o Kieve, *KS*, 12 (1884, 4): 243.

Metropolitan Job Borec'kyj is reported to have founded this women's monastery next to St Michael's Goldendomed (where he resided) in 1621[93]. Peter I, on a visit to Kiev, ordered the nuns to be relocated. At first they dispersed among other monasteries in Kiev, but around 1710 they refounded their monastery in a different section of Kiev, with a church of St John[94]. Due to the run-down condition of the monastery in 1780 its nuns were ordered transferred to the suppressed monastery of Krasnohora near Zolotonoša, which transfer was carried out about ten years later[95].

43. KLYNEC', 10 km from Ovruč; Kiev voev.; Žytomyr obl., Ukraine.
Exaltation of the Holy Cross.

Serafyma Jarmolyns'ka is named superior of Korec' and Klynec' in 1664[96]. According to one work, the monastery is still mentioned in 1740[97].

44. KNJAŽE, 9 km NW of Zoločiv; Lviv obl., Ukraine.
St Paraskeva.

The only sure fact about this monastery is that it was suppressed in 1781[98].

45. KOREC', Volyn' voev.; Rovno obl., Ukraine.
Resurrection.

Prince Bohuš Korec'kyj founded this monastery around 1571. His great-granddaughter Serafyna Korec'ka was its superior in the 1620's and 1630's[99]. After a short period as Catholic in the second half of the eighteenth century, in 1794-1795 it reverted to the Orthodox[100] and sur-

---

[93] This common assertion is questioned, with reasons given, in *Kievo-Zlatoverxo-Mixajlovskij monastyr'* (Kiev, 1889), p. 49-50.

[94] P. L-V, Istoričeskie zametki o Kieve, *KS*, 12 (1884, 4): 238-243.

[95] Cf. *PSPR*, Catherine II, 3: 289-291: Nikolaj DUMITRAŠKO, *Istoriko-statističeskij očerk Zolotonošskogo Krasnogorskogo Bogoslovskogo vtoroklassnogo ženskogo monastyrja* (Poltava, 1859), p. 21-22.

[96] PETRUŠEVIČ, *Svodnaja letopis' 1600-1700*, p. 140.

[97] *Słownik geograficzny Królestwa Polskiego i innych krajów słowiańskich*, 15, pt. 2 (Warszawa, 1902): 85.

[98] Cf. the short notice by Myron POTOPNYK, Neisnujuči žinoči manastyri ČSVV na halyc'kyx zemljax, *Svitlo*, 37 (1974), November, 389.

[99] DENISOV, p. 170.

[100] Cf. N. PETROV, Kratkija izvestija o položenii bazilianskogo ordena i raznyx

vived as a state-supported monastery of the second class. Monastic life was still lived there as late as 1975[101].

46. KOROBIVKA, 10 km SW from Zolotonoša on the left bank of the Dnieper r.; Perejaslav polk; Čerkasy obl., Ukraine.
Annunciation.

Joasaf Rakovyč, superior of the monastery in Mošnohory in the Right Bank, moved his monks here in 1719 in consequence of disputes with Uniates. Soon after, however, the monks returned to their original home, but Joasaf left his three sisters-nuns to live at Korobivka. A community grew up around this nucleus. In 1760, when the monastery burned down, a certain Theodore Kapolje of Pryluky bought land and built a new one not far distant, on the outskirts of Zolotonoša, and Jakiv Ščerbyna, a Zaporozhian Cossack, had the church built for it. The monastery was suppressed in 1817. In the 1830's through the efforts of one of its nuns there was a short-lived attempt to resurrect monastic life here[102].

47. KOROP, Nižyn polk; Černihiv obl., Ukraine.

The only source for the existence of this monastery is a universal of hetman Ivan Mazepa dated 18 August 1693 which approves the foundation in Pečenyky (here called Pečenihy). In the universal the hetman refers to the request of the nuns of Korop to be allowed to move to the property in Pečenyky which was being offered them by the widow Semenova (Samojlovyč), as their location in Korop was too confined, and they had no lands from which to support themselves[103].

48. KOZELEC', on Oster r.; 64 km from Kiev; Kiev polk; Černihiv obl., Ukraine.
St John the Evangelist / Epiphany.

The first references to this monastery date from the early eigh-

---

peremenax v ego upravlenii, ot 1772 g. do 1811 g., *TKDA*, 9 (1868), no. 3: 165-166.

[101] Cf. *Pravoslavnyj visnyk*, 1975, no. 6, p. 6.

[102] M.A. MAKSIMOVIČ, Vospominanija o Zolotonoše, *Žurnal ministerstva vnutrennyx del*, 23 (1848): 419-421. Maksymovyč speaks from personal knowledge of the monastery. Amvrosij was rather confused about this monastery; in his *Istorija*, vol. 4, published in 1812, he says it was already suppressed, but unwittingly has three separate entries for this one monastery (one as Zazulivka, p. 133, one as Zolotonoša, p. 211-212, and one as Korobivka, p. 774), all of which give the same information.

[103] The universal is printed in *UA*, 1: 295-296.

teenth century[104]. In 1786 it was placed on official lists as a third class monastery; twenty years later it was closed[105]. Amvrosij, whom later compilers follow, lists two monasteries here—St John and Epiphany separately, but his notice is almost the same for both[106]. Documents of 1723 and 1757[107] name only one monastery in Kozelec'. The monastery most probably had two churches, or a church with a chapel (*prydil*), which gave it two names.

49.   KRASNOHORA, by Zolotonoša; Čerkasy obl., Ukraine.
St John the Evangelist.

Monks lived in this monastery from 1687 to 1789. In 1789, on the initiative of the metropolitan of Kiev Samuel Myslavs'kyj the nuns of the St John monastery of Kiev were transferred here[108]. There were still nuns here in 1979[109].

50.   KRYLOS, near Halyč; Ivano-Frankivs'k obl., Ukraine.
St Elias.

Kossak cites a notation referring to a women's monastery here, but fails to give the source[110]. In 1763 it was reported of one nun of the Slovita monastery that she was just then under obedience in Krylos[111], which implies that the monastery still existed then.

51.   KULYKIV, 16 km N of Lviv; Lviv voev.; Lviv obl., Ukraine.
St Demetrius.

Again, we have no information regarding the monastery's origins. In 1680 a priest of Vinnycja bought a plaščanycja for the monastery church[112]. In 1743, during a reorganization of monasteries, the nuns of Kulykiv were permitted to go to any of their choice, and the monastery was closed[113].

---

[104] Cf. *Istoriko-statističeskoe opisanie Černigovskoj eparxii*, 5 (Černigov, 1874): 187.
[105] ZVERINSKIJ, 1: 68.
[106] AMVROSIJ, 4: 555, 556.
[107] *OASS*, vol. 3, priloženija, p. cxiii; Nikolaj ŠPAČINSKIJ, *Kievskij mitropolit Arsenij Mogiljanskij i sostojanie kievskoj mitropolii v ego pravlenie (1757-1770 g.)* (Kiev, 1907), p. 228.
[108] *PSPR*, Catherine II, 3: 289-291, 308.
[109] *Pravoslavnyj visnyk*, 1979, no. 8, p. 5.
[110] KOSSAK, p. 205-206.
[111] "Wielebna Anyzyja... obedyencyę sprawuie w Kryłosie", C'OROX, p. 234.
[112] PETRUŠEVIČ, *Dopolnenija 1600-1700*, p. 589.
[113] Archival documents in Slovita, as cited by C'OROX, p. 61.

52. KUTEJNO, 1 1/2 km from Orša on Dnieper r.; Vicebsk voev.; Vicebsk obl., Belorussia.
Dormition / Descent of the Holy Spirit.

In 1631 Anna Oginska Stetkevyč and her son John Stetkevyč founded this monastery on their property on the opposite side of the Kutejno river from the men's monastery also of their foundation[114]. In the seventeenth century this monastery was one of the largest and most prosperous; later it began to decline, but continued to exist into the twentieth century.
This monastery, referred to sometimes as "Oršanskyj monastyr", is not to be confused with no. 78, Orša, an entirely different foundation. The former was always Orthodox, the latter Catholic.

53. LADYN (Ladan), on Udaj r., 17 km from Pryluky; Pryluky polk; Černihiv obl., Ukraine.
Pokrov.

The monastery was founded about 1615 by prince Michael Vyšnevec'kyj for monks[115]. In 1619 his widow Raina permitted Isaiah Kopyns'kyj, ihumen at Hustyn' and later Orthodox metropolitan, who also had other monasteries under his jurisdiction, to transfer the monks from here elsewhere and to transform this into a women's monastery with his sister Alexandra as its first superior[116]. The monastery continued to exist until the twentieth century.

54. LEBEDYN, on Turja r.; Čerkasy obl., Ukraine.
St. Nicholas.

This monastery was founded in 1779 by several nuns from Moldavia, where their monastery had been sacked by the Turks. The monastery grew and prospered throughout the nineteenth century[117].

55. LISOVYČI, on Kotluj r.; Kiev obl., Ukraine.
St George.

In 1654 thirty nuns were said to be living here[118].

---

[114] Document of foundation in *Akty ZR*, vol. 4, no. 230.
[115] Cf. LAZAREVSKIJ, *Opisanie*, 3: 414.
[116] The document issued by Raina Vyšnevec'ka is in *Akty ZR*, vol. 4, no. 216.
[117] L. POXILEVIČ, *Skazanija o naselennyx mestnostjax Kievskoj gubernii* (Kiev, 1864), p. 715-716.
[118] ZVERINSKIJ, 3: 56.

56. LVIV.
St Catherine / St Onuphrius / Presentation in the Temple / St
Paraskeva.

The Stauropegian monastery of Lviv resolved to found a
monastery for nuns next to its monastery of St Onuphrius and in 1590
sent two of its members to metropolitan Michael Rahoza for his ap-
probation. The metropolitan counseled them to seek civil approval first;
this the brotherhood did, and in 1591, during his visit in Lviv, Rahoza
blessed the already started structure[119]. By 1603 the nuns were well
established there[120].

In 1646 the hospodar of Moldavia Basil Lupul made a gift of land
on the outskirts of the town to the Lviv nuns[121]. Kossak[122], followed by
C'orox[123], regards it as a separate foundation, whereas Petruševyč[124] sees
it as a relocation of the brotherhood monastery. There is greater prob-
ability in the second opinion. For one thing, after 1646 one no longer
finds references in sources to "nuns of St Onuphrius monastery",
"monastery of nuns by the Stauropegian church", as one does earlier[125].
Secondly, and with greater force, the documents concerned with Lupul's
grant—his own letter[126], the confirmation of king John Casimir in
1659[127]—speak of a new church and monastery for the Lviv nuns, implying a transferral rather than a totally new foundation. The monastery
died out at the end of the eighteenth century[128].

57. MAHILEV, Mahilev obl., Belorussia.
Savior.

According to Zverinskij, a women's monastery at the church of the
Transfiguration existed next to the men's monastery from 1447[129]. There

---

[119] A. Krylovskij, L'vovskoe stavropigial'noe bratstvo (Kiev, 1904), p. 207, footnote.
Rahoza himself refers to the women's monastery in his charter of authorization, Pamjatniki, 3: 67.
[120] In that year Constantine Kornjakt assigned to the Stauropegian confraternity a
sum from the income of one of his villages, part of which sum was to go to the nuns of
the Lviv monastery, cf. Petruševyč in Zorja Halycka, 26.IX (8.X).1851, p. 652.
[121] Petruševyč, it seems, had seen this document (cf. Svodnaja letopis' 1600-1700, p.
510), but it has not been found published.
[122] Kossak, p. 206.
[123] C'orox, p. 62.
[124] In Zorja Halycka, as above.
[125] As, for instance, Petruševič, Dopolnenija 1600-1700, p. 86.
[126] Petruševič, Svodnaja letopis' 1600-1700, p. 510.
[127] Cf. Akta grodzkie i ziemskie, 10 (Lwów, 1884): 285, no. 4745.
[128] For its final years, cf. Chotkowski, p. 138-142.
[129] Zverinskij, 3: 164.

is a mention of it in 1588[130] and again in a document of 1625, in which its superior Ksenja is named[131]. In 1625 it was certainly Catholic; the confraternity that had formed itself around the church of the Transfiguration had had to abandon it in 1608 to the Uniates[132]. The women's monastery probably ceased to exist soon after; there are many references in succeeding years to the Spas monastery, but all have to do exclusively with monks.

58. MAHILEV.
Epiphany.

The Mahilev confraternity, as was usual, founded a monastery on its property next to the church of the Epiphany in 1619 and some time later, across the street from it, a women's monastery, which never had a separate church. The monastery seems to have prospered while the brotherhood itself was flourishing, but by 1700 had begun to decline. Nevertheless, it continued to exist until 1795, when bishop Athanasius Volxovskij of Belorussia, never well-disposed towards the brotherhood, on being asked for his consent for the repair of the dilapidated monastery, took the occasion to close it and to send the nuns to others of their choice[133].

59. MAHILEV.
St Nicholas / St Anne.

In July 1634 and again in April 1636 Ladislaus IV issued charters, the first to the townspeople of Mahilev, the second to Peter Mohyla, permitting the construction of a church and monastery of St Nicholas in Mahilev on land bought by the townspeople for that purpose. In September 1646 the king issued another charter, consenting to this becoming a women's monastery[134]. In 1664 the monastery was relocated at a place near Mahilev called Xolmy, by a church of St Anne[135], but continued to be called the St Nicholas monastery, as in the register of

---

[130] Cf. *Akty ZR*, 4: 7-8.

[131] Cf. *IJuM*, 8: 413-417.

[132] Cf. *AS*, 2: xxv (Zapiski ihumena Oresta).

[133] Cf. F.A. ŽUDRO, *Bogojavlenskij bratskij monastyr' v g. Mogileve* (Mogilev, 1899), p. 30-36; also *AS*, 2: lxxv, where the dealings of bishop Athanasius are vividly characterized.

[134] The charter of Ladislaus IV of 6 September 1646 is in *AS*, 2: 69-71; also in *IJuM*, 13: 498-499.

[135] The charter of John Casimir approving the transfer, issued on 12 April 1664, is printed in Russian translation in *AS*, 2: 80-81.

revenues and expenditures of the town Mahilev, in which a donation is
noted in 1691 "do monastyrja Nikol'skoho zakonnycam"[136]. It ceased
to exist in the eighteenth century, between 1720 and 1795[137].

60. MAKOŠYN, on Desna r.; Nižyn polk; Černihiv obl., Ukraine.
St Nicholas / Pokrov.

This monastery was founded by Adam Kysil' in 1640. Little is
known about it, but it was in existence until 1786[138].

61. MARAŠČANKA (Marošanka), 15 km SE of Kamjanka Buz'ka;
Rus' voev.; Lviv obl., Ukraine.

Petruševyč merely mentions that a monastery of Basilian nuns existed here[139].

62. MAZYR, on Prypjat' r.; Minsk voev.; Homel' obl., Belorussia.
St Paraskeva.

There was a monastery of nuns here throughout the eighteenth century[140].

63. MENA, on Mena r.; Černihiv polk; Černihiv obl., Ukraine.

The existence of this monastery is documented for 1670[141], but no
further particulars have been found.

64. MINSK, capital of Belorussian SSR.
Sts Peter and Paul.

In Minsk during most of the seventeenth and eighteenth centuries
there was one Orthodox monastery and two Uniate ones. The Orthodox
monastery of Sts Peter and Paul was founded in 1612 by Eugenia
Šembelev close to the men's monastery of the same title and under its
jurisdiction. Eugenia herself became a nun and the monastery's first
superior[142]. The monastery survived until 1796, when it was closed by

---

[136] *IJuM*, 7: 152.
[137] It is named in the charter of Augustus II in 1720, *IJuM*, 12: 364. In 1795 the
Epiphany monastery was the only one of nuns in Mahilev.
[138] ZVERINSKIJ, 2: 279.
[139] PETRUŠEVIČ, *Dopolnenija 1600-1700*, p. 420.
[140] NIKOLAJ, p. 160-161.
[141] XARLAMPOVIČ, p. 279.
[142] Cf. *VZR*, 2: (1863), November, 11-16.

the authorities and its nuns sent to the one in Sluck[143].

65. MINSK.
Holy Trinity.

Although in July 1636 this monastery is called "just recently founded" by a "pani Wiazowiczowa"[144], Wołyniak is no doubt correct in placing the foundation in 1630[145], since already in 1634 Raphael Korsak mentions a Catholic women's monastery in Minsk in a report he prepared[146]. It coninued to exist until 1834, when the Russian authorities took it over for the town hospital.

66. MINSK.
Holy Spirit.

Metropolitan Antony Sjeljava contributed much at the foundation of this monastery in 1650 and summoned Catherine Sapieha from the Vilna Holy Trinity monastery to be its first superior. After these territories came under Russia, the nuns were transferred in 1795 to the Holy Trinity monastery in Minsk[147].

67. MOZOLIV, 10 km from Mscislav; Mscislav voev.; Mahilev obl., Belorussia.
Dormition / Transfiguration.

This monastery was founded in 1675 by Marianna Suxodolska, a wealthy gentrywoman, on her lands[148]. Between 1727 and 1795 it was Uniate[149]. After being turned into an Orthodox monastery in 1795 it remained in existence as a monastery of the third class until the twentieth century[150].

68. MUTYN, on Sejm r.; Nižyn polk; Sumy obl., Ukraine.
Transfiguration.

---

[143] Nikolaj, p. 92-93.
[144] "Dopiero nowo fundowanych", AS, 12: 40-41.
[145] Cf. Wołyniak, p. 73.
[146] EM, 2: 121.
[147] Wołyniak, p. 71-77.
[148] The deed of foundation, as entered in 1767, is printed in IJuM, 14: 511-518.
[149] Cf. LB, vol. 2, no. 248, for an account of how it passed to the Union. Not all of its nuns, however, accepted it, as one of those who did not and who left for Smolensk testified later, cf. OASS, 21: 464.
[150] In AV, 27: 344, there is a mention of a "Možoxovskyj" monastery passing to the

Hetman Ivan Skoropads'kyj in 1718 gave a hieromonk John permission to found this monastery[151]. In 1733 the monks were given the Hamalijivka monastery in exchange, and the nuns from the latter moved here[152]. The monastery was closed in 1786.

69. MYKOLAJIV, on Dniester r., 38 km S of Lviv; Rus' voev.; Lviv obl., Ukraine.
St Nicholas / Ascension.

Brief references are made to this monastery around the middle of the seventeenth century[153].

70. MYKULYNCI, near Zhar r.; Braclav voev.; Vinnycja obl., Ukraine.
Exaltation of the Holy Cross.

In 1716 some nuns settled in what had once been a monastery of monks near the village of Mykulynci until destruction by the Tatars in the middle of the seventeenth century. In 1733 a fire destroyed this new foundation. A new monastery, small and never prosperous, was established then at a little distance away, closer to the village of Rižok. It was officially closed by church authorities in 1748, but some nuns, Uniate and not, continued to live there until 1796[154].

71. NAVAHRUDEK, Navahrudek voev.; Hrodna obl., Belorussia.
Sts Boris and Hlib.

The foundation of this monastery was confirmed by the Congregation of the Propaganda in 1635[155], but nuns were there earlier, at least since 1629[156]. Two hundred years after its foundation, in 1835, the monastery was closed by Russian authorities.

Uniates—an example of the metamorphoses befalling proper names (in this case, obviously, Mozoliv).
[151] ZVERINSKIJ, 2: 210.
[152] LAZAREVSKIJ, *Opisanie*, 2: 354.
[153] The earliest is from 1641, cf. *Arxiv JuZR*, pt. I, 11: 434-435.
[154] SECINSKIJ, p. 339-352, gives the history of the monastery, together with some documents pertaining to it.
[155] *Documenta Pontificum Romanorum historiam Ucrainae illustrantia*, ed. Athanasius G. WELYKYJ, 1 (Romae, 1953): 499-500.
[156] In *OAZM*, vol. 1, no. 573, there is an allusion to certain properties of the metropolitanate being used for a new monastery: "...za obraščeniem tex mest, gde oni proživali, na ženskij monastyr'...".

72. NEMYRIV, 45 km from Vinnycja; Braclav voev.; Vinnycja obl., Ukraine.
St Nicholas.

Originally Vincent Potocki founded this monastery in a woods near Nemyriv for monks. The circumstances under which it became a women's monastery around 1783 are unknown[157]. Authors disagree on whether it was ever Uniate or not[158]. It continued to the twentieth century.

73. NIŽYN, on Oster r., 7 km from Černihiv; Nižyn polk; Černihiv obl., Ukraine.
Presentation.

The Nižyn monastery was founded in the eighteenth century by a widow from the Cossack milieu[159]. It survived the period of suppressions and continued to the twentieth century.

74. NOVA HREBLJA, 17 km S of Berežany; Ternopil' obl., Ukraine.

According to Kossak, this monastery is mentioned in the pomjanyk of Krexiv of the seventeenth century[160].

75. NOVI MLYNY, on Sejm r.; Nižyn polk; Černihiv obl., Ukraine.
Assumption.

It appears that this monastery had a chance beginning. In late 1657 or early 1658 the nuns in Baturyn were given a deed to some property in Novi Mlyny. The superior and some nuns went there, perhaps at first not with the idea of staying permanently or founding a monastery, but to see to matters connected with the property. The superior was now called ihumenja of Baturyn and Novi Mlyny, which confirms the impression that the latter was closely associated with the former. Perhaps some nuns settled there rather soon, as the property was contested, and it may have been necessary for the nuns to enforce their rights by remaining there. But in 1683, as has been related above, the Baturyn monastery burned down, and a definitive transfer occurred at that time of all the nuns to Novi Mlyny. From the names of some of its land and

---

[157] SECINSKIJ, p. 332-336.
[158] I. ČISTOVIČ, *Očerk istorii zapadno-russkoj cerkvi*, 2 (S.-Peterburg, 1884): 375, followed by C'OROX, p. 64, consider it Uniate 1783-1795; SECINSKIJ, *loc. cit.*, doubts it.
[159] Cf. LAZAREVSKIJ, *Opisanie*, 2: 79.
[160] KOSSAK, p. 208.

of its woods this monastery was also known as "Kerbutovs'kyj" and "Bobrykovs'kyj"[161]. It closed down in the nineteenth century, probably in its early part.

76.   OLES'KO, 23 km N of Zoločiv; Rus' voev.; Lviv obl., Ukraine.

Here is another example of a monastery known only, according to Kossak, from the Krexiv pomjanyk[162].

77.   OMBYŠ, on Oster r., 25 km S of Borzna; Nižyn polk; Černihiv obl., Ukraine.

Catherine Uhornyc'ka, widow of the treasurer (*skarbnyk*) of Černihiv, founded this monastery on her property at Ombyš some time between 1625 and 1640. A little later she founded there also a monastery for monks, under the authority of the Lavra of Kiev. At Xmel'nyc'kyj's uprising Uhornyc'ka fled to safer territory. The monasteries were plundered; although the one for monks managed to revive, local inhabitants returning to Ombyš eleven years later (i.e., in 1659) found not a single nun at the women's monastery and the place in an abandoned state[163].

78.   ORŠA, on Dnieper r.; Vicebsk voev.; Vicebsk obl., Belorussia.
        Pokrov.

This Uniate monastery just outside Orša was founded around the middle of the seventeenth century. In 1671 it appears on the list of monasteries of the Catholic metropolitanate[164], but there are few other notices about it. It was suppressed in 1839.

79.   OSTROGOŽSK (Ostrohož), Voronež obl., Russia.
        Dormition / St Paraskeva.

---

[161] Cf. LAZAREVSKIJ, *Opisanie*, 2: 294-296; idem, Akty, p. 60-61. ZVERINSKIJ, 3: 202, in speaking of the Baturyn monastery shows great confusion with regard to the two monasteries of Baturyn and Novi Mlyny, though ultimately his information can be traced to a faulty document (which speaks of hetman Bohdan Xmel'nyc'kyj in 1658) later printed by VASILENKO, 1: 197-199.

[162] KOSSAK, p. 209.

[163] The entire account, based on monastery documents deposited in the Kiev university library is set out in V.A. MJAKOTIN, *Očerki social'noj istorii Ukrainy v XVII-XVIII vv.*, 1, pt. 1 (Praga, 1924): 81-82.

[164] *EM*, 2: 321.

The town of Ostrogožsk was founded around the middle of the seventeenth century. In 1653 the local polkovnyk founded a men's monastery and shortly after also one for nuns[165]. The latter was suppressed in 1786.

80. OVRUČ, Kiev voev.; Žytomyr obl., Ukraine.
Birth of the Mother of God.

Only two early, unconnected notices about this monastery exist. It is named in 1496[166], which places its foundation most probably in the fifteenth century. In a charter of 1531 Alexandra Nemyrovyč was given this monastery to administer[167].

81. OVRUČ.
Sts Joachim and Anna.

One would be tempted to identify this with the preceding monastery were it not that the privilege of grand prince Alexander mentions each as a separate entity. In that document of 1496 princess Daškova is given this monastery—whether as superior or only for revenues is not clear[168]. It may not have survived much longer.

82. PEČENYKY, 53 km from Starodub; Starodub polk.
Assumption.

Maria, widow of the Starodub polkovnyk Semen Samojlovyč, founded this monastery in 1693. It was suppressed in 1786[169].

83. PERESOPNYCJA, Volyn' voev.; Rovno obl., Ukraine.

The monastery of the Blessed Virgin, although later inhabited by monks, was at least for a certain period in the sixteenth century a women's monastery. (Alternatively, there could have existed two monasteries, for monks and for nuns, for a short time). Although in a document of 1504 it is not clear whether Maria Čartorys'ka received the

---

[165] AMVROSIJ, 5: 382-384, says the foundation occurred "okolo 1663 goda", but as there were nuns from Ostrogožsk (called "kievljanki") in Moscow already in 1657 (cf. XARLAMPOVIČ, p. 306), perhaps already at that time a community had begun to form itself there.

[166] Cf. *Akty ZR*, 1: 164.

[167] *Ibid.*, 2: 218-219.

[168] *Ibid.*, 1: 164.

[169] ZVERINSKIJ, 2: 392.

monastery as its superior or only for its revenues[170], in a description of 1545 mention is made of nuns there[171].

84. PIDHAJCI, 28 km S of Berežany; Rus' voev.; Ternopil' obl., Ukraine.

This is one of the monasteries known only from the Krexiv pomjanyk[172].

85. PIDLUBY, SE of Javoriv; Rus' voev.; Lviv obl., Ukraine.

The notice under the preceding number can be repeated here.

86. PIKULICE (Pykulyči), 5 km S of Peremyšl'; Rus' voev.; Rzeszów woj., Poland.

Again, the same notice can be repeated.

87. PINSK, on Prypjat' r.; Brest obl., Belorussia.
St Barbara.

The monastery in Pinsk had a long, but largely unrecorded history. It was founded before 1521. Between 1600 and 1633 it accepted the Union[173]. In the nineteenth century, before suppression, it was again Orthodox.

88. POLOCK (Polack), Vicebsk obl., Belorussia.
Savior / St Sophia.

Of all the women's monasteries in the territory of the metropolitanate of Kiev this one alone survived from pre-Mongolian times to the twentieth century. The foundress was Predyslava—Euphrosine in monastic life—, the daughter of prince Svjatoslav Vseslavyč of Polock. As a young girl she chose the monastic life, living first under the guidance of an aunt who was a nun (after 1116), then as a solitary by the cathedral of St Sophia in Polock, where she occupied herself in copying books. Before 1128 the bishop gave her some

---

[170] *Akty ZR*, 1: 959.
[171] *Pamjatniki*, 4: 188-189.
[172] KOSSAK, p. 209.
[173] PETRUŠEVIČ, *Dopolnenija 1600-1700*, p. 16, says in 1600, but ZVERINSKIJ, 1: 110, asserts that it became Uniate only in 1633. There are no documents from the intevening period that warrant favoring one or the other view.

property outside the town on the Polota river with the church of the Savior where the bishops of Polock were buried for the estabishment of a monastery. Among her first companions were her sister Horodyslava-Evdokija and a cousin Zvenyslava-Evpraksija. Euphrosine died in Jerusalem during a pilgrimage to the Holy Land in 1173[174]. Hardly anything is known of the monastery's history during the next few centuries except that in the thirteenth century another member of the princely house of Polock, Paraskeva-Zvenyslava, is associated with it[175]. From the mid-sixteenth century the community had a rather unsettled life. The nuns abandoned the monastery in 1562 during the war between Poland and Muscovy. When Poland regained Polock Stephen Batory gave the monastery as well as its properties to the Jesuits[176]. The nuns for a time lived dispersed, but Josaphat Kuncevyč, when archbishop of Polock, built a monastery for them by the cathedral of St Sophia and endowed it with some lands of his eparchy[177]. In the seventeenth century the war waged by tsar Alexius against Poland-Lithuania again compelled the nuns to abandon their monastery. In the nineteenth century, after the establishment of Orthodoxy and other vicissitudes, nuns were again settled in the monastery of the Savior by the church built by Euphrosine[178].

89. POLOCK.
St Michael.

---

[174] The chronicle account is found in the Stepennaja kniga, *PSRL*, 21: 206-220. Cf. GOLUBINSKIJ, *Istorija russkoj cerkvi*, 1, pt. 2: 597-600.

[175] Cf. the chronicle of Byxov, *PSRL*, 17: 479-480, and the other Lithuanian chronicles in that volume. Although the compiler of her life obviously got the story confused, it hardly justifies the editors of a second edition of these chronicles (*PSRL*, vol. 32) to identify her with Euphrosine without more ado (cf. the index to this volume which gives "Evfrosinija" followed by page numbers where only Paraskeva is mentioned). Golubinskij and other Russian and Soviet writers ignore her completely.

[176] One cannot agree with L.V. ALEKSEEV, who in *Polockaja zemlja* (Moskva, 1966), p. 211, claims that the Spas church of Batory's grant was not that of this monastery, but another, larger, nearby. It is unlikely that two churches only a few steps apart should both be called Spas. Furthermore, in the profuse writings concerning it that were the sole tangible result of the litigation between metropolitan Florijan Hrebnyc'kyj, who was also archbishop of Polock (1720-1762), who at that late date pressed his claim to all properties taken from the eparchy, and the Jesuits, for the persons who were there on the spot and who had access to town records there is never any doubt that the matter concerned the monastery and the monastery church (this material is collected in APF, Miscellanee Diverse, vol. 19).

[177] The document of endowment, sent to Rome by Hrebnyc'kyj in Latin translation a century later, is transcribed in APF, Miscellanee Diverse, vol. 19, fol. 444-446. Cf. SUSZA, *Cursus vitae et certamen martyrii*, p. 55.

[178] C'OROX, p. 65-66; ZVERINSKIJ, 1:236, and 161-162.

There is one solitary, casual mention of this monastery in the late fifteenth century[179].

90. POLONNE, Zvjahel' dist., Volyn' voev.; Xmel'nyc'kyj obl., Ukraine.
Dormition.

Originally founded for monks, it became a women's monastery around 1612[180]. Towards the middle of the seventeenth century this monastery became Catholic. Already in 1804 there was a proposal to close it[181], but it survived until 1858, Orthodox in its last years.

91. POPIVKA (now Krasnostav), on Turja r., 13 km NW of Volodymyr Volyns'kyj; Volyn' voev.; Volyn' obl., Ukraine.
St Nicholas.

Adam Kysil' founded this monastery on his property Hnojina on an island on which was located a little village Popiv Mlyn or Popivka in 1646[182]; his mother Euphrosine was its first superior. Later in that century it became Catholic. It probably closed in 1836[183].

92. PUŠKARIVKA, 3 km from Poltava; Poltava obl., Ukraine.
Pokrov / Ascension.

Nuns from Podillja founded this monastery in 1676 in the town of Poltava itself; in 1721 it was moved outside the town to Puškarivka. It survived until the late eighteenth century[184].

93. PUSTEL'NYKY, part of the village Radexiv, 32 km NE of Kaminka Buz'ka; Rus' voev.; Lviv obl., Ukraine.

We know of this monastery only from entries that commemorate its nuns in the pomjanyk of Krexiv (seventeenth century) and in that of Derevjany (seventeenth and eighteenth centuries)[185].

---

[179] According to *Sapiehowie* 1:6; "Iwaszko Sapieżyc wkrótce potem otrzymuje jeszcze dwa podobne potwierdzenia, na siolo Boldawicze, na Dźwinie powyżej Polocka, kupli swej od *staricy* (mniszki) monasteru św. Michala w Polocku".

[180] Cf. N.I. Teodorovič, *Istoriko-statističeskoe opisanie cerkvej i prixodov Volynskoj eparxii*, 1 (Počaev, 1888): 236; Zverinskij, 1: 278.

[181] *AV*, 16: 74.

[182] *OAZM*, vol. 1, no. 767.

[183] Cf. Zverinskij, 3: 95.

[184] *Ibid.*, p. 129.

[185] Kossak, p. 209; Iljarion Svjencickyj, *Opys rukopysiv Narodnoho Domu z kolekci-*

94. PYSAREVŠČYNA, Poltava polk; Poltava obl., Ukraine.
Holy Trinity / Transfiguration.

The foundation date of this monasery is unknown, but it was
already in existence in 1679[186]. Originally it was located at Velyki
Budyšča, then moved to Pysarevščyna nearby, which circumstance has
given rise to a variety of names for the monastery and great confusion
in the authors who mention it. Although it had a long existence, into the
twentieth century, little is known of its internal history[187].

95. RIPJANKA, 12 km SE of Kaluš; Ivano-Frankivs'k obl., Ukraine.
Dormition / Holy Trinity.

In her list of monasteries C'orox lists Rypjana and Rypjanka, both
in Halyčyna, but in different districts[188]. Rypjanka is taken from
Kossak[189], while Rypjana is due to Holubec'[190]. Unfortunately, Holubec'
based his own listing on a careless reading of the *Svodnaja letopis'*. This
last work transcribes an inscription in a Gospel book donated in 1689 by
two nuns, Natalia and Pankratija, to the "Rypjanskyj" monastery,
which Petruševyč explains as being located in the village of Ripjanka, in
the woods of the Stanyslaviv district[191]. The monastery was closed in
1756.

96. ROHATYN, 68 SE of Lviv; Rus' voev.; Ivano-Frankivs'k obl.,
Ukraine.
Ascension.

A rather curious document of 1631 has the monks of Univ refusing
to have anything to do with the two monasteries of Rohatyn which the
nuns wanted to give over to them[192]. These monasteries must have been
very small and poor, nevertheless the Ascension monastery managed to
survive until 1784[193].

---

ji Ant. Petruševyča, 3 (Ukrajins'ko-rus'kyj arxiv, 7; U L'vovi, 1911): 105-106.
   [186] From that year there is a settlement of boundaries between its holdings and those
of a neighbor, cf. *Aktovyja knigi Poltavskogo gorodovogo urjada XVII-go veka*, ed. V.L.
MODZALEVSKIJ, 3 (Černigov, 1914): 104.
   [187] ZVERINSKIJ, 1: 269; DENISOV, p. 679-680.
   [188] C'OROX, p. 66.
   [189] KOSSAK, p. 209.
   [190] M. HOLUBEC', Materijaly do katal'ogu vasylijans'kyx monastyriv u Halyčyni,
AOSBM, 3, no. 1-2 (1928): 170.
   [191] PETRUŠEVIČ, *Svodnaja letopis' 1600-1700*, p. 225-226.
   [192] *Ibid.*, p. 68-69.
   [193] C'OROX, p. 66.

97. **ROHATYN.**
Transfiguration.

This other monastery of Rohatyn was closed in 1768[194].

98. **ROZHIRČE, 22 km SW of Stryj; Rus' voev.; Lviv obl., Ukraine.**

For the foundation date of the monastery in Rozhirče only a wide
span of time can be indicated: between 1693 and 1761[195]. In 1761 it was
small and poor. In 1782 it was on the list of monasteries to be suppressed
and actually faded away by 1789[196].

99. **RUSEC'.**

There is a mention of this monastery, with nine nuns, in 1774[197].

100. **SASIV, on Buh r., 9 km SE of Zoločiv; Rus' voev.; Lviv obl.,
Ukraine.**

The existence of this monastery is known from the intention of
metropolitan Athanasius Šeptyc'kyj to close it, expressed already in
1743, but carried out only in 1759[198].

101. **ŠELEXOVE (Šelexiv), Xmel'nyc'kyj obl., Ukraine.**

There is evidence for the existence of this monastery in the eighteenth century[199].

102. **ŠKLOV, on Dnieper r.; Vicebsk voev.; Mahilev obl., Belorussia.**
Dormition.

According to Petruševyč there was a women's monastery in Šklov
already before 1665; in all events, by 1682 it was well established[200]. The

---

[194] *Ibid.*
[195] At the synod of the Peremyšl' eparchy in 1693 only two women's monasteries were
noted, Smil'nycja and Javoriv (*LE*, 4: 117), while bishop Onuphrius Šumljans'kyj added
also Rozhirče in a report written in 1761 (published by A.D. z VALJAVY, Sostojanie Eparxii
ruskoi Peremyskoi pered stoma lity, *Halyčanyn*, 2 [1863]: 86).
[196] CHOTKOWSKI, p. 142.
[197] C'OROX, p. 67.
[198] *Ibid.*
[199] *Ibid.*, p. 68.
[200] PETRUŠEVIČ, *Dopolnenija 1600-1700*, p. 879. Cf. *IJuM*, 27: 202-204, which concerns a grant of property made to it.

last mention of it occurs in the charter of Augustus II of 1720 which confirmed the rights of Orthodox monasteries[201].

103. SLOVITA, 25 km SW of Zoločiv; Rus' voev.; Lviv obl., Ukraine; Holy Cross.

The monastery of Slovita is one of only two in Halyčyna that survived the suppressions of the late eighteenth century and continued to exist until the 1940's. It is first mentioned around 1581[202]. Beginning with 1600 its history is well documented. At the end of the eighteenth century it reached a point of near extinction, but from the 1820's began to revive. It was large and flourishing until its violent end in the 1940's[203].

104. SLUCK, Minsk obl., Belorussia.
St Elias / Savior.

This monastery was founded in the fifteenth century for monks. In 1611 it was transformed into a women's monastery, which existed until 1855[204].

105. SMIL'NYCJA, near Staryj Sambir; Rus' voev.; Lviv obl., Ukraine.

The earliest notice about this monastery is from 1644; according to it a stone church had been built there by bishop Athanasius Krupec'kyj of Peremyšl'[205]. In 1789 the buildings were all in a bad state, and the monastery was abandoned[206].

106. SOSNYCJA, Černihiv polk; Černihiv obl., Ukraine.
St John the Evangelist.

The hieromonk Myron Orlovs'kyj in 1690 founded a skyt, which came to be called Myronovs'kyj after him, at a little distance from Sosnycja; the skyt was dependent on the Holy Trinity monastery of Černihiv. In 1751 ihumenja Maria Lazarevyč with thirteen nuns came from the Borejky monastery in Belorussia and asked archimandrite Iraklij

---

[201] Cf. *Arxiv JuZR*, pt. 1, 4: 403-405.
[202] Ivan KRYPJAKEVYČ, Serednevični monastyri v Halyčyni, *AOSBM*, 2, no. 1-2 (1926): 93.
[203] C'OROX, p. 69-73. Some documents are printed on p. 231-237.
[204] NIKOLAJ, p. 117-119.
[205] PETRUŠEVIČ, *Svodnaja letopis' 1600-1700*, p. 95.
[206] CHOTKOWSKI, p. 142-143.

Komarovs'kyj of the Černihiv monastery to be permitted to settle in the skyt, which in the meanwhile had been abandoned[207]. The women's monastery there, however, was also of short duration: it was closed in 1786.

107. STANYSLAVIV (now Ivano-Frankivs'k), Rus' voev.; Ivano-Frankivs'k obl., Ukraine.
Dormition.

Throughout the eighteenth century references are made to this monastery[208], but neither its origins nor the date of its closing are known.

108. STARYJ SAMBIR (Stare Misto), Rus' voev.; Ternopil' obl., Ukraine.

There are only bare mentions of this monastery in 1744 and 1782. Under the second date it appears on a list monasteries in Halyčyna that were to be closed. As no one was well-informed about the condition of these monasteries, and as already in 1761 there is no mention of Staryj Sambir in a report of bishop Onufrij Šumljans'kyj of Peremyšl'[210], it probably ceased to function well before 1782.

109. SUDOVA VYŠNJA, on Vyšnja r.; Rus' voev.; Lviv obl., Ukraine.

The pomjanyk of Krexiv of the seventeenth century includes a list of nuns from this monastery[211].

110. ŠUMAROVO, 6 km NE of Mhlyn; Starodub polk; Brjansk obl., Russia.
Pokrov.

Elena Roslavec', widow of a merchant, founded this monastery around 1690 and became its first superior. It was closed in 1786[212].

---

[207] Cf. *OASS*, 31: 175-177. Rather confused accounts about this monastery are given by AMVROSIJ, 5: 71-72, and later compilers.

[208] The earliest mention is from circa 1710 (SECINSKIJ, p. 348), and the latest from 1782 (C'OROX, p. 67).

[209] C'OROX, p. 67 (1744); CHOTKOWSKI, p. 136 (1782).

[210] A.D. z VALJAVY, Sostojanie Eparxii, *Halyčanyn*, 2 (1863): 86.

[211] KOSSAK, p. 205.

[212] Cf. Vadim L'vovič MODZALEVSKIJ, *Malorossijskij rodoslovnik*, 4 (Kiev, 1914): 349; ZVERINSKIJ, 2: 414.

111. ŠUMS'KE, Ternopil, obl., Ukraine.

Only the bare existence of a monastery here is known[213].

112. SUMY, on Pslo r.; Sumy polk; Sumy obl., Ukraine.
St John the Baptist.

Though this monastery is ususally referred to as "Sums'kyj", it was actually located two kilometers from Sumy, in the village Luky. Archbishop Filaret Gumilevskij wrote that it was founded in 1687 by the polkovnyk of Sumy Herasym Kondratevyč[214], but nuns from Sumy came to Moscow for alms already in 1658[215]. The monastery was officially closed in 1786, though in fact it continued for a few more years, since nuns from other suppressed monasteries were sent here to end their days.

113. TEREBOVLJA, 32 km S of Ternopil'; Rus' voev.; Ternopil' obl., Ukraine.

There is a mention of this monastery in 1663[216].

114. UNIV (now Mižhirja), Rus' voev.; Lviv obl., Ukraine.
Transfiguration.

Documents and inscriptions in books testify to the existence of the Univ monastery in the seventeenth and eighteenth centuries. The earliest is an inscription dated 1644 on a liturgical book stating that it was placed in the church by the nun Evdokija[217]. Only a few other references to the monastery may be found—such as one in a 1650 will of a certain Suzanna Vercyns'ka, who with her daughter and grandchildren found refuge there during Xmel'nyc'kyj's wars[218]. But the monastery continued its unnoticed existence to the second half of the eighteenth century: the register of funerals at the Univ archimandria notes the death in 1761 of ihumenja Paraskevija of the Transfiguration monastery.

---

[213] ZVERINSKIJ, 3: 213. WOŁYNIAK, p. 169, and C'OROX, p. 68, also mention it, without adding anything.

[214] *ISOXE*, 1: 251.

[215] XARLAMPOVIČ, p. 346.

[216] C'OROX, p. 68.

[217] Ivan BUCMANJUK, *Univ i jeho monastyri* (Žovkva, 1904), p. 75-76 (also for the 1761 notice).

[218] *Arxiv JuZR*, pt. III, 4: 520.

115. UTIŠKIV, 24 km NW of Zoločiv; Rus' voev.; Lviv obl., Ukraine.
Lists of monasteries repeat a mention of one here[219].

116. VICEBSK, Vicebsk voev.; Vicebsk obl., Belorussia.
Birth of the Mother of God.

Zverinskij gives this monastery the title of St John the Baptist[220]. But the source on which he bases his information calls it "Prečystenskij", and only editorial notes refer to it as "Predtečenskij"[221]. It certainly existed in 1553, but nothing of its previous or later history is known.

117. VICEBSK.
Descent of the Holy Spirit.

Zverinskij claims that this monatery was founded in the fourteenth century by Olgerd[222], whereas C'orox has it existing only from 1697 as a foundation of Theodore Lukovs'kyj and Uniate throughout its existence[223]. As regards Zverinskij, his source seems to be the chronicle of Vicebsk, since he lists that in his bibliography. The passages to which he refers, however, speak only of a church of the Holy Spirit[224] and are, moreover, late and unreliable. He states, further, that this monastery is named in 1723 in a list of monasteries of the Orthodox Kiev eparchy. Again, his source says nothing of the kind[225]. C'orox's statement concerning the foundation fares no better. The person concerned was not Lukovs'kyj (Łukowski) but Łukomski and he received permission from the archbishop of Polock to found a monastery for Basilian *monks* in 1697[226].

However, such a monastery did exist in the eighteenth century; it was Catholic[227]. After the destruction of the Union in 1839, Orthodox

---

[219] C'OROX, p. 68, Ivan KRYPJAKEVYČ, Serednevični monastyri v Halyčyni, *AOSBM*, 2: no. 1-2 (1926), 93, and KOSSAK, p. 210, all list it, but the ultimate source for all is *L'vovjanyn*, 1862, p. 90, which is not readily found for consultation.

[220] ZVERINSKIJ, 3: 135.

[221] *Akty ZR*, 3: 47, and p. 5 of notes at back, footnote to no. 12.

[222] ZVERINSKIJ, 1: 140-141.

[223] C'OROX, p. 59.

[224] Cf. ·*Sbornik letopisej, otnosjaščixsja k istorii južnoj i zapadnoj Rusi*, p. 210, 217-218.

[225] Cf. *OASS*, vol. 3, priloženija, p. cxiii.

[226] Cf. Tadeusz WASILEWSKI, Łukomski Teodor Felicjan, *Polski słownik biograficzny*, 18: 561. C'orox was not the first, however, to make this mistake. The original document has not been published, as far as it can be ascertained.

[227] The earliest reference in sources is from 1713, cf. *IJuM*, 21: 165-169. Florijan

nuns were introduced here, but a few years later, about 1844, the monastery was definitively closed.

118. VILNA (Vilnius), capital of Lithuanian SSR.
Holy Trinity.

Relatively much has been written about the Holy Trinity monastery in Vilna, but it has not been established when the women's monastery dependent on it was founded. There are references to the latter from 1589[228], but there is also a casual mention that it existed earlier at another location[229]. Around 1610 the monastic reforms of Rutskyj began to be felt here, and the monastery prospered, also materially. It was one of the more observant as well as economically prosperous Uniate monasteries throughout its existence. In 1839 it was turned into an Orthodox monastery and in 1841 it was closed[230].

119. VILNA.
Holy Spirit / Annunciation.

After the Union of Brest the Holy Trinity brotherhood of Vilna broke up into two—one of uniates and one of dissidents, each claiming legitimate succession. The Orthodox organized themselves into the Holy Spirit brotherhood, named so after their church, built in 1596-1597, and founded another monastery, or rather, two monasteries, one for monks and one for nuns. The women's monastery throughout its existence had never more than a handful of nuns, but it had its own little church of the Annunciation. It was closed in 1795[231].

Hrebnyc'kyj mentions it in his report to Rome on the state of the Kiev and Polock eparchies in 1765: in Vicebsk "extat pariter Monasterium Monialium Basilianarum paenes lapideam Ecclesiam Sancti Spiritus, in fundo episcopali erectum" (*EM*, 4: 373). Thus it seems that an archbishop of Polock helped to found this monastery, but nothing indicates who and when.

[228] Cf. the privilege of Sigismund III confirming the rights of the Holy Trinity confraternity of Vilna, dated 21 July 1589: "Černcom též i černycam v koždom tydnju, vodluh premožen'ja bratskoho, na stravu davaty majut" (in *ČOIDR*, 1859, 3: 23-28, and *AV*, 9: 142). The nuns in 1656 stated that Sigismund III confirmed some of the monastery's properties before the Union (1596), *AV*, 9: 408.

[229] In a letter of Paul Sapieha, dated 10 August 1598, *Archiwum domu Sapiehów*, 1 (Lwów, 1892): 194.

[230] Cf. O.V. ŠČERBICKIJ, *Vilenskij Svjato-Troickij monastyr'* (Vil'na, 1885), p. 126-133.

[231] Cf. D. SCEPURO, *Vilenskoe Svjato-Duxovskoe bratstvo v XVII i XVIII stoletijax* (Kiev, 1899), introduction, *passim*. The monastery might have existed slightly longer, however, because there is still mention of it in a letter of ihumen Daniel of Vilna to the archbishop of Minsk Victor Sadkovskyj dated 25 November 1795 (*AS*, 11: 212).

120. VINNYCJA, on Boh r.; Braclav voev.; Vinnycja obl., Ukraine.
Annunciation.

This monastery was founded in 1635 by Michael Kropyvnyc'kyj for
the Orthodox. In the eighteenth century it was, in the classic phrase,
"zaxvačen uniatami" and remained in their possession until 1795, when
it again changed hands, becoming a state-supported monastery of the second class. In 1845 it was moved to Brajiliv[232].

121. VLODAVA (Włodawa), on Buh r.; Lublin woj., Poland.

There is a brief mention of this monastery by Petruševyč[233].

122. VOLJA ARLAMIVS'KA, near Vyšnja r.; Rus' voev.; Lviv obl.,
Ukraine.

A monastery is said to have existed here in the seventeenth century[234].

123. VOLODYMYR VOLYNS'KYJ, Volyn' obl., Ukraine.
St Elias.

The Catholic metropolitan Felician Volodkovyč founded this
monastery in 1772[235], but issued the document of erection only in 1794.
He contended that this was a refounding, as a monastery had originally
been built there by the Lithuanian prince Švitrigaila in the fifteenth century[236]. In 1804 a report submitted to the Senate in St Petersburg recom-
mended that it be closed[237], but only a fire in 1833 put a definitive end
to it[238].

124. VOLSVYN, near Sokal'; Belz voev.; Lviv obl., Ukraine.

A monastery is supposed to have existed here at one time[239].

---

[232] Cf. SECINSKIJ, p. 249-256, with documents from its archives, p. 257-268.

[233] PETRUŠEVIČ, Xolmskaja eparxija, p. 242.

[234] According to KOSSAK, p. 205, this monastery is mentioned in the pomjanyky of
Krexiv and Ščeploty.

[235] Cf. EM, 5: 279, where Volodkovyč writes on 14 April 1773 "Monasteriolum S.
Eliae, quo sit anno erectum".

[236] Ibid., 6: 409-411. Hence this gave him an opening for litigation with others who
had established rights over this property.

[237] AV, 16: 74.

[238] Cf. WOŁYNIAK, p. 166.

[239] It has passed from list to list (KOSSAK, p. 205, KRYPJAKEVYČ, p. 97, C'OROX, p. 60)
without any documentation.

125. VYŠHOROD, 12 km N of Kiev on Dnieper r.; Kiev obl., Ukraine.
St Nicholas.

It was in the church of this monastery that the icon now known as the Vladimir Mother of God was venerated until Andrew Bogoljubskij carried it off. The account of that happening in some chronicles mentions nuns in Vyšhorod[240].

126. XOLM (Chełm), Lublin woj., Poland.
Assumption.

Jakiv Suša, bishop of Xolm, is credited with founding this monastery in the 1650's by the church of the Assumption and endowing it with land[241]. The monastery was officially closed in 1723, but a community continued to exist here until after 1779[242].

127. XOROŠEVE, 10 km from Xarkiv; Xarkiv polk; Xarkiv obl., Ukraine.
Ascension.

Settlers in Slobids'ka Ukraine from Poland-Lithuania founded this monastery around 1656. In 1786 it became a state-supported monastery of the second class, continuing to exist until the twentieth century[243].

128. ZAHVIZDJA, 3 km from Ivano-Frankivs'k; Rus' voev.; Ivano-Frankivs'k obl., Ukraine.
Holy Trinity.

The earliest documentation for the existence of this monastery is an inscription in an Epistle book given in 1669 to its church by an "otec' Ioann"[244]. It was suppressed in 1789[245].

129. ŽOVKVA (now Nesteriv), 32 km N of Lviv; Rus' voev.; Lviv obl., Ukraine.
Exaltation of the Holy Cross.

---

[240] Cf. Letopis Avraamki (PSRL, 16: 310), and Stepennaja kniga (PSRL, 21: 193, 232); POXILEVIČ, p. 2.

[241] P.N. BATJUŠKOV, Xolmskaja Rus' (Pamjatniki russkoj stariny v zapadnyx gubernijax, vol. 7; S.-Peterburg, 1887), p. 100.

[242] Cf. V.M. PLOŠČANSKIJ, Prošloe xolmskoj Rusi po arxivnym dokumentam XV-XVIII v. i dr. istočnikam, 2 (Vil'na, 1901): 74.

[243] Cf. ISOXE, 1: 109-134.

[244] PETRUŠEVIČ, Svodnaja letopis' 1600-1700, p. 162.

[245] CHOTKOWSKI, p. 142.

Town registers refer to this monastery in 1627[246]; its foundation date is unknown. In 1718 the monastery burned down[247], but it must have been rebuilt, as C'orox cites a document in the archives of the monastery of Slovita which mentions the Žovkva monastery in 1743[248].

130. ŽYDYČYN, on Styr r., 7 km N of Luc'k; Volyn voev.; Volyn' obl., Ukraine.
Holy Spirit.

A monastery existed here for a short time around 1621. In that year the nuns were evicted, and it is not known if they ever returned[249].

DOUBTFUL MONASTERIES

1. ČARJEJA, Vicebsk obl., Belorussia.

There is a mention of an "Jhumenia czereyska Białey Cerkwi" from 1717[250]. Perhaps it should read "Jhumen czereyski": a Basilian monastery was located here.

2. DERMAN' (now Ustens'ke Druhe), Rovno obl., Ukraine.

This was not a monastic foundation, but a transitional place to stay for Uniate nuns from suppressed monasteries, chiefly Korec', at the turn of the eighteenth century. During their stay in Derman' the nuns taught girls[251].

3. DIVYČE, on Zbruč r.

According to a vague local tradition, at one time there was a women's monastery here[252].

4. DUSOWCE (Dusivci), on San r., 13 km S of Peremyšl'; Rzeszów woj., Poland.

This locality figures in C'orox's list, on the authority of the

---

[246] As cited by Sadok BARĄCZ, *Pamiątki miasta Żółkwi* (2nd ed., Lwów, 1877), p. 51.
[247] *Ibid.*, p. 219.
[248] C'OROX, p. 61.
[249] Cf. *Arxiv JuZR*, pt. I, 6: 503-504.
[250] In an inventory of populated estates in the district of Orša, *IJuM*, 12: 183.
[251] C'OROX, p. 60. Cf. *AV*, 16: 81.
[252] SECINSKIJ, p. 299-300.

Schematismus of the Peremyšl' eparchy of 1879, p. 153[253]. The page number should be 53, but, in any case, there is no mention of any monastery.

5. DZISNA, on confluence of Dvina and Dzisna r.; Vicebsk obl., Belorussia.

Zverinskij repeats Amvrosij in listing a women's monastery here, but without sources and without any indications as to when it could have existed[254].

6. IHUMEN, SE of Minsk.

Only on the strength of its name, which has also the variant Ihumenja, is it believed that a monastery existed here[255].

7. KIEV—"na Klovi".

Zverinskij calls this a women's monastery on the basis of a notice found in the Hypatian chronicle: "i požhoša monastyr divyčeskij svjatoho Stefana i derevni herman"[256]. The reading as he gives it, however, is faulty, and more recent editions emend it[257].

8. KRAJSK, 97 km N of Minsk; Minsk obl., Belorussia.

A hasty reading changed this from a monastery of monks in Amvrosij to one of nuns in Zverinskij[258].

9. KREXIV, 12 km SW of Nesteriv (Žovkva); Lviv obl., Ukraine.

Kossak, followed by C'orox, includes this in his list, on the tenuous grounds that since the Krexiv pomjanyk lists the names of many nuns, a women's monastery must have existed there[259].

10. MONASTYRS'KE (now Marksove), on Boh r., 22 km from Nemyriv; Vinnycja obl., Ukraine.

---

[253] C'OROX, p. 61.
[254] ZVERINSKIJ, 3: 200; AMVROSIJ, 4: 38.
[255] ZVERINSKIJ, 3: 69.
[256] *Ibid.*, p. 78. The quote is from *PSRL*, 2: 281.
[257] For one example: the 2nd edition of vol. 2 of *PSRL* has "i požhoša monastyr' Stefanec' derevni" (p. 222).
[258] AMVROSIJ, 4: 791; ZVERINSKIJ, 3: 83.
[259] KOSSAK, p. 205; C'OROX, p. 62.

Local tradition recounted the existence of a monastery here in the eighteenth century[260].

11. PARYZIV (Parypse?).

A monastery is supposed to have existed in Paryziv in the eighteenth century, but it has been impossible to identify this locality (seemingly in the Xolm eparchy)[261].

12. POLTAVA, Poltava obl., Ukraine.

Amvrosij lists a monastery of the Exaltation of the Holy Cross here[262], but no official lists or other sources name it.

13. PUŠKARKA (Puškarnja), Sumy obl., Ukraine.

Amvrosij lists this as a monastery of the Kiev eparchy[263]. However, the only monastery of similar name was Puškarivka outside Poltava.

14. SOKAL', on Buh r., 90 km N of Lviv; Lviv obl., Ukraine.

Although C'orox claims the authority of the Schematismus of the eparchy of Peremyšl' for 1879 for the existence of this monastery, the latter work mentions only Basilian monks in Sokal'[264].

15. TURIV.

A St Barbara monastery appears in a few lists, but the notices regarding it are extremely hazy and without a sound basis, so that its existence can well be doubted[265].

16. VYTOVKA (now Žovtneve), on the mouth of the Boh r.; Mykolajiv obl., Ukraine.

Zverinskij lists a monastery here, but there is no evidence for its existence[266].

---

[260] Secinskij, p. 331-332.
[261] According to C'orox, p. 65, it is mentioned in Maximilian Ryllo's diary. Cf. Petruševič, *Xolmskaja eparxija*, p. 242.
[262] Amvrosij, 4: 873.
[263] *Ibid.*, 5: 582.
[264] C'orox, p. 67; *Sxymatism vseho klyra ruskoho-katolyčeskoho Bohom spasemoi eparxii peremyšl'skoj na hod ot rožd. Xr. 1879* (Peremyšl', 1879), p. 344-345.
[265] Cf. Zverinskij, 3: 35, who draws all his information from Nikolaj, p. 161.
[266] Zverinskij, 3: 39.

17. ZIBOLKY (Dzibolky, now Pidlisne), 14 km E of Nesteriv; Lviv obl., Ukraine.

Kossak claims that a women's monastery in Zibolky is mentioned in the Krexiv pomjanyk of the seventeenth century[267]. However, a brief historical account of the churches of Zibolky, though cited by C'orox to support the claim, mentions only a Dominican monastery, not any monastery of ''Greek'' nuns[268].

---

[267] KOSSAK, p. 205.
[268] C'OROX, p. 61; *Sxymatism eparxii peremyšl'skoj 1879*, p. 203-204.

CHAPTER II

THE FOUNDING OF MONASTERIES

The proper setting of our study is the period from the revival of monastic life after the Mongol invasions to the suppressions of the late eighteenth century. Even within this segment the earlier centuries provide scant material. This entire period was not uniformly favorable to the founding and development of monasteries nor was it a period of steady advancement of the monastic life.

Rather, until the late sixteenth century there existed practically a vacuum as far as women's monasteries are concerned. The late sixteenth, all of the seventeenth, and the first years of the eighteenth century show in comparison remarkable vitality and growth. Then, in the eighteenth century, a progressive decline sets in, the official suppressions of the enlightened sovereigns Catherine II and Joseph II being only, in not a few cases, the coup de grace to many a monastery already on the point of extinction.

For the earlier period few sources on monastic life have survived. This is due partly to the scant remaining documentation on church life in general. But it also reflects the stagnation of monastic life in Ruthenian lands during the fourteenth through the sixteenth centuries. Properties continued to be called "monasteries" when the presence of monks or nuns there was not even a memory. We know at least the approximate date of founding of most monasteries which existed in the seventeenth and eighteenth centuries; these dates do not go further back than 1566[1]. If, and whatever monasteries existed earlier, in the fifteenth and early sixteenth centuries, they had only a brief, passing existence.

---

[1] Only 10 monasteries were founded earlier than that. Polock is a unique case, but one wonders if its existence was uninterrupted. Six monasteries did not survive to the end of the sixteenth century. Of the three remaining (Černihiv, Mahilev-Transfiguration, Pinsk), evidence for their existence previous to about 1580 is based only on local tradition unsupported by documentation.

The few sources at our disposal refer to small monasteries, not outstanding for their observance. This early period obviously did not provide conditions favoring the growth of monasteries. Monastic life reflected the decadence of church life in general.

The seventeenth century saw a resurgence of church life and culture, itself chiefly religious, in the lands of the Kievan metropolitanate. Political and social ferments culminated in the rising of Xmel'nyc'kyj (1648) and in the creation of the hetmanate state. Large-scale settlement of Left Bank Ukraine followed. Not only was Slobidščyna, in the Muscovite state, colonized then, but many new settlements arose in the Černihiv and Poltava territories of the hetmanate. The vitality of these various movements redounded on monastic life and was reflected in the founding of many new monasteries.

Founders

A first question regards the founders of monasteries: who they were and with what intent they acted. The condition so praised by the monk-compiler of the Primary Chronicle—''many monasteries are built by kings and nobles and the wealthy, but they are not like those built through tears, fasting, prayer, vigils''[2]—is hardly ever present.

In fact, one can note, stretching concepts and terms, only four examples with nuns themselves as foundresses, and in three of them it is a matter of fugitive nuns from elsewhere. The Poltava (Puškarivka) monastery was founded by nuns from Podillja in 1676. It seems probable that these came from some locality suffering from Turkish occupation after the fall of Kamjanec' Podil's'kyj to the Turks in 1672. In similar manner, the monastery in Lebedyn south of Kiev was founded by nuns fleeing from the Turks, this time from Moldavia, where their monastery had been pillaged. In 1750 a group of 14 nuns, 3 novices, and 3 girls came to Černihivščyna fleeing from persecution—from Latins and Uniates, the cry was. But investigation of the documents shows it to have been only from the heirs of their founders who wanted to reclaim, by whatever means, the land given to the monastery[3].

In the regions these nuns chose for their new homes they found persons who provided for them. In Lebedyn it was the local proprietor, Fr.X. Lubomirski, a great propagator of Orthodoxy at the expense of

---

[2] Under the year 1051 (6559), in the edition of Lixačev, 1: 107.
[3] Cf. *OASS*, 31: 175-177, 547-548.

the Uniates, though himself a Latin Catholic. In Černihivščyna the archimandrite of the Holy Trinity monastery of Černihiv, who soon after was nominated archbishop of Černihiv, Iraklij Komarovs'kyj, settled the nuns from Borejky in an abandoned skyt (a very small monastery in a solitary place, corresponding to the Russian *pustynja*) near Sosnycja.

Only in the case of Žydyčyn do we find nuns themselves really making the foundation. The exact year of it is not known, but it was probably shortly before 1621. In that year the nuns filed a complaint against the hostile actions of the Žydyčyn archimandrite. In it they describe the origins of their monastery: "[the archimandrite of Žydyčyn raided] their house by the church of the Holy Spirit in Žydyčyn, which they had built with their own money and from begging, with the help of their friends"[4].

Of the monasteries, about the origins of which we know nothing, there must also have been some that were founded by the nuns themselves. In Rozhirče, on the Dniester river, there was a small, poor community of nuns in the late eighteenth century, living in a previously constructed and then abandoned cave monastery[5]. It seems plausible to assume that an anchorite settled there, and then a few others joined her.

A peculiar type of foundation is what can only be called private monasteries, of which we have two examples. The first evidently was short-lived. In 1637 the home of Candida Langyš in Lviv was granted certain immunities because she and some companions were leading there a community life according to the rule of St Basil[6]. As further references to it have not been found, no doubt it lasted only during the lifetime of Candida, who was the daughter of a prominent member of the Lviv Stauropegian Confraternity. The second example is the monastic community at Bystrycja. The widow of a protopop of Hadjač, Anna Borzanovs'ka, took on a quasi-monastic life, and soon others joined her[7]. The monastery thus begun survived into the nineteenth century.

Who were the founders then? In the setting of those times it is obvious that they had to be persons (or, also, associations) with sufficient wealth not only to construct a monastery, but also to endow it with

---

[4] *Arxiv JuZR*, pt. I, 6: 504.
[5] An illustrated description of the monastery is given by V. KARPOVYč, Skal'nyj monastyr u Rozhirči, *AOSBM*, 3, no. 3-4 (1930): 562-573.
[6] The hramota granting the immunities is printed by KRYLOVSKIJ, p. 114-115.
[7] It does not appear in the list of the (Orthodox) Kiev eparchy in 1723, to which territorially it then belonged, when it had already been in existence at least 14 years, cf. OASS, 3, Priloženija, p. cxi-cxiii, but it is named in later lists, cf. the one from 1757 printed by ŠPAčINSKIJ, p. 229.

means of support. In this period that meant primarily real estate, either
arable fields and similar land or town lots and buildings which could
assure the monastery of sustenance.

Because the monastic life was considered especially God-pleasing,
pious people sought to participate in its merits if not by embracing it
themselves, then by founding monasteries or by ensuring their economic
security. This is especially evident in the first half of the seventeenth
century, when religion and religious questions were prominent in Ruthenian lands no less than in other European countries.

Thus Michael Kropyvnyc'kyj, in making an additional donation to
the Vinnycja monastery which he had founded, says he undertook it as
a good deed, that God might be continuously praised there and that
prayers might be offered for him and his wife, his ancestors and his pro-
geny[8].

The foundation grant to the Barkalabava monastery of Bohdan
Stetkevyč, whose family had founded a number of other Orthodox
monasteries and churches, is likewise worth noting. He says first that he
and his deceased wife had together resolved to build churches and found
monasteries on their properties, for the greater glory of God. Then he
adds specifically of the Barkalabava monastery: "In carrying out this
old resolution of mine, I do it not because of the persuasion or convic-
tion of others, but of my own firm resolve, freely, in the hope that the
Lord will be merciful to me both here in this world and in the future
life, and that through the prayers of pious persons dedicated to God I
may participate in God's unfailing promises and in exchange for tem-
poral goods receive eternal ones, and may leave for myself, for my wife,
and for my descendents prayers offered to God and an undying remem-
brance"[9].

The Gentry As Founders

In the late sixteenth and early seventeenth centuries, until they
became totally latinized, members of the Ruthenian nobility and gentry
often founded monasteries on their lands. The church and monastery of
Sts Florus and Laurus in Kiev were built by the Hul'kevyč family, which
had extensive possessions especially in the Kiev territory, on its property
in 1566[10].

---

[8] SECINSKIJ, p. 257-261.
[9] *Akty ZR*, 5:68-69
[10] *Akty JuZR*, 2:78.

Jasnohorod was situated in lands belonging to the Ostroz'kyj family, and the monastery there was founded by a member of that family. From 1592 we have the deed of foundation given by prince Constantine Ostroz'kyj to the nuns of the monastery he founded near Dubno. In it he expressed the wish that they "might live in the shelter of our ancestral land and might pursue their salvation in peace under our protection"[11].

Soon another wish came to be expressed in these deeds of foundation: that the monastery might be a stronghold of the Orthodox faith. Such a wish, and indeed condition, may be found in the grant of foundation dated 29 September 1631 given by Anna Oginska Stetkevyč and her son John to the Kutejno monastery near Orša:

> This our charter in all its points depends on these two paragraphs, that this women's monastery of Kutejno and its superior with the sister-nuns remain under the authority, obedience, and blessing of the holy see of Constantinople, and that the superior with the sister-nuns continue unfailingly to live the common life[12].

A similar condition is expressed by Anna Stetkevyč's other son Bohdan at his founding of the Barkalabava monastery[13].

One of the most prominent magnates of his time, Adam Kysil', in 1646 founded and endowed a monastery on his properties in Volyn' at Popivka. He was impelled to this, he says, by the recollection of the zeal for religion of his acestors and by the reflection that there were few monasteries for those well-born women of the Greek rite who wanted to enter the service of God[14]. He founded also the Makošyn monastery for nuns in Černihivščyna, as well as a monastery for monks in Nyzkynyči.

The monastery in Brahin was founded by prince Adam Korybut Vyšnevec'kyj and his wife Alexandra Xodkevyč in 1609. On the extensive properties of the Vyšnevec'kyj family in the Left Bank several monasteries were founded at about the same time, among them one for nuns at Ladyn. Another member of the Xodkevyč family, Anna, sister of the Lithuanian hetman Jan Karol Xodkevyč and wife of Bohdan (Bohuš) Korec'kyj, was also a foundress. In the characteristic milieu of such families in those times marked by the reformation and counter-

---

[11] *Arxiv JuZR*, pt. I, 6:90.

[12] *Akty ZR*, 4:523-524. The same act of foundation is also in *VZR*, 3 (1865), March, 6-13.

[13] *Akty ZR*, 5:68-72.

[14] *OASS*, 1:282.

reformation she passed from Orthodoxy to Calvinism to An-
titrinitarianism and, it was said, also to Judaism, then back to Orthodoxy. Towards the end of her life (she died in 1626) she founded a
monastery in Bilylivka on the family properties[15]. Her husband's father
Joachim had earlier, in 1571, founded a women's monastery in Korec'
itself.

Another family with holdings in Volyn', the Četvertyns'ki, founded
a monastery in Četvertnja in 1618. Prince Gregory Četvertyns'kyj and
his wife donated the land with its easements (uhodja), while his aunt,
Maria Hulevyč, wife of Adam Balaban, took it upon herself to have the
monastery and the church built[16].

On the Uniate side, Gregory Tryzna founded a monastery in Bycen'
which his daughter Euphrosine entered. Shortly afterwards, however,
the place of the nuns there was taken by Basilian monks, the monastery
becoming the novitiate house for them.

It was not rare for people of means, gentry and townsmen, to
found monasteries in this period. A functionary of the Crown, Michael
Kropyvnyc'kyj, founded the Vinnycja monastery in 1635[17]. In the
eastern regions Catherine Uhornyc'ka, the widow of an official, founded on her property at Ombyš a women's monastery, as well as one for
monks, around the year 1640[18]. The list would be greatly extended were
one to include the founders of men's monasteries.

Some foundresses became nuns and, as could be expected, the first
superiors of their monasteries. Examples of this are the Orthodox Minsk
Sts Peter and Paul monastery, founded by Eugenia Šembelev in 1617,
and the Catholic monastery in Navahrudek, founded by Christine
Borovs'ka in 1635. Several other women who wanted to become nuns
joined Christine Borovs'ka in founding the monastery. Metropolitan
Rutskyj endowed it with properties which the metropolitanate possessed
in that town[19].

Occasionally the foundation of a monastery served also personal
convenience. In 1675 Mariana Suxodolska founded a monastery on her

---

[15] The particulars about her given here seem to be, on the one hand, common
knowledge, but on the other, difficult to trace to their source: an account written out by
metropolitan Peter Mohyla, printed in *Arxiv JuZR*, pt. I, 7:66-67. Cf. *Słownik geograficzny Królestwa Polskiego i innych krajów słowiańskich*, 5:163.

[16] The foundation grant is in *Arxiv JuZR*, pt. I. 6:471-473.

[17] SECINSKIJ, p. 249-250.

[18] MJAKOTIN, 1, pt.1:81.

[19] This time the history of the founding is set out on the occasion of conflicting claims
to possession of some property in Navahrudek, see *OAZM*, 2:183.

property Mozolovščyna in the Mscislav voevodship. She was motivated, she says, by zeal for the glory of God, that the services of the Eastern Greek Church might be celebrated in perpetuity there and prayers offered for her family and her own soul when she died. She bequeathed her possessions to the monastery and intended to live out her life there—not as a nun, but as a laywoman-boarder[20]. This was a not uncommon practice in those times; other examples we shall note later.

Cossack Founders

One group of monastery founders can be singled out in the late seventeenth and early eighteenth centuries—the families of Cossack officials (staršyna). They were also prominent as benefactors of monasteries, and not infrequently members of these families themselves entered monasteries.

Here we shall note only some of the Cossack foundations. In 1693 the nuns of Korop turned to the widow of the Starodub polkovnyk Semen Samojlovyč (son of hetman Samojlovyč) with a request for land to found another monastery. The widow, Maria Sulyma, decided to found a monastery on her property in Pečenyky, to endow it, and to build a church for it[21].

A prominent example of a Cossack foundation is the Hamalijivka monastery. In 1702 Anton Hamalija, on the general staff of the hetmanate, founded a church of St Charlampius and, it seems, already then a monastery on his property. For his support of Mazepa he was exiled to Siberia in 1710 (but returned to Moscow two years later), and his properties were given to the new hetman Ivan Skoropada'kyj[22]. The hetman's enterprising and energetic wife Nastasja Markovna made the prosperity of the monastery her concern. Through her efforts the monastery was granted various lands, among them her father's properties after his death in 1712[23], and the properties of Andrew Horlenko, another of Mazepa's followers[24]. She obtained in 1714 the confirmation

---

[20] The deed of foundation, precise and detailed as was usual, may be found in *IJuM*, 14:511-518.

[21] *UA*, 1:296; cf. LAZAREVSKIJ, *Opisanie*, 1:144-145. Semen Samojlovyč, eldest son of hetman Samojlovyč, died in 1685 at 25 years of age; his widow was a "šljaxtanka" (*ibid.*, p.21-26).

[22] Cf. MODZALEVSKIJ, *Malorossijskij rodoslovnik*, 1:241.

[23] *Ibid.*, 3:388.

[24] *Ibid.*, 1:306.

of Peter I for all of these possessions for the monastery[25]. Hetman Skoropadas'kyj, who died on the return journey from a visit to Moscow in 1722, was buried in the warm church of the monastery[26]. In spite of, or perhaps because of all she obtained for the monastery, before her death in 1729 Markovna specified in her will that the nuns of Hamalijivka should make an exchange of monasteries with the monks of Mutyn. This stipulation was carried out after her death[27].

Some foundresses from Cossack families themselves intended to lead a monastic life. The Hluxiv monastery owed its origins to the widow of a Cossack official, Agatha Kymborovyč, Athanasia in monastic life[28]. It seems that the monastery in Nižyn began in a similar manner. It was founded by Anna Bryslavs'ka, also of a Cossack family, though it is not certain whether she herself was a nun there[29].

Of some monasteries Cossack officials may be regarded as second founders. In 1698 general judge Basil Kočubej transferred to the locality Pysarevščyna a monastery situated originally not far away, by the river Vorskla[30]. In 1721 the Poltava polkovnyk Ivan Černjak moved the nuns from the Pokrov monastery located in Poltava itself to his property in Puškarivka nearby[31].

Although we do not know the reasons for the transfers, it appears from the nature of both cases that they were carried out to ameliorate the conditions of the monasteries. The Poltava monastery did not possess a large plot in the town itself. The relocation, with the construction of a new stone church by the polkovnyk, which demonstrates his generosity and care, was from the material point of view definitely an advantage.

---

[25] Cf. E.V. BARSOV, Opisanie aktov arxiva Markeviča otnosjaščixsja k istorii južnorusskix monastyrej, ČOIDR, 1884, 2:27.

[26] The procesion, in which the nuns took part, that met the funeral cortege and the funeral in the Hamalijivka monastery are described by an eyewitness, Skoropads'kyj's secretary Mykola (Nikolaj) XANENKO in his Diariuš (published Moskva, 1858), p. 73-74.

[27] Cf. PSPR, (ser.I), 8:27.

[28] Cf. Ol. HRUŠEVS'KYJ, Het'mans'ki zemel'ni universaly 1660-1670 rokiv, Istoryčno-heohrafičnyj zbirnyk, 1 (1927): 72; VASILENKO, 1:358-361.

[29] Cf. M. Domontovič, Černigovskaja gubernija (Sanktpeterburg, 1865), p. 681. He, and others after him, write that her husband was the polkovnyk of Starodub, but there was none of that name, cf. LAZAREVSKIJ, Opisanie, 2:79. Perhaps he was a minor Cossack official of the Starodub polk.

[30] ZVERINSKIJ, 1:269, mentions the existence of a cave on the presumed site of the monastery. If his information is correct, we may have here in Poltavščyna a formation of a monastery similar to that in Roznirče in Halyčyna: an anchorite settled in a cave, others grouped themselves around her, and eventually a regular monastic community developed.

[31] Cf. AMVROSIJ, 5:652.

Brotherhoods `As Founders

Monasteries were also founded by associations. Sometimes these were informal groups of townspeople who collectively founded a monastery and supplied it with means of support. The St Nicholas monastery of Mahilev provides one example of this. A group of townspeople from the section of Mahilev known as Hryvljany bought some plots of land there and on them built a church and a monastery. They obtained permission to buy further plots to enlarge the church property and to hold two fairs a year, on the two feasts of St Nicholas (9 May and 6 December) for the support of their foundation. The charter of Ladislaus IV of 1646 by which approval is given for the women's monastery says:

> We confirm and strengthen our consent to the construction of the above-mentioned church and monastery as well as to the unhindered purchase by the people of Hryvljany for the enlargement of that church and monastery... Just as in our first privilege, as we saw how our townspeople of Hryvljany out of their deep piety from their own means bought land and plots in Hryvljany for putting up that church and monastery, in order that they might have some kind of support from us, we permitted them to hold at that church of St Nicholas two fairs, that is, on the solemn feasts of St Nicholas according to the old calendar in the spring and in the fall, so we confirm all these things with this our privilege for all times[32].

Two brotherhoods founded women's monasteries in addition to their monasteries for monks: the Vilna Holy Spirit brotherhood and the Lviv brotherhood of St Onuphrius. In Vilna it may have been due, more than anything else, to rivalry with the Uniate Holy Trinity brotherhood and monasteries, across 'the street from which dissatisfied *bratčyky* set up their own Orthodox stronghold.

Hierarchs and the Foundation of Monasteries

The Lviv brotherhood, in founding a women's monastery, turned to metropolitan Rahoza for his advice and blessing. We are thus led to

---

[32] *AS*, 2:70-71.

consider the role that hierarchs played in the founding of monasteries. Although some hierarchs are credited with founding monasteries, an attentive study of sources leads to the conclusion that such generous credit is, alas, usually unwarranted.

Occasionally this mistaken notion is easy to trace and correct. Thus, when Zverinskij says that the archbishop of Černihiv Lazar Baranovyč founded the monastery in Šumarovo[33], he really means that Baranovyč was the hierarch who authorized the foundation. The actual founder was Helen Roslavec', widow of a merchant and the monastery's first superior[34].

A more complicated case is the foundation of the Catholic monasteries in Minsk and Orša. Metropolitan Antony Sjeljava is usually given the credit[35]. His connection with the Orša monastery can almost definitely be discarded. Neither among his letters to Rome is there any mention of this monastery[36], nor is the monastery mentioned in his will, in which he leaves various sums of money to other monasteries with which he had ties[37]. As far as the Minsk Holy Spirit women's monastery is concerned, it is true that he had a new building put up[38], but in his will he calls Zuzanna Gąsiorowska the foundress of the monastery[39].

On the other hand, although we do find references in official letters to metropolitan Rutskyj as founder of the monastery in Navahrudek[40], as the account of its origins above showed he was not its founder in a true sense. Rutskyj gave it official ecclesiastical sanction and had it confirmed by Rome and was an early benefactor.

It is commonly and confidently asserted that Job Borec'kyj founded a women's monastery next to the St Michael's Zolotoverxyj monastery in Kiev around the time of his consecration as metropolitan in the renewed Orthodox hierarchy in 1620. But a historical survey of that monastery, a publication of the monastery itself, states that no evidence exists to warrant regarding him as founder and that the women's monastery existed already before his time[41].

---

[33] ZVERINSKIJ, 2:414.

[34] MODZALEVSKIJ, *Malorossijskij rodoslovnik*, 4:349.

[35] For instance, by WOŁYNIAK, p. 71, 78.

[36] His letters are in EM, vol.2.'

[37] The will is printed in *IJuM*, 2:255-286. It is summarized in *OAZM*, 1:293-298.

[38] There is a mention of this in the brief biography from the Greek College, *EM*, 2:177.

[39] *IJuM*, 2:260. Later she tried to reclaim part of the grant she had made to the monastery, and the nuns took the matter up in court, cf. *Sapiehowie*, 3:116-117.

[40] Cf. *Documenta Pontificum Romanorum historiam Ucrainae illustrantia*, 1:499-500.

[41] *Kievo-Zlatoverxo-Mixajlovskij monastyr'*, p.49-50.

Only two foundations by bishops remain. The monastery in Xolm, various authors assert, was founded by Jakiv Suša in 1654[42]. A lack of sources prevents us from examining this in detail. In the latter part of the eighteenth century metropolitan Felicjan Volodkovyč, who also retained the eparchy of Volodymyr, built a monastery for nuns in Volodymyr Volyns'kyj by the parish church of St Elias[43]. Although Volodkovyč claimed that a women's monastery had existed there earlier, had there ever been any such, even the memory of it was lost by his time. The pastor of St Elias was the dean of the Volodymyr cathedral chapter[44]. As could be expected, the Volodymyr chapter, supported by Volodkovyč's coadjutor Antony Mlodovs'kyj, reacted and prolonged litigation ensued[45]. The suspicion arises that at least one of the motives of the foundation was the metropolitan's desire to take the church from the chapter.

The monasteries of Korobivka and Ladyn, both located in Poltavščyna, have similar origins one century apart. Around 1615 Isaiah Kopyns'kyj, at that time superior of the monastery in Hustyn' and later metropolitan of Kiev, began the building of the Ladyn monastery on lands belonging to the Vyšnevec'kyj family. It was meant for monks, but early in its existence Isaiah changed his intentions and obtained from his benefactress, Raina Korybut Vyšnevec'ka, approval to transform it into a women's monastery, with his sister Alexandra as the first ihumenja[46].

In 1719 the ihumen of a monastery in Mošnohory, a hilly region south of Kaniv in the Right Bank, thought of transferring it to the Left Bank and began to build one near the village of Korobivka. He too soon changed his mind, before even the monastery was finished, and it was then given over to a community of nuns, with one of his sisters, Manassija, as the superior[47].

Procedure of Founding

As regards the actual procedure of founding, on the basis of acts of foundation we see that as a rule first the authorization ("blessing") of a

---

[42] Cf. BATJUŠKOV, p.100; PLOŠČANSKIJ, 2:73-74.

[43] Cf. EM, 6:413-414.

[44] Since 1608, cf. Arxiv JuZR, pt.I, 6:386-388.

[45] Volodkovyč's letters are full of complaints about this, see for instance, EM, 6:458-460 (no. 283-284).

[46] Vyšnevec'ka's consent to the formation of a women's monastery is in Akty ZR, 4:503-504.

[47] AMVROSIJ, 4:211-212.

hierarch was sought. For Uniate monasteries this was formally laid down as a rule at the fifth congregation of the Basilian monks in 1629 in Žyrovyci: "We determine that monastery buildings, whether of monks or of nuns, may not be built without the express permission of the metropolitan or his coadjutor"[48]. Only the metropolitan is mentioned here because at this time he—Rutskyj—was also protoarchimandrite. Monasteries of nuns, however, always had dealings with local bishops and with the metropolitan only if they were located in his eparchy.

As regards Orthodox monasteries, a few examples will best illustrate this point. The foundation document for Novi Mlyny, dated 22 June 1657 and issued by Christopher Sylyč from Brahin, says, for instance:

> With the blessing and permission of... Silvester Kosov, by God's grace Orthodox metropolitan of Kiev and Halyč and all Rus', having received his blessing and permission for this holy deed, I grant in perpetuity my own plot of ground...[49].

At times Orthodox founders turned directly to the patriarch of Constantinople for the authorization, as in the case of the founding of the monastery in Četvernja in 1618, when it was difficult or impossible to have recourse to a local Orthodox bishop. This holds for the period 1596-1633, when the Orthodox hierarchy was not officially recognized in the Polish-Lithuanian Commonwealth and was greatly reduced.

Generally the permission of civil authorities also had to be obtained. The universal of hetman Demjan Mnohohrišnyj for the foundation of the Hluxiv monastery in 1671 may serve as an example. The hetman wrote:

> Since the illustrious and most reverend... Lazar Baranovyč, archbishop of Černihiv, Novhorod, and lord and pastor of the whole Siver, seeing the piety of the reverend nun Athanasia Jevfymovna, at her request has permitted her, with his blessing, to found the monastery of the Transfiguration of the Lord on her own land in the town of Hluxiv...; then we too, acceding to the will of our... pastor... have confirmed his letter and have permitted the founding of the above-mentioned monastery[50].

---

[48] As no.16 of the second session, *AS*, 12:34.

[49] LAZAREVSKIJ, Akty, p.60. Sylyč meant his foundation for monks and gave the deed to the ihumen of Baturyn, with the injunction to found a monastery on that property. The latter, however, promptly turned the deed over to the nuns of Baturyn, who then founded the monastery in Novi Mlyny.

[50] VASILENKO, 1: 361.

In another instance, hetman Mazepa gave his authorization for the founding of the Pečenyky monastery provided that the archbishop of Černihiv gave his[51].

The founding of monasteries in Poland-Lithuania needed first the authorization of the king. We have several examples of charters granting such authorization. A hramota of Ladislaus IV of 1635 permits the founding of the monastery in Vinnycja[52]. From 1648 there is a charter of the same king permitting the Orthodox to build a church and/or a monastery of monks or of nuns in Lupalov, a suburb of Mahilev[53]. In both cases the properties on which the monasteries were to be built were under the jurisdiction of the towns.

The one notable exception to the need for royal confirmation were monasteries founded on the property of the szlachta, on which the owner could freely build or found whatever he chose without any restrictions. Explicit mention was made of such exemption, especially when it was important in a particular case. As we have seen above, the foundress of the Sts Peter and Paul monastery in Minsk was a townswoman, Eugenia Šembelev. In 1612 she did not find it possible to obtain permission from the authorities to found an Orthodox monastery in Minsk. As she recounts in her will, written in 1637, she gave money for the foundation to Anna Oginska Stetkevyč, who, as her founding of the Kutejno monasteries makes evident, was a fervent Orthodox[54]. Anna Stetkevyč then acquired property in Minsk, founded the monastery, and turned the deed to it over to Eugenia and her compaions. In the deed she emphasized her rights to found the monastery: "utilizing my freedom as szlachta, that eveyone can do what he likes with his property, immovable and movable, to give it to whomever he likes, by sale or gift, to will it to a church or a monastery"[55].

A largely unanswered question regards the persons who actually began monastic life in a new foundation—its first nuns. Someone deciding to build a monastery must have known for whom he was building it. One account that does provide some information is related in the foundation charter of Barkalabava. The founder, Bohdan Stetkevyč, specified that the ihumen of Kutejno should take counsel with the superior and all the sisters of the Kutejno women's monastery. From among these sisters should be chosen someone pious and capable

---

[51] LAZAREVSKIJ, *Opisanie*, 1: 144-145.

[52] *IJuM*, 25: 259-262.

[53] SECINSKIJ, p. 249-250.

[54] Printed in *VZR*, 2 (1863), November, 11-16.

[55] *Ibid.*, October, p. 11.

for the superior of the new monastery as well as others, "as many as may be necessary", to accompany her[56]. This no doubt was the procedure in other new monasteries which had ties with older ones. It is known, for instance, that four nuns from the Vilna Holy Trinity monastery were sent to start the Holy Spirit foundation in Minsk. Otherwise, a monastery began with local women who were attracted to that kind of life.

Prerogatives of Founders

It was the accepted custom that founders in their deeds of foundation specify obligations on the part of the nuns (such as certain prayers for the founder and his family) and lay down certain regulations. Such founders' rules (ktytors'ki ustavy; ktytor means founder or, more broadly, benefactor) are valuable in giving us a glimpse of the internal life of a monastery—provided, of course, that they were kept[57]. Specific items will be discussed later, but here their spirit can be analyzed in a preliminary manner.

For the Orthodox founders of the seventeenth century—and most deeds of foundation come from them—it was a great preoccupation that their foundations should remain forever Orthodox. This finds expression, for instance, in directives for the removal of those superiors who should become Uniate, as we find in the rules of Barkalabava and Mozoliv[58]. The Barkalabava founder's rule especially insists on this point and repeatedly stresses that the monastery chaplain too should be only a priest who recognizes the authority of the patriarch of Constantinople. This is a reflection of the general struggle between Orthodoxy and Union that dominated the period from the union of Brest at the end of the sixteenth century to the unions of the eparchies of Peremyšl', Lviv, and Luc'k at the turn of the seventeenth-eighteenth centuries.

Perhaps it also provides one explanation for the vigor of monasticism at that time. In a period of intense, if rather unthinking and explosive religious feeling, stimulated by ceaseless litigations over properties, demands about rights or protection of rights, heightened by the Cossack wars[59], it is not strange that such manifest expressions of

---

[56] *Akty ZR*, 5: 69.

[57] It is always hazardous to reconstruct actual conditions from the letter of the law.

[58] *Akty ZR*, 5: 70 (Barkalabava); *IJuM*, 14: 515-516 (Mozoliv).

[59] Yet one should not view this period exclusively as one of conflict. Any true picture must include examples such as the following. In 1702 an Orthodox *burmistr* (town official)

religious convictions as monasteries were built and peopled more than in calmer periods. On the other hand, an effort was often made to ensure that the life in monasteries would be in accordance with certain fundamental principles of monastic life, especially common life. These are set out in founders' rules; that they bore good fruit, especially in the immediate period, will be shown in other chapters of this study.

of Mahilev, M. Kaškevyč, in his will, in which he left various sums of money to numerous Orthodox churches and monasteries, included also this entry: "do Żołkwi, ...na cerkiew... złotych trzysta, na wyżywienie oycom, czyli też popom, złotych tysiąc, niech będzie czy uniacka, czy iaka" (*IJuM*, 11: 214).

CHAPTER III

THE ECONOMICS OF MONASTERIES

The best documented aspect of monastic life is that related to various economic matters. This is not surprising, since this side of monasticism often requires an involvement of civil authorities (or emanates from them) and legal formalities. Economic transactions and economic status, therefore, are fixed in public records and in fortunate cases are published. Such matters are also intrinsically important: without a sound economic basis monasteries simply dissolved in a very short time.

The work of the nuns themselves in the period under study (seventeenth-eighteenth centuries) was negligible towards the support of the monasteries and will be treated later, with other facets of the internal life of monasteries. The only exception are very poor and very small monasteries, in which the work of the nuns was the main source of income. This was the case with the monasteries of Halyčyna at the end of the eighteenth century[1] and no doubt earlier, throughout their existence.

Now we shall treat of sources of income, the wealth of monasteries and their material condition, and their relations with civil authorities regarding this aspect of monastic life. We shall take monasteries by regions and chronologically within the regions.

Comparisons are not easy to make. First of all, our data on the wealth of monasteries is far from complete. It is still more difficult to interpret it. In addition to the obvious difficulty of determining even the approximate value of the innumerable terms of currency and measure which, besides, were not stable even in any one region, there is also that of comparing different forms of economic life. Although everywhere ownership of land was a basis of wealth, feudal obligations, for instance, were not the same in the early eighteenth century in eastern

---

[1] As reported by government officials, see CHOTKOWSKI, p. 140.

Belorussia and in the Starodub polk—to keep only to the same time and to neighboring territories with frequent contacts between them, though situated in different states. Monasteries in the towns of the grand duchy of Lithuania collected rents from buildings owned in the towns, while those in Left Bank Ukraine fees from flour mills.

To begin with, because it is a phenomenon that appears in the early part of our period, monasteries were not only objects of the Christian charity of the populace, but also sources of income for certain individuals. Some monasteries were in the personal possession of individuals or the hereditary possession of certain families. The granting of ecclesiastical properties to laypeople by the Polish kings was only too common in the sixteenth century.

However such situations arose, we have a vivid description of what they entailed. In 1545 a description of the fortresses of Volyn' and of their holdings was compiled. It was observed that formerly some monasteries had been benefices at the king's disposition, from which he received not a small income, but now they were held by others.

> The first is the monastery of the Holy Virgin at Peresopnycja, which the late prince Czortoryiski the starosta of Luc'k had sought for his mother to live and to be sustained there to the end of her life; she was supposed to become a nun. And prince Czortoryiski kept the monastery for himself, and now his sons hold the monastery for themselves. And to this monastery belongs the village Hrabovo, in which there are one hundred people, the dues from which yield a koloda of honey and ten kopy of money[2].

There follows a description of other holdings of the monastery. Then, after mentioning other monasteries, the author of the description gives his reflections on the matter:

> We consider, with regard to all these monasteries, that their holders asked for and retain them not for any glory of God and prayers for the king, but on account of their great sin and avarice, because whatever benefits and income used to accrue to the church of God, and from which the brethren and the monastery servants were sustained and offered incessant prayers for the king, they now have turned it over to their own use[3].

---

[2] *Pamjatniki*, 4: 188. A *koloda* was a measure of liquids, principally honey, and sometimes other foodstuffs. A koloda of honey contained about 120-140 liters. *Kopa* means 60; here it refers to 60 Lithuanian units of currency (groši). A kopa of Lithuanian money was always equivalent to 2 1/2 Polish zloty.

[3] *Ibid.*, p. 189-190.

At Ovruč in the late fifteenth century two monasteries were held by laypeople, to whom they were granted by the great prince[4], and there were any number of others for which no documentation exists. The St Florus monastery in Kiev was held in a similar manner by the Hul'kevyč family until 1632, when Ivan Bohuš Hul'kevyč, himself then a monk at Sluck, ceded his rights over it to Agatha Humenyc'ka, the ihumenja of the monastery. By the seventeenth century, though, this particular means of exploiting monasteries for one's gain had almost disappeared, though a few examples of men's monasteries still crop up.

Belorussian Monasteries

Thanks to the great number of official records pertaining to Belorussian lands which were published in the last century, we have a more complete picture of the economic conditions of monasteries in Belorussia than in other Ruthenian territories.

One of the most detailed reports about a monastery's holdings is also the earliest. A full listing of the properties of the Savior monastery in Polock was drawn up in 1580, when both the monastery and its properties had already been confiscated. But it reflects the situation prior to 1563, when the entire Polock province was taken by the Muscovites, who held it until 1579. The report notes repeatedly that most of the settlements described in it have now been deserted or the lands usurped by the local gentry. In the case of one village it states explicitly that all but two of its twenty household had been dispersed because of the war. The description can in no sense be considered typical; of the few women's monasteries existing around the middle of the sixteenth century no other had holdings nearly as extensive. However, it is one of the rare items of information of that period and gives a complete account of at least the material status of the Polock monastery[5].

The monastery owned twenty-six small villages. In only four cases is the obligation of work mentioned and when it is, it consisted of two weeks in the spring (in two instances) and also in the fall (in the other two instances). The obligations consisted rather in dues of produce and money. The dues in nature were as follows (totals for all the villages): 34 pudy of honey, plus, from two villages, half of their annual production; 112 korcy of rye; 63 korcy of barley; 19 1/2 units of flax; from

---

[4] *Akty ZR*, 1: 164.
[5] It is printed in *IJuM*, 2: 286-316.

three villages also one fourth (every fourth sheaf) of the harvest; 90
bundles of wood; 300 logs[6]. Beaver trapping for the monastery is mentioned twice and fishing four times. The rents in money amounted to
almost 13 kopy. The monastery was thus well provided for.

The villages provided also for the support of various officials of the
monastery, who received money or produce. There is one mention of a
"bobrowniczy Jhumienniny"—the man who trapped beavers for the
monastery. The monastery must have employed many others to administer its extensive lands, collect the rents from them, and perform the
various works—a collector, "birczy Jhumienniny", is mentioned.

Although the nuns at this time lost their monastery, they somewhat
later resettled in Polock itself, next to the cathedral of St Sophia. The
archbishop of Polock Josaphat Kuncevyč built a monastery for them
with an orchard by it, endowed it with properties belonging to the eparchy, and assigned to it an annual contribution from the eparchy's
revenues of grain and other produce[7]. The monastery's fortunes seem to
have soon revived. Metropolitan Antony Sjeljava mentions that in Rutskyj's time yet he, then archbishop of Polock, borrowed from it 600
kopy of Lithuanian money[8].

When a monastery was founded by a wealthy family or individual it
was given at the outset sufficient possessions for its support. Sometimes
an annual income in money—the interest on a sum or revenues from
some property—or an annual supply of provisions was given. Such
means of support were not very secure, since they could easily be
stopped from one year to the next. Not that a deed to a property always
gave greater security. The property could always be contested or
usurped, and since courts in the Polish-Lithuanian Commonwealth left
the execution of their decrees to the plaintiffs, reclaiming one's property
or goods was no easy matter.

There is an example of nuns turning to their founder to ask for a
larger endowment because the original foundation was insufficient to
meet the monastery's needs. Bohdan Stetkevyč, who circa 1641 had
founded the monastery at Barkalabava, had endowed it with 6 voloky[9]
of arable land, 6 voloky for pasture, a mill, with fishing facilities in the

---

[6] A *pud* was equivalent to about 16.38 kg. *Korec'* was a unit of measure of grains,
containing about 100 kg.

[7] A Latin copy of his endowment of 1621 is in APF, Miscellanee diverse, 19, fol.
444-446.

[8] *IJuM*, 2: 269-270.

[9] A *voloka*, like most measures in eastern Europe, did not have stable value. In
Lithuania it equalled a little over 21 hectares.

millpond and in a stream as well as in the Dnieper. In 1643 he gave another piece of ground for a vegetable garden to the sisters there, "seeing the poverty of the land of the Barkalabava nuns..., complying with their request"[10]. In 1652, on behalf of the same monastery, which had grown quickly in size, the son of the founders was asked to permit the transfer of half the land given previously to the Bujnyči monastery, which request was granted[11]. The consequences of his property transfer a century later will be treated below.

The foundress of the Mozoliv monastery, Marianna Suxodolska, gave over to it her entire inheritance: three villages, the inhabitants of which had obligations both of rents and of work, and various types of easements. She retained for her own use all movable property and money, but after her death all this too was to go the monastery[12].

The holdings of extinct monasteries were assigned at times to existing ones. In 1609 Barbara Sapieha—Vasilissa in the monastery—, superior of the Holy Trinity monastery in Vilna, received for the benefit of the monastery the holdings of a former monastery near Braslav[13]. In 1614 the king gave her for the support of her community the monastery in Lješč[14], but she renounced its possession in favor of the metropolitan and the Basilian monks in 1633[15].

This Uniate monastery of Vilna enjoyed the support of a number of prominent families. The Holy Trinity church and monasteries had traditionally enjoyed the patronage of the Sapieha family. Paul Sapieha mentions in a letter to Christopher Radziwill in 1598 earlier family grants as well as his own, which included also provisions for the nuns[16].

. When Vasilissa Sapieha entered his monastery she renovated it from her own funds[17]. Her uncle Leo Sapieha, voevoda of Vilna and hetman of the grand duchy of Lithuania, and her brother Paul Sapieha, vice-chancellor of Lithuania, both endowed the monastery with lands.

Anastasia Tryzna Zawisza, wife of the voevoda of Vicebsk Jan Zawisza, gave the Holy Trinity monastery, where perhaps her aunt Euphrosine Tryzna had spent a short time as a nun, a large building in Vilna[18].

---

[10] *AV*, 11: 133.
[11] *AS*, 2: 71-74.
[12] *IJuM*, 14: 511-518.
[13] *Akty JuZR*, 2: 53-54.
[14] Cf. *OAZM*, 1: 200, where some damage to that property is described.
[15] APF, Scritture riferite nelle Congregazioni generali, 306, fol. 446.
[16] *Archiwum domu Sapiehów*, 1: 194.
[17] *Sapiehowie*, 1: 246.
[18] *AV*, 9: 408.

Some of their gifts and other possessions of the monastery in 1639 are listed in a confirmatory charter of Ladislaus IV: two land properties, four large buildings in Vilna, as well as the monastery enclosure proper[19]. Three of the buildings had been bought by the monastery, which indicates that it had appropriately large funds, the gifts of these and other wealthy families. In this period we can note that Eugenia Catherine Vyšnevec'ka, for example, left 1000 Polish zloty for the monastery[20]—a sum sufficient to buy more than one large building.

Monasteries turned frequently to civil authorities for a confirmation of rights or for the granting of immunities. In conjunction with the confirmation of possessions or separately authorities often freed monasteries from various obligations. The confirmatory charter cited above to the Vilna Holy Trinity monastery exempted the buildings owned by the monastery from the quartering of officials during court assizes and other assemblies that gathered in the capital of the grand duchy.

Monasteries situated in Lithuania suffered from the wars between Muscovy and Poland-Lithuania. We have already noted how the war conducted by tsar Ivan IV affected the Polock monastery. A century later, when Alexius attacked Lithuania, the nuns at Polock were again displaced. They sought refuge in the west[21] and when they returned in 1667 they discovered that all their documents, which had been in the keeping of the Polock town secretary, had perished. In 1670 we hear of them living in great poverty and need[22].

This war caused hardships to all Uniate monasteries in Lithuania. The nuns of the Holy Trinity monastery in Vilna also lost all their documents, as they were crossing the Vilja river, fleeing before Muscovite troops which took Vilna in 1655. The nuns themselves got across safely, but the large, heavy coffer with their documents sank. They seem to have settled for the duration of the hostilities on their property near Ošmjanka (southeast of Vilna): they entered a formal

---

[19] *AS*, 10: 268-270; repeated by John Sobieski in his charter of 1688, *AV*, 9: 264-267. The building given by Anastasia Tryzna was sold in 1740 for 2000 Pol. zl., *AV*, 9: 329-332.

Another branch of the Tryzna family remained Orthodox, and another Anastasia Tryzna left a bequest to the nuns of the Orthodox Holy Spirit monastery in Vilna, *AV*, vol. 11, no. 68.

[20] Cf. *AV*, vol. 11, no. 66.

[21] Where in particular is not evident. Upon returning to Polock, the ihumenja said they had returned "s kraiow Litewskich", *IJuM*, 26: 166.

[22] They speak of their own condition: "U velykom ubostve i nedostatku meškajučy" (*ibid.*, 25: 238).

declaration and description of their lost documents in the town records of Ošmjanka in 1656[23]. The nuns from the Minsk monastery of the Holy Spirit took refuge on their property near Hrodna in 1655[24].

This state of unsettlement lasted as long as the Muscovite occupation of Lithuania, since Alexius gave orders that no Uniates be permitted to remain[25]. When the sisters thus left their monasteries for several years, during their absence the monastic property must often have been looted and damaged. The account of the fortunes of the Pinsk monastery is especially interesting because it was related by the superior of the St Barbara monastery Euphrosine Tryzna. She describes the attempts to convince the nuns to abjure the Union; her own constancy and courage, as well as that of the other sisters, appear clearly in the account. They came out safely, but their monastery and church were set on fire[26].

A circumstantial picture of how the war affected Orthodox monasteries is provided in the case of Kutejno and Barkalabava. Alexius entered Lithuanian territory in 1654; in August he took Mahilev and in September Smolensk. Two nuns from the Kutejno monastery accompanied the vicar of the Kutejno men's monastery Dorotej to the tsar in Smolensk to ask for a protective letter for their monasteries and properties. This the tsar granted, extending it to all people who might seek refuge from the hostilities at the monasteries[27].

Soon afterwards the tsar's forces attempted to take the town of Byxov, twelve miles form Barkalabava. The nuns of Barkalabava turned to the tsar for protection from the soldiery, who issued orders in compliance with the request[28]. When the Muscovite forces were forced to retreat somewhat, the monastery sent some of its members to Byxov to ask that the defensive forces, in issuing out of Byxov, should not pillage the monastery. A local official sent four men to the monastery for its protection, but kept five nuns in Byxov as hostages. Of the four men sent to guard this monastery, two went off somewhere, and the other two were captured by the Muscovites[29].

However, things did not go too badly for this Orthodox monastery.

---

[23] Cf. *AV*, 9: 408.

[24] Cf. *Sapiehowie*, 2: 139.

[25] See his instructions to the voevoda of Vilna, *AI*, 4: 261.

[26] Euphrosine's letter to bishop Jakiv Suša of Xolm in a Latin version is in *LB*, 1 97-100.

[27] Cf. *Akty JuZR*, 14: 207-210.

[28] *Ibid.*, p. 365-368.

[29] *Ibid.*, p. 444-445.

Once the Muscovites were installed in those parts, in 1655 a letter was sent to Alexius on its behalf by the commander of the forces Ivan Zolotarenko, which asked for alms for the monastery[30]. The tsar began to supply it with annual provisions. Nor were other means wanting to it. A certain Fedka Mixajlov, while in the tsar's army and under siege in Mahilev, had his fishing boats robbed. The nets turned up in the Barkalabava monastery. He requested the tsar to order their restitution, and a dispatch to that effect went out to the monastery[31].

In 1656, during his campaign, Alexius visited the monastery at Kutejno. As a result, by his orders the monastery was to receive annually from the state treasury 300 rubles and 330 quarters of rye[32]. In 1660 at the request of its ihumenja Fotynja Kyrkor and the other sisters, they were granted annually 3 pudy of wax for candles and 2 pails of church wine and for the sisters 350 rubles and 300 quarters of rye[33].

This monastery frequently sent out nuns to beg alms in Moscow. The first mention of this is from 1658[34]. In 1674 it was permitted to make two such trips yearly—more frequently than other monasteries, because it described itself as oppressed by enemies and the only refuge of the Orthodox in its region[35]. In 1679, though, it was prosperous enough to buy a property of four voloky and three lots in the town of Orša from the Dominicans there[36]. Up to the end of the seventeenth century its alms-begging trips to Moscow are mentioned frequently.

We can describe one such trip, made in 1691 by two nuns of the monastery accompanied by two servants. During their stay in Moscow, which lasted two weeks, the nuns received daily 4 kopeks, 1 tankard of mead, 2 tankards of beer, and food. Both upon arrival and upon departure each nun received three rubles and a pair of sable skins. For their monastery they were given sable skins worth 30 rubles. On their return trip they were supplied with the same daily provisions as during their stay in Moscow and also with conveyance as far as Smolensk[37].

In succeeding reigns restrictions were placed on seeking alms in Muscovy. The frequent trips of Kutejno nuns into Russia provoked in

---

[30] *Ibid.*, p. 721-722.

[31] *Ibid.*, p. 859-862.

[32] Mix. Osip. Bez-Kornilovič, *Istoričeskija svedenija o primečatel'nejšix mestax v Belorussii s prisovokupleniem i drugix svedenij k nej že otnosjaščixsja* (Sanktpeterburg, 1855), p. 200-201.

[33] *AI*, 4: 457.

[34] Cf. Xarlampovič, p. 94.

[35] *Ibid.*, p. 353-354.

[36] Cf. *IJuM*, 26: 379-384.

[37] Cf. *OASS*, 5, pribavlenija, p. cl.

1742-1743 an investigation of the monastery's properties, income, and needs, as well as of the annual provisions made by Alexius but stopped several decades earlier. A plan was devised to provide it with specific amounts of money and flour annually[38], which was approved with the proviso that the monastery never have more than seventy-four nuns (the number there at that time)[39].

Large and small donations and legacies in money were left, especially to the town monasteries in Lithuanian lands. At times they illuminate the entire milieu from which they spring in a mode quite at odds with the one made familiar by a long series of historians. When Vilna was occupied by the forces of Alexius (1655-1661), an Orthodox merchant of Vilna, Samuel Bočočka, disposing of his earthly goods in 1657, left sums to various church institutions. These included the two monasteries of monks and of nuns by the Holy Spirit church, but also the Catholic monastery of nuns of the Holy Trinity[40]. Actually, during this period this women's monastery was unoccupied; its Uniate nuns returned only after the Muscovites were forced to withdraw in 1661.

Another will, dated 1663, was written by another Samuel, Fylypovyč, a town councillor of Vilna and a Uniate (we can determine the last fact on the basis of his choice of a place of burial: the Holy Trinity church). He piously made gifts to the two monasteries of the Holy Trinity, but did not omit the nuns by the church of the Holy Spirit either[41].

But no doubt the most extraordinary document of all is the will of a Vilna townsman, Kondrat Parfianovyč, written in 1664. He was Orthodox (he asked to be buried in the Holy Spirit church), but his daughter Marusja was at this time living under the care of the sisters "by the Uniate church of the Holy Trinity". Moreover, she had expressed a desire to become a nun herself, there, at Holy Trinity, a wish he quite approved of. Besides making provisions fo her, he also left sums to the Orthodox nuns of Holy Spirit (40 zl.) and to the Uniate nuns of Holy Trinity (25 zl.)[42].

Sometimes the sums left to women's monasteries were fairly large. Michael Hutorovyč, a town official of Mahilev, in 1702 left in favor of the Barkalabava monastery 600 zl. for the church, 300 zl. for the nuns, and 300 zl. for memorial services (*sorokousty*), and similar bequests for

[38] *Ibid.*, 16: 73-74; 23: 34-38.
[39] *PSPR*, Elizabeth, 3: 141.
[40] *AV*, 9: 491.
[41] *Ibid.*, p. 494.
[42] *Ibid.*, p. 499.

the Kutejno and Sluck monasteries[43]. Donations with the obligation of prayer in return were common. In 1763 the wife of a starosta gave the Vicebsk Holy Spirit monastery 200 talers, while the nuns obligated themselves to prayers for the souls of her parents[44].

At times donors left money or lands jointly to several monasteries which had ties among them. In 1669 the ihumen of the Holy Trinity monastery of Vilna obligated himself to pay over to the women's monastery its part of a legacy[45]. The Orthodox monastery of the Holy Spirit in Vilna received generous endowments from the Radziwill family. Maria Lupul, daughter of the hospodar of Moldavia Basil Lupul and widow of Janusz Radziwill, hetman of Lithuania, carrying out her deceased husband's wishes in 1659 gave the two monasteries by the church of the Holy Spirit 150.000 Polish zloty—a very large sum, though how much of it went to the nuns is not known. In her own will, written on the same date in 1659, she left equal sums to the two Holy Spirit monasteries of Vilna and, among other bequests, sums to the women's monasteries of Minsk (Sts Peter and Paul) and Sluck[46].

As concerns dowries in Uniate monasteries, the Synod of Zamość specified a sum, but in fact it was determined by time and place[47]. In Lithuania the practice was common, differently than in western Ukraine, as we shall see. According to the prescriptions of the Synod, novices were to pay for their board[48]. Examples of this occur: we find a novice at Holy Trinity in Vilna bequeathing her inheritance to the monastery, except for 1000 zl. set aside for the expenses of her novitiate[49]. There are also frequent references to the "wyprawa"—an outfitting with the things a nun might need[50].

A similar practice was general in Orthodox monasteries. In the

---

[43] *IJuM*, 11: 212.

[44] *Ibid.*, 19: 116-119.

[45] *AV*, 11: 189-191.

[46] *Ibid.*, p. 149; 12: 585-592.

[47] The sum was 1500 zloty (about 200 talers), see *SPR*, p. 110. The sum is rather high; actual amounts recorded in various documents all revolve around this figure and sometimes are even higher. At Vilna in the 1730's a dowry of 2000 zl. is recorded. At the entrance of Constance Jelenska 1000 zl. was given to the monastery, 500 zl. was spent on her outfitting when she received the habit, and of the remaining 500 zl. part was used by Constance for medicines and the rest paid over to the monastery, see *AV* 11: 493-494 and 498-501. At Vicebsk in 1750 the dowry was 150 talers (*IJuM*, 18: 417-420), while in 1761 it was set at 300 talers (*IJuM*, 19: 104).

[48] "Tempore probationis suis pecuniis alatur", *SPR*, p. 111.

[49] *AV*, 9: 462.

[50] *Ibid.*, 11: 304.

testament of the foundress of the Sts Peter and Paul monastery in Minsk is a list of sums the first nuns brought in (which includes, in every case, also a silver spoon)[51]. The sums were large. It is stated that the money was used to buy properties for the monastery, while the remainder was loaned on interest.

* * *

Loaning money was a frequent economic enterprise of Lithuanian monasteries. The amounts a monastery loaned indicate the economic well-being of the monastery. It is difficult to say, though, whether making loans was a profitable transaction. Although as a rule some property—land or a building—was handed over to the lender in temporary possession as surety until the loan should be repaid, it often happened that this property was retaken by force by the original owner without the loan and the accruing interst ever being repaid.

A few examples of loans, which we shall give below, will give some idea of the financial condition of monasteries. The height of prosperity for most monasteries falls in the seventeenth century, and it is then that the most and the largest loans were made.

The date of the loan is not always noted. We have very often not the original agreement, but a description of it made when reclaiming the loan through the courts. No doubt there were debtors honest enough to repay loans. What we observe, though, are such frequent refusals of repayment that we can only wonder why the monasteries continued to make such unprofitable transactions. Even if in court the case was adjudicated in the monastery's favor, it did not mean that the monastery won it. As has already been mentioned, no provision was made in the Polish-Lithuanian Commonwealth for organs to carry out judicial decrees. It was up to the creditor to find ways and means to recover the money and court costs. In the majority of cases this was a hopeless undertaking.

Together with the long period of wars (1648-1721) and the falling value of currency, property disputes with the ensuing damages and court costs brought even once flourishing monasteries to ruin. In this, it should be stressed, they shared the conditions and fate of other institutions of the Commonwealth. Records of these cases throw light on the economic conditions of monasteries and provide also some information

---

[51] *VZR*, 2 (1863), November, p. 14.

on other aspects of monastic life. At times only references to lawsuits are found, or only one moment of their course, but in a few cases available materials provide us with a good idea of what they entailed.

Only a few notices about loans and their consequences can be given here. In 1652 the Vilna Holy Trinity monastery had made a loan of 3000 zl. The debtor died without repaying the loan and his heirs refused to acknowledge it. The monastery brought the matter up repeatedly in the courts and always received a verdict in its favor, which, however, never had practical consequences. The debt was finally settled in 1672 through the mediation of friends[52].

The Navahrudek monastery brought suits frequently against its debtors. Its rights were confirmed and fines were laid on the debtors, but whether the loans were repaid is doubtful. In 1645 it was in court over a loan of 3004 kopy of Lithuanian money[53], in 1659 and 1662 over a loan of 353 zl.[54], in 1664, 1665 over a loan of 965 zl.[55]

The debtors were generally local gentry. Official institutions, though, were no surer risks. Around 1711 the Vicebsk Holy Spirit monastery loaned 7213 zl. to the town of Vicebsk. Town officials not only refused to pay back the loan, but did not even answer the court summons[56]. Thus, although loaning money on interest was a source of income for monasteries, it was not without risks and often dragged a monastery into a costly, sometimes ruinous lawsuit.

The extent of one monastery's loans form a twenty-year period show its prosperity. The monastery is Holy Trinity of Minsk, and the years are 1645-1665. The loans are: 20 kopy of Lithuanian money—1645; 100 kopy—1645; 600 Polish zloty—1652; 550 zloty—1655; 40 zloty—1661; 26.000 zloty—before 1665[57]. This information comes only from published materials; it is very likely that other loans were made. The sums a monastery could loan are sometimes surprisingly large. The Hrodna monastery made a loan of 2000 talers (about 12.000 zl.) on interest to the Jews of Hrodna in 1678[58].

The tendency of disputed claims to drag on is evident, and at times

---

[52] See *AV*, 15: 174-176, 248-250, 267-268; 11: 205-207, for various stages in the case. The last, which is the settlement of 1672, recounts how it began.

[53] *Ibid.*, 15: 11-12.

[54] *Ibid.*, p. 65-67.

[55] *Ibid.*, p. 137-138.

[56] *IJuM*, 21: 165-169.

[57] *AV*, 15: 18, 31-32 (1645); 45-46 (1652); 92-93 (1655); 93-94 (1661); 262-263 (1665).

[58] *Ibid.*, 29: 51-53.

they continued not just for years, but for decades. In the 1660's Magdalene Gosiewska, wife of the treasurer (podskarbij) of Lithuania, borrowed 18.000 zl. from the Holy Spirit monastery of Minsk, on the security of her estate. Soon, however, she took back her estate, which after her death passed to an heir, Benedict Sapieha. He began to repay the borrowed money, but not for long. Although the monastery pressed its rights, it did not succeed in reclaiming either the money or the property[59]. In 1711 the monastery again brought claims, this time already against Benedict Sapieha's heirs, who too had begun to repay the debt but had not continued for long[60]. In 1718 the tribunal awarded the monastery half the estate[61]. This too did not work out. From 1738, though, we have what is apparently the final document of the affair, a peaceful settlement with the payment of 30.000 zl. to the nuns[62].

The extent to which monasteries, following the trend of society as a whole, were enmeshed in lawsuits is still better realized when we note that at the same time the same monastery had several such cases in the courts. In 1711 it also brought a complaint against a gentry family for failure to repay 1000 talers (about 6000 zl.)[63], and in 1723 against a Jew of Minsk for a debt of 45 talers (about 315 zl.)[64]. Nor does this complete the list—it is only what available documents provide us with.

In 1670 metropolitan Gabriel Kolenda, who was at the same time archbishop of Polock, brought a suit on behalf of the Polock nuns against Chrysostom Nemyrovyč-Ščyt, who had appropriated for himself one of the monastery's villages. Although the verdict was in the monastery's favor, it was not the end of the case: at the next assizes Nemyrovyč-Ščyt was to present his "justification"[65].

Property disputes between monasteries arose more than once. One that went on for a considerable time involved the Barkalabava monastery and the monks of Bujnyči, both founded by the Stetkevyč family and both belonging to the Kutejno grouping of monasteries. It all originated in a charitable deed early in the history of the monasteries. The founders had granted the Bujnyči monastery a very large property—100 voloky, and that monastery possessed other means as well. The Barkalabava monastery, which grew in size very quickly, had a much

---

[59] *Ibid.*, 8: 171; *Sapiehowie*, 3: 116-117.
[60] *AV*, 8: 173.
[61] Cf. *Sapiehowie*, 3: 358.
[62] *AV*, 11: 485-489.
[63] *Ibid.*, 8: 170-171.
[64] *OAZM*, 2: 52.
[65] *IJuM*, 25: 236-239.

smaller endowment. Taking all that into account, the ihumen of these
monasteries, Joil Trucevyč, asked the Stetkevyč family—and obtained
from them—that half of the grant to Bujnyči, 50 voloky, be assigned to
the Barkalabava monastery instead. He claimed that the monks of Bujnyči were in perfect agreement with such an arrangement. Their
superior, however, lost no time in raising a protest, demanding the property back. Nothing further was done about it, and the matter lay dor-
mant for a hundred years, with the nuns in possession of their 50
voloky. But in the 1740's the monks of Bujnyči again claimed possession
of the land and occupied it by force. This gave rise to a legal battle,
"klotnia prawna" as the parties call it, not only before civil courts in
Lithuania, but also before the Kiev consistory. The whole affair, which
at times degenerated into acts of violence, had no other outcome than
expenses for both sides. In the end the quarrel was settled by in-
termediaries. In 1759 the land was surveyed anew, and another equal
division was made, with 50 voloky going to one monastery and 50
voloky to the other[66].

* * *

An inventory of the Barkalabava monastery property made on that
occasion lists the 50 voloky (over 2500 acres), of which 30 were arable,
and two villages with 83 serfs. Rents amounted to about 172 zl. About
one of the villages the inventory noted that the villagers were to render
as much pryhon (corvée) as would be dictated by necessity. No doubt
the same prescription applied also to the other village[67]. At the end of
the eighteenth century the property of this monastery was still about the
same[68].

---

[66] An account of the original division of property, differing somewhat in details and
chronology, is set out in the deed of Joil Trucevyč of 1652, printed in *AS*, 2: 74-76 (also in
IJuM, 14: 137-141). The legacy grant of Stetkevyč is doubtless more reliable (*AS*, 2: 71-74,
and *IJuM*, 14: 141-146). The act of the division of property is in *IJuM*, 14: 135-137. The
first protest of the Bujnyči monastery is recorded in *AS*, 2: 77-78. The early phases of the
litigation between Barkalabava and Bujnyči one hundred years later, many documents
from which have been published, are recounted in the decision of metropolitan Timothy
Ščerbac'kyj of 3 March 1752 (*AS*, 2: 114-115; *IJuM*, 15: 369-372). This remained ineffective. The following year the nuns took their complaint to the town tribunal of Staryj Byxov, the decision of which, found in *IJuM*, 15: 408-423, includes many circumstantial
details on the determined manner in which both parties carried on the dispute. The later
phases are described in the document on the division of property between the two
monasteries, *IJuM*, 16: 283-288 (also in *AV*, 12: 142-152; *AS*, 2: 125-130).
[67] The inventory is found in *IJuM*, 16: 288-295.
[68] AMVROSIJ, 3: 428.

The economic condition of the Barkalabava monastery lends itself to comparison with that of the monastery or Orša not very far away. This latter was much smaller in number of members: its average was about ten to Barkalabava's fifty and more. At the end of the eighteenth century the monastery in Orša had 55 serfs, about 150 morgs (265 acres) of arable land and about 120 morgs of woods, pasture, and other, besides 15 morgs by the monastery; in addition, the monastery possessed some lots in Orša[69]. This might seem to be sufficient, but metropolitan Hrebnyc'kyj in 1756 describes the monastery as on the verge of economic ruin[70]. Even if Hrebnyc'kyj's description tends to extremes (he had his own reasons to paint the picture in the darkest colors), the impression remains that here as in numerous other monasteries a critical economic situation was brought on by sheer incapacity to manage things well.

Further comparisons can be made with two other monasteries. The Vicebsk Holy Spirit monastery at the end of the eighteenth century had from its lands and capital an annual income of 338 rubles, which was not sufficient for its maintenance and which was supplanted by donations[71]. One of the poorer town monasteries of Belorussia was the Epiphany monastery of Mahilev. When it was closed in 1795 its funds amounted to only 158 rubles and 5 kopeks. It owned some land, but had no labor force, and in its last years the nuns lived mostly from their handwork and from donations[72].

Finally, we can say something about the state of monastery buildings and churches. With regard to the churches, it was not rare for a monastery to have several, from its very beginnings. The monastery at Barkalabava, founded about 1641, ten years later already had two, of the Ascension and of the Birth of St John the Baptist[73]. The Kutejno monastery not far away by 1743 had three churches, one of them with a prydil (side chapel)[74].

An interesting description of a monastery enclosure exists: the Polock monastery by St Sophia in 1637. The main building, obviously of wood, had several rooms, an entrance hall, and a veranda. Nearby was the refectory with another room; close to it were the kitchen and the bakery with a cellar and storerooms for grain. Another cabin faced

---

[69] WOŁYNIAK, p. 78.
[70] *EM*, 4: 373.
[71] WOŁYNIAK, p. 165.
[72] ŽUDRO, *Bogojavlenskij bratskij monastyr'*, p. 31, 35.
[73] *AS*, 2: 73.
[74] *OASS*, 23: 36 (from a detailed description of the monastery drawn up in 1743).

the bakery, with a storeroom and a small animal shed. Next to the buildings was a vegetable garden and an orchard, and further a brewery, a bathhouse, a cowbarn, a stable, and several sheds for storing hay and straw. An enclosing wall ran around this entire property[75].

Even partial and casual descriptions may throw an interesting light on various facets of monastic life. At the monastery of Orša the wooden building had seven cells, plus a kitchen and a refectory. The nuns' quarters reflect the same conditions as their property described above—by the end of the eighteenth century everything was greatly dilapidated[76]. If one compares this Uniate monastery with the nearby Orthodox monasteries of Barkalabava and Kutejno with their fifty and more nuns, everything here speaks for the fact that the Union was in these parts much weaker than Orthodoxy.

On the other hand, in Vicebsk the Holy Spirit monastery and its church were both in stone, one of the best constructions in town [77]. In Hrodna the nuns at first lived in a rented house by one of the town's churches, but rather soon moved to their own monastery, which is already mentioned in 1651[78]. It was badly damaged in a fire in 1720, but metropolitan Leo Kyška rebuilt the monastery and the church in stone[79].

Halyčyna

We possess some information about the early fortunes of several monasteries in Halyčyna. The origins of the Slovita monastery are obscure, but we know of its conditions in the seventeenth century. The monastery had suffered from two Tatar incursions at the end of the sixteenth century[80]. Its rebuilding owed much to the starosta of Lviv, Stanislaus Boniface Mniszek. He gave permission to use timber from the Slovita woods for the rebuilding of the monastery and then assigned to the monastery an ownerless property together with a mill and pastures and vegetable gardens[81]. A century after the ruinous attacks at Slovita

---

[75] *IJuM*, 29: 19.

[76] Wołyniak, p. 78-79.

[77] Cf. *Geografičeskij slovar' rossijskogo gosudarstva*, 1 (Moskva, 1801): 881.

[78] Cf. *OAZM*, 2: 150 (copy of a 1651 document confirming the monastery's possessions).

[79] E. Orlovskij, *Očerk istorii goroda Grodny* (Grodna, 1889), p. 44.

[80] Antonij Petruševič, Slovickij ženskij monastyr' Činu Sv. Vasilija V. i ego devičoe vospitališče, *Zorja Halycka*, 3/15 February 1851, p. 110.

[81] His charters, from Slovita monastery archives, are printed in C'orox, p. 235-237.

the Tatar menace still remained. In 1692 Tatars pillaged Žovkva, at which time seven nuns died in the fire set to the town[82].

In general, the economic fortunes of monasteries in Halyčyna are little known; it can safely be asserted, though, that they were not flourishing. The monasteries reflect the economic and social conditions of the Ruthenian population of Halyčyna. The few isolated notices which have come down only confirm this impression. The little monastery in Bus'k, for istance, founded without properties, was soon after given a vegetable garden and some woods, which provided some of the monastery's necessities[83]. In the first half of the seventeenth century some notable bequests to monasteries were made, as the one to Mykola-jiv in 1641[84], but they dwindled to insignificant pittances or ceased altogether later.

The nuns themselves likewise brought in little to their monasteries. In Slovita, we know from a visitation of 1763, a nun who brought in a dowry was a rare exception[85].

In spite of the strict injunctions of the Synod of Zamość concerning dowries, the same situation as at Slovita must have existed in the rest of the little monasteries of western Ukraine. The Synod had been concerned about adequate maintenance of the nuns, so that it would not be necessary for each one to worry about providing herself with the necessities of life. But the women who entered these monasteries did not have the means to bring in dowries. At Lviv there was an attempt to enforce this regulation, at least in the eighteenth century. The sums brought in as dowries vary from 1000 zl. (the most common) to, in one case, 7000 zl.[86].

Even of the Lviv monastery few other details are known, though earlier, in the seventeenth century, it must have been prosperous. Basil Lupul, hospodar of Moldavia, was a benefactor of the Stauropegian confraternity of Lviv and included in his benefactions the women's monastery founded by the confraternity, giving it land on the outskirts of Lviv[87]. Other gifts from him, of money and of religious objects,

---

His grants were renewed by his heirs, cf. PETRUŠEVIČ, *Svodnaja letopis' 1600-1700*, p. 585.

[82] PETRUŠEVIČ, *Svodnaja letopis' 1600-1700*, p. 235.

[83] *Ibid.*, p. 11 (the endowment of "Stanisław hrabia z Tarnowa, kasztelan Sędomirski, Buski starosta", dated 25 August 1602).

[84] PETRUŠEVIČ, *Dopolnenija 1600-1700*, p. 220.

[85] Cf. the catalog of nuns in C'OROX, p. 233-234, where in almost every case it is noted, "posagu żadnego niema".

[86] The sums are noted for most nuns in a list drawn up around 1800, *ibid.*, p. 237-240.

[87] Cf. the charter of John Casimir given to the Lviv nuns by which their land was

followed. In the nineteenth century the nuns in Slovita possessed icons with Rumanian inscriptions, and Petruševyč suggests that they had been brought to Slovita from Lviv when the Lviv monastery died out at the end of the eighteenth century[88].

In general, the sisters in Halyčyna supported themselves by hand-work and from alms[89]; we shall treat of this in greater detail when we speak of the occupations of the nuns and of common life. Since the monasteries were poor, they were also small. The monastery in Javoriv was a wooden house with two larger and two smaller rooms[90]. There were relatively many monasteries in Halyčyna, as a glance at the list will show. A great number of them, however, passed away leaving only the barest of traces, and in all of them, it seems, the nuns barely eked out a miserable existence.

If the causes for this are sought, certainly the principal one lies in the character of the Ukrainian society in Halyčyna in the seventeenth and eighteenth centuries. There was neither a wealthy gentry class nor a prosperous town class. Even the Stauropegian confraternity by the mid-seventeenth century had lost its early drive.

The most telling evidence are the official figures collected in the 1780's, which permit us to make comparisons with Latin women's monasteries in the same territory. According to estimates made by government officials the properties of the Basilian women's monasteries in Halyčyna amounted to 11.988 fl.; the annual revenues of the Lviv monastery (11 nuns) was a little over 196 fl. At the same time the estimated value of the properties of the Poor Clares in Lviv (35 nuns) was 61.380 fl; the annual income from that was 2412 fl. 34 kr. And this was far from being among the wealthiest Latin convents in Halyčyna. The Brigittines in Lviv (20 nuns) possessed properties valued at over 85.350 fl., and other convents possessed far more[91].

Volyn'

One of the earliest documented foundations in any Ruthenian region is that in 1592 by prince Constantine Ostroz'kyj of a monastery

---

freed from taxes and other contributions, *ibid.*, p. 227-229.

[88] PETRUŠEVIČ, Slovickij ženskij monastyr', p. 128.

[89] Investigations in the 1780's made this abundantly clear, cf. CHOTKOWSKI, p. 103.

[90] *Ibid.*, p. 128. The monastery owned some land (cf. C'OROX, p. 241-243, for two grants of 1636 and 1639), but the nuns always lived "z dzieła rąk swoich [printed 'moich'] y iałmużny", as the foundress testified in her testament in 1664 (p. 245).

[91] All these figures are cited by CHOTKOWSKI: p. 145 (Basilians), 35, 39 (Poor Clares),

on a little island near Dubno in Volyn'. What the property contained is just as undefined as its size—"field and everything"—but a later description says the island was very low and just large enough for the monastery buildings and a small orchard and vegetable garden[92]. Later Ostroz'kyj gave the monastery other property nearby.

Another prominent founder in Volyn', Adam Kysil', endowed his monastery in Popivka with a village and ponds and mills, as well as an interest of 700 zl. annually from his estate. He also promised to build a stone church and to furnish it[93].

Monastery buildings were simple. The Korec' monastery was a wooden house, rebuilt only in 1754-1767 in stone in two storeys together with a stone church[94]. The Dubno monastery is described in detail in an 1818 visitation, but from this we can judge of its appearance much earlier, as the monastery had not changed with the years, but had only deteriorated. It was built in the form of a three-sided rectangle in one storey with eighteen cells in the middle section, while the side wings were occupied by a kitchen, a refectory, and storerooms. At the date of the description the dowries of the nuns living there were recorded as being from 150 to 900 rubles[95].

Podillja

When we turn to Podillja, we again see that at their beginnings monasteries were well provided for. A member of a wealthy gentry family, Michael Kropyvnyc'kyj, in 1636 bought a plot of land in Vinnycja, built there a monastery with a church, and assigned it an annual contribution of 300 Polish zloty[96]. Four years later he added to that a fishpond which, he said, could function in rainy years and repeated the annuity of 300 zloty[97]. In Vinnycja we have also an interesting case of the town administration endowing the monastery with a hayfield in 1642[92]. Eventually it was litigation that brought the monastery to ruin.

109-110 (Brigittines).

[92] *Arxiv JuZR*, pt. I, 6: 90. Cf. J. SKRUTEN', Vizyta dubens'koho monastyrja SS. Vasylijanok 1818 r. *AOSBM*, 2, no. 3-4 (1927): 356-357.

[93] *OAZM*, 1: 282.

[94] Cf. AMVROSIJ, 4: 647.

[95] SKRUTEN', p. 355-359.

[96] WOŁYNIAK, p. 163-164.

[97] His deed is in SECINSKIJ, p. 257-261.

[98] *Ibid.*, p. 251.

It enjoyed prosperity for over a hundred years. But then the new owner of its founder's estate refused to pay the stipulated annual sum and usurped some of the monastery's holdings as well. The monastery took the matter to court, with the result of being reduced to such penury that the nuns even abandoned it for about six years, from 1780 to 1786.

From around 1792 there exists a description of this monastery. The wooden church with three domes dated from 1723; evidently the first church, put up by the founder a century before, had burned down. Next to the church was a belfry with two bells. The monastery proper, also of wood, with seventeen glass windows, had twelve cells, a refectory and a kitchen, and two storerooms. A palisade fenced in the monastery enclosure from the front and a plaited fence on the other sides. On the monastery land there was also a priest's house, sheds, and ten peasants' cottages (but already in 1764 the monastery had only six serfs)[99].

The material well-being of another Podillja monastery, that at Mykulynci, was also assured at the beginning. The local landowner, Nicholas Kryns'kyj, repaired the church and the cells of an abandoned monastery there, gave the sisters some land in the vicinity, helped them with produce (however much of grain and oil they might need) and money, permitted them to take timber from the woods for all their purposes and to catch in the local pond four buckets of fish every Saturday[100]. That was around 1716. In 1733, however, the monastery burned down, and this time Kryns'kyj opposed its rebuilding, nor did the nuns themselves find the means to rebuild it. Not far away they managed to put up a small chapel and little huts for individual cells[101]. Only in 1745 did Kryns'kyj permit them to use a hayfield to which they had had access before.

In 1747 the monastery was ordered closed by a church official from Braclav because of a lack of necessary material provisions, but some nuns persisted in staying there until the end of the century. They did handwork, but to subsist they had to rely on alms and for this they went begging in the neighborhood. The monastery buildings consisted of seven wretched cells, a refectory with a small and poor chapel and no enclosure—in fact, the path from the woods to the two neighboring villages Mykulynci and Rižok ran between the huts. Church vessels, books, and vestments were bought for money the nuns obtained by begging[102]. The chapel in 1785 was in such a dilapidated condition that the

---

[99] *Ibid.*, p. 266-267.
[100] The endowment document, *ibid.*, p. 343-344.
[101] *Ibid.*, p. 340-341; Wołyniak, p. 259.
[102] Secinskij, p. 345-348.

visitator forbade services to be held there. Not long afterwards, however, the land passed to a new owner, and with his help and the help of the local villagers the church was completely restored and reconsecrated[103], though the monastery was definitively closed a few years later.

Kiev

In Kiev the monasteries were rather prosperous. The beginnings of a revival of its monasteries falls in the early seventeenth century. The monastery of St. Florus was then thoroughly restored by its ihumenja Agatha Humenyc'ka. Here is how the material restoration is described in a charter confirming the monastery's immunities issued by Ladislaus IV in 1636:

> [Agatha Humenyc'ka] took over the old and dilapidated church under her care, restored and renewed it, and adorned it in every manner as was most fitting; then she obtained both by request from pious people and by purchase for ready money several lots contiguous to it, because the place was very confined; then she enclosed it as was becoming with a fence, and further she built some cells and had some pious nuns settle in them[104].

In the seventeenth century Kiev monasteries often sent members or emissaries to Moscow for alms. Liturgical books and other church supplies were often requested and given, as for the Kiev Ascension monastery. In 1671 it received vestment materials, wine, incense, wax, and a set of liturgical books, meant to be complete, but because not all were in stock in Moscow limited only to an altar Gospel, a služebnyk, and a common menaion[105]. Late in the seventeenth and early in the eighteenth centuries, rather than being allowed to send people on such trips to Moscow, these monasteries were assigned money and supplies from local state funds. Trips to Russia came to be undertaken rather to protect a monastery's interests than to seek new gifts. We see this in petitions taken to Moscow and then St Petersburg by the ihumenja of Sts Florus and Laurus monastery in 1725[106]. The monastery's rights to prop-

---

[103] *Ibid.*, p. 342.
[104] *Akty JuZR*, 2: 97.
[105] Ėjngorn, *ČOIDR*, 1898, 4: 784-785.
[106] *OASS*, 5: 463-464.

erties in Kiev were at stake, as well as a subsidy every four years from
Moscow. The outcome of this trip is unknown. It is highly unlikely that
the subsidy, originally assigned to the Kiev Ascension monastery, was
ever renewed. The properties too probably remained with their new
owners—the Kiev municipality and a parish church.

Already in 1683, in response to a request from the Ascension
monastery, local funds were assigned for the building of a warm church
(for winter use) and for the repair of a well[107]. The properties of this
monastery are enumerated in a confirmatory charter of 1688: five
villages and a mill[108]. This rather contradicts a statement made in the
same charter, echoing the petition of the nuns, that they "live on
Christ's name and their own toil". On 1 December 1687 hetman Ivan
Mazepa issued a universal confirming the properties of this same
monastery, of which his mother at that time was ihumenja. In the Kiev
polk the monastery had been in possession of the village Podhoryšče for
a long time; the universal orders its "subjects" to fulfill all their obligations. The widow of a polkovnyk had given the monastery a village and
another smaller settlement, both deserted now, concerning which the
universal gives the monastery the right to settle people there. In addition, the monastery possessed two small villages in the Perejaslav
polk—one where it had its own farmstead (xutor) and one which it had
bought[109].

A schematic drawing of the Ascension monastery grounds gives us a
good idea of what it looked like toward the end of its existence. The
drawing was made in 1713-1715, after the nuns had been moved, but
before the buildings were razed. The enclosure was dominated by the
large, many-domed and many-apsed main church built by Mazepa. Even
on the plan it shows features common to the baroque churches of the
period. A semi-circle of cells went around one end of the enclosure, with
the refectory in the middle. A wall enclosed the entire complex[110].

---

[107] *Dopolnenija k Aktam istoričeskim*, 10 (Sanktpeterburg, 1867): 311.
[108] *AI*, 5: 288-291.
[109] *Akty ZR*, 5: 213-214.
[110] The particular of the Lavra and the Ascension monastery appears on a plan of the
properties of the *Pustynnyj* St Nicholas monastery in Kiev and is reproduced by Fedir
ERNST, Kyjivs'ka arxitektura XVII viku, *Kyjiv ta joho okolycja v istoriji i pam'jatkax*
(Zapysky Ukrajins'koho Naukovoho Tovarystva v Kyjivi, 22), p. 153. The great Ascension
church appeared in the panegyrical engraving of Ivan Mihura offered to hetman Mazepa
in 1706. The six churches built by Mazepa that appear in the engraving are redrawn in V.
SIČYNS'KYJ, *Istorija ukrajins'koho mystectva*, 1 (New York, 1956): 115. The Ascension
church is the first from the right. N. MAKSIMOVIČ, Vydubickij monastyr', *Kievljanin*, 1841,
p. 25, fn. 10, published the contract of 17 March 1701 between the superior of Ascension,

The Kiev St John monastery was to be given annually, beginning in 1758, 100 rubles and 100 quarters of flour[111]. An indication of prosperity is the fact that in 1786, when the state took over monastic properties in Ukraine, the serfs of the St Florus monastery numbered 3905[112].

Hetmanate

The monasteries in Left Bank Ukraine for the most part arose or developed in the hetmanate period. They, and those in Kiev, had frequent dealings with hetmans and lesser Cossack officials, especially in the seventeenth century. Monastery properties were not only left undisturbed in spite of the new conditions of land ownership, but even increased their holdings. The hetmans confirmed what the monasteries already possessed; their charters of confirmation inform us about the properties of monasteries and their growth.

The concept of obtaining a reconfirmation of holdings continued to obtain here as it had under the kings of Poland-Lithuania. Two series of such confirmations can be cited as examples. The Černihiv monastery received confirmations of its holdings from the polkovnyk of Černihiv Joanikij Sylyn who was carrying out directives of Bohdan Xmel'nyc'kyj, and from hetmans George Xmel'nyc'kyj (1659-1662) in 1660, Ivan Brjuxovec'kyj (1663-1668) in 1663, Ivan Samojlovyč (1672-1687) in 1672, Ivan Mazepa (1687-1709) in 1689, Ivan Skoropads'kyj (1708-1722) in 1710, Daniel Apostol (1727-1734) in 1729[113]. For the monastery of Novi Mlyny we have universals of Bohdan Xmel'nyc'kyj, Demjan Mnohohrišnyj (1668-1672) from 1689, Ivan Samojlovyč from 1676, Ivan Mazepa from 1688[114]. As can be seen, each such document dates from early in a hetmanate.

Monasteries applied also to tsars for reconfirmation of their

---

M.M. Mazepa, and the Vydubyc'kyj monastery outside Kiev for manufacturing bricks on the land of the latter for the new church.

[111] *PSPR*, Elizabeth, 4: 328-329.

[112] Volodymyr Ivanovyč ŠČERBYNA, Narysy z istoriji Kyjiva, *Novi studiji z istoriji Kyjiva* (U Kyjivi, 1926), p. 13.

[113] The first is mentioned in a charter of tsar Alexius in Vasilenko, 3: 458. All the rest are published on p. 459-466.

[114] The Xmel'nyc'kyj universal has not survivied, but its existence is proved by contemporary references to it, see LAZAREVSKIJ, *Opisanie*, 2: 295. It was issued actually to the Baturyn monastery, but the one at Novi Mlyny may be regarded as its continuation—it retained all the properties of the former. The other universals are published by LAZAREVSKIJ, Akty, p. 62-65.

holdings. The tsars issued their charters on the basis of those of the hetmans. On the one hand, it was expected of monasteries to submit the universals they received to Moscow for confirmation. We learn indirectly that according to the articles of Hluxiv (1669) if a hetman or other official issued a universal granting or confirming properties to anyone, confirmation of this was then to be sought of the tsar, who was bound to give it[115].

On the other hand, applications to Moscow were seldom made promptly. In a confirmation charter for the Hluxiv monastery dated 3 July 1709 it is stated that all the previous confirmations of hetmans have been presented and are now confirmed by Peter[116]. Since it was already thirteen years even of the sole reign of Peter I, it is clear that the monastery had considered the universals of the hetmans sufficient. Now, however, on the eve of the battle of Poltava, the nuns thought it best to ensure themselves of the undisturbed and secure possession of their holdings by obtaining charters from both sides. One can give examples of belated applications from other monasteries: the properties of Baturyn were confirmed by Alexius in 1672[117], those of Novi Mlyny by Ivan and Peter in 1690[118].

In one instance we have a reference to a "žalovannaja gramota" also of the tsarina, given to the Ascension monastery in Kiev[119].

A rare type of endowment by tsar Alexius was made to the Černihiv monastery of St Paraskeva in 1663: two mills at a nearby village[120]. At this time properties in Ukraine were seldom apportioned by the tsar himself.

Recourse was often had to hetmans and to other officials by both parties in the collisions between monasteries and their neighbors. If we consider how relatively often staršyna and rank and file Cossacks are forbidden in the charters of hetmans and tsars to invade monastery property, we must conclude that it was not rare for them to do so. Reiterated commands of hetmans to Cossacks—as well as to other local

---

[115] The confirmatory charters of Alexius frequently mention these conditions: "A v gluxovskix i v ninešnix postanovlennyx statjax, kakovi učineni na rade mež Putivlja i Konotopa napisano: komu getman i staršina za uslugi dadut melnicju i derevnju i universali svoi dadut, i na tie maetnosti našy velikogo gosudarja, žalovannie gramoti, po čelobitju davat'." (In a charter for the monastery of Novi Mlyny, Vasilenko, 1: 198).

[116] Ibid., p. 356-358. On p. 360-363 are printed universals given to this monastery by Mnohohrišnyj in 1671 and by Mazepa in 1688 and 1690.

[117] Ėjngorn, ČOIDR, 1899, 2: 1010.

[118] Printed in Vasilenko, 1: 194-197.

[119] Mentioned in a universal of Mazepa, Akty ZR, 5: 217.

[120] Cf. Lazarevskij, Obozrenie, p. 26.

inhabitants—not to encroach on the properties of monasteries are frequent in the universals given to the latter.

Ivan Mazepa in 1688 addressed a universal to the Perejaslav polk in which he repeated the complaints made by the superior (his mother, Maria Magdalene) of the Kiev monastery of the Ascension concerning one of the monastery's properties in that polk. The local Cossacks had taken for themselves one part of the land, and the inhabitants of nearby Baryšpil' another part, plowing in the fields and mowing the haypastures. The hetman severely ordered both groups of poachers to desist; the Cossacks were to be content with their own land[121].

On the other hand, monasteries tried to take lands on which Cossacks, who were free of all feudal duties, had settled and to enserf them. The economic-statistical census of 1723 was carried out in the hetmanate to investigate the complaints of Cossacks and the legitimacy of land ownership. At Pečenyky, for example, the monastery had seized the land of the local Cossacks and had settled peasants on it[122]. At Šumarovo the inhabitants declared about the five Cossacks homesteads in the village:

> Their grandfathers and fathers had been Cossacks, and they themselves had been on campaigns in military service; then when the late Lukjan Roslavec was sotnyk, and his mother was ihumenja of the Šumarovo monastery, at her request Lukjan made them subject to the monastery[123].

Complaints were also directed to the hetman by peasants whose lands had been seized by monasteries. In one such case, when the ihumenja of Novi Mlyny had seized the woods and other possessions of one of the monastery's neighbors, he at first turned to the Nižyn polkovnyk, who issued a "letter" that these should be returned. The letter proved to be of no effect, so the free peasant turned to hetman Skoropads'kyj for redress[124].

A few confirmatory charters of hetmans can be examined in greater detail for the sake of comparison. That the grants given to monasteries by hetmans were not negligible can be seen by examining the charter given by Ivan Samojlovyč to the monastery in Novi Mlyny in 1676. In it, as is usual, all the monastery's possessions are listed, but that is not what is of special interest. Parenthetically it can be observed that one of

---

[121] *Akty ZR*, 5: 217-218.
[122] LAZAREVSKIJ, *Opisanie*, 1: 145.
[123] *Ibid.*, p. 308.
[124] *Ibid.*, 2: 296-297.

its four mills was bought by the monastery itself, which demonstrates
that it had sufficient capital besides lands. Of the property, then, more
than half had been given it by hetmans, "because preceding hetmans,
ever zealous for the glory of God, because of the destruction of the
women's monastery of Baturyn[125], to support it and the one known as
Bobrykovs'kyj, have endowed it with"—and here follows a listing that
amounts to a ferry, two villages with various types of land, several
mills. A few lines further down we learn how the land came to be at the
disposal of the hetmans: a mention of one of the villages reads "the
village of Otjuša with the lands of the szlachta". It had, therefore,
belonged to szlachta who had fled to the Right Bank in 1648; the hetmans distributed such land to staršyna and monasteries. That not
everyone was happy with this turn of affairs can be inferred from the
final words of the universal: "We especially order the village communities not to refuse every kind of obedience and duty to the reverend
superior and nuns of the above-mentioned monastery"[126].

Not only land, but also other economic benefits were assigned to
monasteries. From a universal of George Xmel'nyc'kyj of 1659 we learn
that his father, in granting some land to a certain Ivan Avramovyč,
specified that the fees received from a ferry across the Desna river
should go to the Černihiv monastery of St Paraskeva. Hetman George
Xmel'nyc'kyj himself assigned the fee in flour from a mill, due to the
hetman, to the same monastery[127].

Aside from grants of property, notice should also be taken of other
gifts and benefactions to monasteries, though of these we do not have
the same abundance of records. The noted ktytor of churches and
monasteries Basil Dunin-Borkovs'kyj, polkovnyk of Černihiv, in the
1680's renovated the St Paraskeva monastery of Černihiv and put up an
enclosure around it[128].

Hetman Skoropads'kyj, seeking confirmation for the properties of
the Hamalijivka monastery acquired through his, and especially his
wife's, efforts[129], stated that he wanted to assure the nuns there of suffi-

---

[125] Around 1666 the Baturyn monastery was pillaged by Tatars, its superior later
reported in Moscow. Cf. ĖJNGORN, ČOIDR, 1899, 2: 1010-1011.

[126] LAZAREVSKIJ, Akty, p. 63-64. The entire process of a small farmstead of szlachta
ownership becoming a large and prosperous village in the possession of a monastery—in
this case Hluxiv—is described in the 1729 census of land holdings, Vasilenko, 1: 49-50.

[127] LAZAREVSKIJ, Obozrenie, p. 25-26.

[128] Cf. Afanasij ŠAFONSKIJ, Černigovskogo Namestničestva topografičeskoe opisanie,
ed. M. SUDIENKO (Kiev, 1851), p. 271.

[129] For how her efforts were regarded, see OASS, 10: 79. The process of acquiring

cient food and clothing. The monastery owned five mills, most of them with several wheels, to which were attached farmsteads with fields, pastures, copses, and woods, another mill without further specifications, two wheels in yet another mill, one glassworks with fields and other land, and four villages with all their lands, one of them having also numerous small lakes. The "pospolyti ljudy" (the population other than the Cossacks settled there) of the villages had obligations of work towards the monastery. This was in 1718[130]. In 1720 another glassworks was established nearby, and hetman Skoropads'kyj obliged the glazier to pay the monastery 100 zloty and provide it with as much glass as it needed[131].

This monastery was considered very wealthy, and its holdings can serve as a basis of comparison with those of others. Thus the monastery at Hluxiv was obviously less affluent. In 1709 it had only one village with its various kinds of land (arable, pastures), with "pospolyti ljudy", and one mill, all of this being the original grant of the foundress and first superior, given in 1671[132]. What this meant in terms of the actual provisions and funds for the needs of the monastery, though, cannot be determined.

The Černihiv monastery, although it had properties on a par with Hamalijivka, received little benefit from them, due to poor administration, or so at least reported the bishop of Černihiv Nikodym Srebnyc'kyj in 1744[133]. His report is corroborated by a comparison of two economic descriptions, of 1729 and 1765. In the former the monastery is listed as holding eight villages in the Bilous sotnja with 156 obligated households. By the time of the 1765 description in the same sotnja it had only four villages with 53 households[134].

Mills could be an important source of income. The monastery in Pečenyky reported in 1740 that from its flour wheels it received at least 50 quarters of flour a year and 10 rubles from its fuller's wheel[135].

Ferries were another source. At Makošyn the ferry across the Desna river brought the monastery 500 rubles per summer[136], while the

---

land for this monastery may be observed by comparing MODZALEVSKIJ, *Malorossijskij rodoslovnik*, 1: 306; 3: 385, 388; 4: 462, 464, as well as *UA*, 1: 3, 68, 399.

[130] This is quoted in a charter of Peter I, dated 1718, VASILENKO, 1: 316.

[131] Cf. Vadym MODZALEVS'KYJ, *Huty na Černihivščyni* (Kyjiv, 1926), p. 20.

[132] VASILENKO, 1: 356-358, 360-361.

[133] Cf. *OASS*, 19: 508, where a list of the properties is also found.

[134] VASILENKO, 3: 43 (1729); LAZAREVSKIJ, *Obozrenie*, p. 22-23 (1765).

[135] LAZAREVSKIJ, *Obozrenie*, p. 23.

[136] Cf. Ju. VYNOHRADS'KYJ, Serednja Černihivščyna naprykinci XVIII ta na počatku XIX v., *Istoryko-heohrafičnyj zbirnyk*, 2 (1928): 191.

monastery at Novi Mlyny owned a ferry across the Sejm river by Baturyn[137].

This last monastery remained prosperous to its very end. Although we do not have a full list of its possessions in 1781, when statistics were being gathered prior to the confiscation of monastery property, we learn that the nuns lived on income derived from its villages, and that the monastery had 445 serfs. At the monastery there was one wooden church, and another was being built (the nuns could not have foreseen that the monastery would soon be closed). The ihumenja's part of the monastery had six rooms, and there were ten cells for the nuns (of whom there were over twenty)[138].

In contrast, the monastery of Šumarovo is described at this same period as dilapidated and on the verge of collapse. The nuns supported themselves by operating a distillery, using grain and wood given in alms and selling the spirits in the village[139].

Slobidščyna

With wooden construction prevailing, fires everywhere were a frequent bane. It was not every monastery that could recuperate its fortunes after such a devastation and no monastery could do so immediately. We have two examples of this from Slobidščyna. The Ostrogožsk monastery burned down in 1702, about forty years after its foundation. In place of its original two churches only one was rebuilt, two years later; to replace it a stone one was built by the local people in 1780. The nuns by that time were supported in large part by alms from the local people[140].

The monastery of Xoroševe near Xarkiv held in possession the village Xoroševe. It knew troubled times in the early eighteenth century from marauding Cossacks and Tatars. The monastery had two churches, of the Ascension and of St Michael the Archangel. The first was thoroughly restored in 1742, eighty years after it was built, with a new

---

[137] Cf. Vasilenko, 1: 194-195.

[138] Lazarevskij, Opisanie, 2: 299. Cf. Neskol'ko cyfr iz statistiki russkoj cerkvi 18-go stoletija (s 1742 po 1786 g.), TKDA, 1867, 2: 492. The church, built in the 1780's, a small, elegant structure in the form of a Greek cross ending in four apses still stood in the 1960's. A photograph of it may be found in M. Capenko, Po ravninam Desny i Sejma (Moskva, 1967), p. 27 (commentary, p. 24). No other trace of the monastery remains.

[139] Cf. Lazarevskij, Opisanie, 1: 309.

[140] Geografičeskoe opisanie rossijskogo gosudarstva, 4: 947.

foundation and a new roof. Unfortunately, it was not lasting. Two years later the entire monastery—the two churches, the cells, and the enclosure fence burned down. The sisters received permission from the metropolitan of Belgorod to collect money for the rebuilding of their monastery, in 1744 and again in 1749[141]. The letter of 1749 informs us that the harvest had been poor, and the sisters were in great need. Some kind of cells must have soon been rebuilt; until they were, the nuns dispersed to the homes of relatives[142]. Construction of a new principal church, this time in stone, was begun in 1754 and finished four years later. It is worth noting that in authorizing the new construction metropolitan Joasaf Horlenko of Belgorod specified that the domes on the church were to be topped by four-ended crosses. A second, warm church was built only in 1785. A few years later a wooden fence was put up around the monastery, grainstores and a cellar were added, and guestrooms built[143].

* * *

While a few women's monasteries possessed great wealth—Sts Florus and Laurus of Kiev, for instance—the economic means of most were modest, and of some downright inadequate. The story of monasteries in all these territories is surprisingly the same. At founding and in the first period of their existence they received generous endowments, but mismanagement and other causes reduced their means, sometimes drastically.

The economic standing of a monastery determined the number of members the monastery accepted. In the conditions of the time and place means of sustenance had to be procured before more members could be taken in. The situation in Russia and in western Europe was not very much different. Where the monasteries did not adhere to this—that is, where numbers exceeded the funds of the monastery—common life necessarily was abandoned, the nuns were reduced to misery, and the monastery underwent a lingering death.

---

[141] The two letters of permission are printed in *ISOXE*, 1: 115-117.

[142] The author of the Kvitka family chronicle recorded that his aunt Maria (later ihumenja of the monastery) and another nun came and lived with them until the cells were rebuilt, *ibid.*, p. 120.

[143] *Ibid.*, p. 118-124.

CHAPTER IV

RELATIONS WITH HIERARCHS AND WITH OTHER MONASTERIES

The life of the nuns in any monastery reflected to a certain extent dependence on the hierarchy, observance of monastic rules and of the regulations of higher authorities, and very often also the characteristics of a particular grouping of monasteries.

Dependence on Hierarchs

With regard to dependence on hierarchs, it is important of course to know whether a monastery was Orthodox or Unitate, and while this is usually obvious, there are a few doubtful cases. These regard mostly the date, at least approximate, when an Orthodox monastery became Uniate. Events external to the monastery are not a sure guide. Although the Lviv eparchy with its bishop Joseph Šumljans'kyj officially accepted the Union in 1700, all its monasteries did not, or did not immediately draw the necessary consequences. At the Slovita women's monastery its pomjanyk, written in 1724, mentions the Uniate metropolitan George Vynnyc'kyj (1708-1713), but also the Orthodox metropolitan Joseph Krokovs'kyj (1708-1718)[1]. This shows at least confusion and hesitance.

As a second step, it is not always an easy matter to determine which hierarch was acknowledged as a monastery's ecclesiastical superior. Apart from the difficulty of determining the territory of eparchies, one cannot be guided by the principle that all monasteries were under the authority of their local bishops. That may have been church law, but practice was different, and the latter is discovered only by examining the situation of individual monasteries.

---

[1] PETRUŠEVIČ, Slovickij ženskij monastyr', p. 112.

Uniate monasteries seem to have been under their local bishops—at least, there are no records of any conflict between hierarchs concerning jurisdiction over them. In the case of Orthodox monasteries, the charters of authorization for their founding are one indication. Apart from the very fact that issuing a charter was already a mark of authority over a monastery, there may be an explicit mention in the charter. When Dionisius Balaban, metropolitan and also administrator of the Luc'k-Ostrih diocese, blessed the founding of the monastery in Drohyčyn, he made it dependent on the Luc'k bishop[2].

Founders often stated on which hierarch their monastery was to be dependent. At a time when one of the arms used against the Uniates was the accusation of breaking away from their lawful pastor, the patriarch of Constantinople, Orthodox founders strained to emphasize that their monasteries were to be in perpetuity under the obedience of "our lawful pastor, the most holy patriarch of Constantinople". Then they also named the hierarch who was to exercise effective authority over the monastery and again they stressed his ties with Constantinople. The founders of the Mozoliv monastery, making it dependent on the metropolitan of Kiev, emphasized that he was named ("podavany²") by the patriarch of Constantinople[3].

As with Mozoliv, so also in the case of other monasteries in Belorussia, often not the local hierarch, but the metropolitan of Kiev was named as their ecclesiastical superior. Thus the foundress of the Sts Peter and Paul monastery of Minsk says she proceeded "with the blessing" of the metropolitan of Kiev[4]. And the founders of the Kutejno monastery stated categorically that "no metropolitan, nor any bishop of Belorussia, save for the Kievan metropolitan, are to have any affairs or pretexts regarding our Kutejno women's monastery at Svystoly for all time"[5].

This led, as one can easily surmise, to tension between the local bishop and the metropolitan, especially when the two found themselves in different states. In 1710 the matter reached Stephen Javors'kyj, at that time the higest church authority in Russia with the title of exarch, to whom Belorussian monasteries had evidently complained of their local bishop. Javors'kyj confirmed the "ancient" rights of the Kievan

---

[2] "Ten monaster, iesli za pomocą Bożą stanie i zakonnice w nim się umnozą, ma mieć dependetią od Nas, iako loci ordinario y po nas będących", *AV*, 33: 399.

[3] *IJuM*, 14: 513.

[4] In her testament, *VZR*, 2 (1863), November, 11.

[5] *Akty ZR*, 4: 523.

metropolitans over these monasteries and forbade the bishop of Belorussia to exercise any jurisdiction over them[6].

The monasteries named in this case were Barkalabava, Kutejno, and Mozoliv, but the sentence was of wider application. Whether the monastery of St Nicholas in Mahilev, which exceptionally was placed at its founding under the jurisdiction of the bishop of Mscislav, Orša, and Mahilev (at that time Sylvester Kosov)[7], came under this ruling is not known. But of others we see, for instance, that the Sluck monastery in 1724 was dependent on the metropolitan of Kiev. In that same year, when the bishop of Belorussia Sylvester Četvertyns'kyj excommunicated a group of priests and monks and the ihumenja of the Kutejno monastery, the persons concerned appealed to metropolitan Vanatovyč. He declared the ban null, on the grounds that it was an intrusion on the part of Četvertyns'kyj, since the monasteries were subject to the metropolitan[9].

The matter of conflicting jurisdictions was finally settled after the partition of Poland in 1772, when this territory was taken by Russia; all the monasteries were then definitively placed under the jurisdiction of the local bishop. Prior to that the bishop of Belorussia and Mahilev, as he was called, was able for short periods to assert his authority[10]. In 1756 the Kiev metropolitan granted full jurisdiction over the Barkalabava monastery (consequently also over Kutejno) to the bishop of Mahilev, which he still retained three years later[11]. In spite of this, matters continued to be sent to Kiev for settlement[12].

---

[6] *AS*, 5: 75-76.

[7] *Ibid.*, 2: 70.

[8] A visitation to look over its material and economic state took place "with the blessing" of the metropolitan of Kiev Varlaam Vanatovyč, cf. SNITKO, Opisanie dokumentov, p. 153.

[9] The two sentences are in *Arxiv JuZR*, pt. I, 4: 412-416 (Četvertyns'kyj's) and 416-419 (Vanatovyč's).

[10] The bishop Theodosius Vasylevyč confirmed a charter given to the Mahilev Epiphany monastery by previous metropolitans, but he signed himself "namesnyk mytropolii kievskoj", as did others in similar situations, cf. *IJuM*, 10: 497. A report to the Holy Synod in 1743 concerning the Kutejno monastery stated that it was under the jurisdiction of the metropolitan of Kiev, cf. *OASS*, 23: 36.

[11] Cf. *IJuM*, 16: 284. The ihumenja of Barkalabava, in making a legal declaration, stated that she was acting "za wolą y błagosłowienstwem ias. wielm. imsci xiędza Jerzego Koniskiego, biskupa białoruskiego y mohylowskiego, pana pasterza y dobrodzieia naszego, plenariam potestatem y zwierzchnosc nad monasterami naszemi Buynickim y Barkałabowskim, od iasnie wielmożnego w Bogu nayprzewielebnieyszego imsci xiędza Timofieia Szczerbackiego, metropolity kiiowskiego, in scriptis ieszcze w roku tysiąc siedmset piędziesiątym szostym miesiąca Julii dwudziestego szostego dnia, maiącego".

[12] The document cited in the previous note refers to this.

In other regions too monasteries were placed under the metropolitan of Kiev. Margaret Dyškevyč in her testament left the monastery of Javoriv not under the protection of the bishop of Peremyšl', in whose eparchy it was situated, but under that of Peter Mohyla[13].

The extent of the authority of hierarchs over monasteries—or at least the extent to which they exercised it—can likewise be determined only by examining actual practice. Examples are not frequently met with; evidently women's monasteries were a minor concern of the hierarchs.

The sort of interventon on the part of bishops that did occur can be seen in two examples from the first half of the seventeenth century. The first concerns Josaphat Kuncevyč. He first built a monastery by the cathedral of St Sophia in Polock and collected there the nuns who had lived dispersed since 1580. Then he asked metropolitan Rutskyj to send from the Vilna Holy Trinity monastery, located in the metropolitan's diocese, a superior and another sister who might instruct the Polock nuns in religious observance[14]. The second concerns the investigation on the part of metropolitan Antony Sjeljava in 1650 of accusations made against the nuns of Hrodna. In answer to a complaint of some Jews of that town that the nuns had baptized a Jewish girl still a minor the metropolitan called upon the archimandrite of Vilna to investigate the matter. The nuns showed extreme reluctance in heeding the summons that required their superior to go to Vilna, and the metropolitan felt obliged to excommunicate her[15].

We have already mentioned some dealings of hierarchs with monasteries, such as examining disputed property boundaries between two monasteries. Besides the case between Barkalabava and Bujnyči described in Chapter III, one can cite also the mediation of metropolitans Balaban and Vanatovyč in a dispute between the monasteries of Novi Mlyny and Baturyn men's. The hierarchs had no more success than civil authorities in reconciling the claims of the two

---

[13] Cf. C'OROX, p. 245.

[14] He himself tells of this in his grant of 1621 to the monastery, cf. the Latin copy in APF, Miscellanee diverse, 19, fol. 445 v: "Et volendo pro pastorali sollicitudine mea, illas ad religisiorem reducere aliquomodo, et reformare statum; extructo Monasterio prope Ecclesiam meam Cathedralem S. Sophiae, illas ad illum Monasterium congregavi et transtuli, et Superiorissam cum Socia, ad effectum reducendi illas ad religiosam observationem ex Monasterio Vilnensi Sanctissimae Trinitatis, ab Illustrissimo Domino Metropolitano expetii".

[15] The whole affair is recounted in *OAZM*, 1: 291-293.

monasteries[16]. Recourse was also had to hierarchs by the laity in their complaints against monasteries, but it did not always have a happy outcome for the complainant[17]. From formulas in official documents we learn that at least in the Uniate metropolitan eparchy the assent of the metropolitan was asked before carrying out major financial transactions[18].

In the seventeenth century the patriarchs of Moscow on some rare occasions exercised direct authority over some monasteries. Its character is exemplified in a letter of patriarch Adrian to Maria Magdalene Mazepa, ihumenja of the Kiev Ascension and Hluxiv monasteries[19]. In 1692 the ihumenja had been to Moscow to seek alms from the tsars and while there, as the letter notes, had asked the patriarch's blessing for herself and her sisters. In response the patriarch wrote a letter of spiritual advice. At its very end he added that the ihumenja had informed him that the Hluxiv monastery was located by a noisy marketplace and surrounded by taverns, and that she was endeavoring to transfer it to a more tranquil spot, with the consent and approval of hetman Mazepa (who had built the Assumption church at the new location) and of the metropolitan of Kiev Varlaam Jasyns'kyj. The patriarch then took it upon himself to permit and order ("blagoslovljaem i stroiti tamo... povelevaem") the relocation.

Rules

On occasion in documents concerned with women's monasteries one encounters phrases such as "the rule of St Basil", "the statutes of the holy fathers", or that the sisters in a newly founded monastery are to live "according to the rule of St Basil", or they follow "the rule of St Basil"[20]. The above phrases do not refer to a text of a rule of St Basil,

---

[16] Balaban's decision of 1658 is in LAZAREVSKIJ, Akty, p. 61-62, and a report of a commission set up by Vanatovyč in 1730 ibid., p. 66-70. There too, on p. 62, is an order of hetman Mnohohrišnyj, on the lines of Balaban's, to put an end to false claims, while a charter of tsars Ivan and Peter in VASILENKO, 1: 195, mentions an attempt by Mazepa in 1690 to settle the matter.

[17] Cf. LAZAREVSKIJ, Opisanie, 2: 298, for one such recourse to the Kiev metropolitan in 1727.

[18] So in a deed of sale of one large building in Vilna in 1740 which brought the monastery 2000 Pol. zl., AV, 9: 329.

[19] Printed in Arxiv JuZR, pt. I, 5: 345-348.

[20] For example, from the foundation grant of 1612 for the monastery of Sts Peter and Paul in Minsk, "vodle zakonu, poradku i ustavu žytija svetoho vasylyja", VZR, 2 (1863),

but are a way of designating the traditions of eastern monasticism as they were commonly understood. In the titles of books from various monasteries there is never even a small volume of excerpts or paraphrases of St Basil and very little of other eastern monastic fathers—though granted that we have few lists, especially complete ones[21].

Furthermore, the above phrases taken in context clearly do not refer to written works. In the foundation grant for the Barkalabava monastery it is stated, for example, that the superior should carry out the duties of her office "according to the statutes of the ancient holy fathers and the blessed nuns of old"[22], that is, she should act in harmony with sound monastic tradition.

This is not to say that written rules were entirely lacking. There was at least one Orthodox and one Uniate rule. Both are connected with Vilna monasteries and both were composed at about the same time. Both were written for monks, but since the monasteries concerned had women's monasteries associated with them, the rules must have been known also to the latter; for the Uniate one we have direct evidence of

---

November, 12; from the testament of the foundress of the Javoriv monastery in 1644, "według Reguły Sw. Bazylego", C'OROX, p. 243.

Related to this is the designation of the nuns themselves as of the "rule" or of the "order of St Basil the Great". This was a term used in Poland-Lithuania to distinguish all eastern nuns (and monks) from those of the Latin rite and was used by all to refer to both Uniates and Orthodox. Two sets of examples from two localities illustrate this; in each, one monastery is Orthodox and one Uniate. A court document of 1672 has the following phrase: "Ja Anastazya Tekla Kotłowna—starsza ze wszystkiemi pannami zakonnemi świętego Bazylego wielkiego monastyra Wileńskiego, przy cerkwi Tróycy świętey w uniey będącego" (*AV*, 11: 205); another court document, of 1678, has similar wording—"Ja, Elizabeta Wasiliewiczowna—starsza klasztoru Wileńskiego panien zakonu Bazylego świętego" (*ibid.*, p. 220-221), and even if we did not know that she was superior at the Holy Spirit monastery, it is said so explicitly on p. 222. In similar fashion we have the following: from a will of 1677, "wielebnym pannom zakonnym zakonu Sw. Bazylego Wielkiego monastyru Orszanskiego, w iedności sw. z kościołem rzymskim zostaiącym" (*IJuM*, 26: 359, footnote); and in a court document of 1719, "monastyr Kuteięski Orszanski zakonu swiętego Bazylego W-go" (*ibid.*, 30: 86). From another region, the founder of the Vinnycja monastery calls it "rehuly svjatoho Vasylyja" in 1639 (Secinskij, p. 258).

[21] With regard to the works of St Basil there is one possible exception. An ascetical homily of his in manuscript was found in the St Florus monastery in Kiev, bound with a seventeenth century manuscript of St Ephrem. However, the description does not say whether the St. Basil copy, or the binding, is of the same century or later. See N.I. PETROV, Opisanie rukopisnyx sobranij, naxodjaščixsja v gorode Kieve, *ČOIDR*, 1897, 2: 253.

[22] "Vodluh postanovlenija drevnyx svjatyx otcov i svjatoblyvyx davnyx inokyn", *Akty ZR*, 5: 70.

this. A comparison of the two rules would have been interesting and valuable, but the Orthodox one is an extremely rare work.

The archimandrite of the Orthodox Holy Spirit monastery of Vilna Leontij Karpovyč was the author of *Kynobion, ily izobraženie Evanhel'skoho Inočeskoho Obščohožytija ot Svjatyx Otec vokratci sobrano* printed at Jevje at the Vilna brotherhood typography in 1618[23]. This work could have been known at least in the women's monasteries of Holy Spirit in Vilna and Sts Peter and Paul in Minsk.

For Uniate monks a rule was written at about the same time by Rutskyj. Perhaps already at that time it was adapted for nuns, though such an adaptation was printed only in 1771 by Felicianna Sorokivna, superior of the Holy Spirit monastery in Minsk under the title *Ustawy Śgo. Oca. Ngo. Bazylego Wgo. tudzież uwagi i nauki duchowne przez S.J.J.X. Józefa Welamina Ruckiego metropolitę całej Rusi zebrane i klasztorowi Mińskiemu Panien tegoż zakonu podane, dla większej wygody teraz wydrukowane w Wilnie w Drukarnie J.K.M.XX. Bazylianów*[24]. There is a contradiction in the heading, inasmuch as the Holy Spirit monastery was founded thirteen years after the death of Rutskyj (1637). The manuscript of that monastery, however, was supposed to have been written in the hand of Catherine Sapieha and thus could have been brought by her from Vilna.

These rules, as has been said, are an adaptation of the ones Rutskyj gave his monks; whether the adaptation was made by him or by some other person is impossible to determine. It is interesting to observe that both he and Karpovyč claim to be only transmitting ancient monastic rules. Like the phrases quoted earlier about the rule of St Basil, these appeals to the ancient monastic authorities reveal the same orientation: an emphasis on ties with tradition. In spite of that, Rutskyj's rule, in fact, is quite removed from the text of St Basil[25], and, one suspects, so was Karpovyč's.

Another point open to speculation is the extent to which these rules were known and used. There is probably an indirect reference to Rutskyj's rule when in 1724 metropolitan Kyška prescribed that the ''rule of

---

[23] Cf. I. KARATAEV, *Opisanie slavjano-russkix knig napečatannyx kirillovskimi bukvami*, 1 (Sanktpeterburg, 1883): 345.

[24] They were printed in Polock in 1807 and in Rome in 1854, when an Italian translation was also put out. The only copy of the 1771 edition was found in the Lviv Church Museum, no. 5421, cf. A. ŠEPTYC'KYJ, *Vytjah z pravyl sv. Otcja našoho Vasylija Velykoho* (Žovkva, 1909).

[25] A study of the various influences on it has been made recently by Porfirij Vasyl' PIDRUČNYJ, *Narys zakonodavstva Vasylijans'koho Čynu Sv. Josafata* (dissertation, Pontifical Oriental Institute, Rome, 1976).

St Basil'' be read four times a year in the refectory of the Minsk Holy Spirit monastery[26]. And there is another in 1744 when metropolitan Athanasius Šeptyc'kyj similarly prescribed for the Hrodna monastery the reading at meals of lives of the saints and of the rule of St Basil[27]. The rule of St Basil in both cases must mean either a manuscript copy of Rutskyj's rule for nuns, or the printed one for monks.

All other rules and regulations emanated from persons outside the monastic milieu, but having authority under one head or another over monasteries. First come the rules given by the founders of monasteries, the so-called *ktytors'ki ustavy*. In this period they appear as integral parts of foundation grants, though by the seventeenth century they lacked the detailed prescriptions older ustavy had had[28] and limited themselves to laying down some general principles.

Such founders' statutes all prescribed more or less the same fundamental norms of monastic life. The two specific items most frequently mentioned were observance of common life and election of the superior by the nuns themselves. Some of these ustavy confined themselves to general statements; others proceeded to specify particulars.

An especially interesting ustav is the testament of Eugenia Šembeleva, the foundress of the Sts Peter and Paul monastery in Minsk. She herself had entered the monastery and had been superior there. The testament was written in 1637, twenty-five years after the foundation of the monastery. Based as it is on prolonged personal experience and knowledge, it no doubt reflects well the condition and spirit of the monastery at that time. The following are her dispositions about the election of the superior: the sisters are to elect in common agreement and without consulting any religious or laity a superior from among their own number without regard to her conditions of birth or the amount of dowry she had brought in, but one who is devout, prudent, knowledgeable in running a household, who desires good for the monastery and for all the sisters[29]. The explicit exclusion, even in a consultative capacity, of all extraneous persons in the elections was probably directed primarily at the brotherhood with which the monastery had ties.

Common life is emphasized in the charters of the founders. Soon after Constantine Ostroz'kyj founded the Dubno women's monastery he

---

[26] Acta Kisciana, 6, fol. 268.

[27] Cf. *OAZM*, 2: 91-92.

[28] Cf. older ustavy given to men's monasteries, *Akty ZR*, 3: 22-25; *AS*, 9: 16-22, 58-63.

[29] *VZR*, 2 (1863), November, 12.

associated it with that of the monks, with the injunction that it observe
common life. In a charter given to the latter monastery by which common life was introduced there the prince described at length what common life is "according to the rules of St Basil and the holy fathers".
The same manner of life was to prevail at the women's monastery[30].

In the charter given to the Kutejno monastery it is specified that the
sisters may elect to the office of superior either one from among
themselves or else a nun from some other monastery, provided that the
other monastery too observe common life[31]. The founders evidently did
not want an ihumenja used to a less observant from of monastic life in-
troducing similar relaxations in theirs.

In addition to injunctions about prayers for the founder and his
family, some other general specifications about prayer were made. These
generally stipulated that all rites and practices of the "holy Eastern
Church" should be observed. This appears in the foundation document
of Vinnycja: the founder's grant holds as long as the sisters remain "in
pious orthodoxy" ("pry pravovyreju blahočestyvoju"), keep to the
traditional rites of the Church, and observe the old calendar[32].

The most important influence on the regulations of Uniate
monasteries was the synod of the Kievan metropolitan province headed
by metropolitan Leo Kyška held in Zamość in 1720. The Synod set
down some rulings which concern women's monasteries; these relate
above all to the observance of enclosure. The nuns were not to go out
of the monastery except in the gravest of necessities, and no externs, except those whose services were needed, were to enter it[33]. On this point
the hierarchy simply adopted Tridentine legislation concerning women
religious without regard for the different historical development and the
different character of monasticism at home. In addition, the Synod left
detailed directives for visitators of monasteries[34].

Since what interests us is monasticism as it was lived and not ideal
and perhaps unrealized systems described in rules, it is most useful to
look at the separate points of the Synod's regulations in connection with
the topic to which they apply. At this point, however, we can compare

---

[30] *Arxiv JuZR*, pt. I, 6: 93-95.

[31] *Akty ZR*, 4: 522.

[32] SECINSKIJ, p. 258-259.

[33] *SPR*, p. 110-112. That some such regulations were necessary is shown if only by the
fact that in the past even hierarchs seemed to be unaware of what was proper and gave
banquets for rowdy guests on monastery grounds, cf. an account of one such in *Litterae
Basilianorum*, 1: 152-156.

[34] *SPR*, p. 140-142.

the Synod's prescriptions with those of some visitations of monasteries that followed it.

Visitations

The Synod of Zamość called for visitations in each eparchy at least once every two years, to be made either by the local hierarch or by visitators designated by him. It specified that women's monasteries were to be included in the visitations, as they were wholly under the authority of the bishops[35]. Visitations did occur, but hardly biennial ones; references to them are not at all frequent.

The practice actually was not new with the synod. In 1710, for instance, we hear of preparations for a visitation of monasteries in Vilna (Holy Trinity) and Minsk (Holy Trinity and Holy Spirit), as well as in Vicebsk (Holy Spirit). Whether the one of Vilna and Minsk was carried out, though, remains uncertain. Already in 1709 the protoarchimandrite, Leo Kyška, however, was prevented from making it himself because of the general chapter of the Basilians at Biała and sent delegates instead, who, however, were not accepted by the nuns[36]. Early in 1710 Demetrius Zankevyč, Basilian superior in Navahrudek, asked to be assigned to carry it out, but his request was denied, since the nuns reiterated that they would accept as visitator only the metropolitan or the protoarchimandrite[37]. Somewhat later protoarchimandrite Kyška wrote that the visitation would be carried out by him after Easter[38]. But again other matters detained him, and the metropolitan named the superior of Vilna, Antony Zavadz'kyj, as visitator, giving him at the same time specific instructions[39]. Nothing indicates, though, that the nuns had been persuaded to accept a mere delegated visitator.

---

[35] *Ibid.*, p. 97.

[36] Acta Kisciana, vol. 6, fol. 55-56. Kyška here copies Vynnyc'kyj's "Instrumentum pro visitatione monasteriorum Minscensium monialium datum Superiori Vilnensi" dated 29 April 1710, where much of the background is recounted. Mention is made there also of an earlier visitation.

[37] This is noted by Kyška under 4 January 1710, *ibid.*, fol. 1.

[38] *Ibid.*, fol. 28r.

[39] These regard the material condition of the monastery, monastic discipline, and confirmation of elections: "Aby . . . w sprawy y munimenta weyrzał, splendory cerkiewne konnotował, prowenta, maiętności, y to wszystko co do dobrego porządku bedzie należało, sporzadził, Przełożoney w oboygu Conwentach Minskich, kanonicznie przez vota sekretne Wielebnych Panien Bazylianek obrane, do dalszey Dispositiey Naszey konfirmował, y utwierdził osobliwie zas w klasztorze Panienskim Wilenskim porządku wnętrz-

The visitation of the Vicebsk Holy Spirit monastery in that same year was carried out, however, and there exists a circumstantial account of it. In this case protoarchimandrite Leo Kyška delegated two Basilian monks of Vicebsk to carry it out. (The rector of the Jesuit college had been asked, but had declined the charge). Visitations appear to have been due not to a regular practice, but to circumstances that called for an intervention. At this time the Vicebsk monastery was in a turmoil because one of the nuns had submitted a long list of accusations against the superior. The investigation carried out at the visitation proved them to be unfounded[40].

Although in these examples the protoarchimandrite is seen as taking a great deal of initiative, the visitations were due actually to the metropolitan, George Vynnyc'kyj, in whose eparchy the monasteries were located. This is evident from the letter of authorization he issued for the visitation of the Minsk monasteries.

After the Synod of Zamość we hear of a visitation of the Minsk Holy Spirit monastery in 1724[41]. In 1744 there was a visitation of the Hrodna monastery carried out at the behest of metropolitan Athanasius Šeptyc'kyj; after its completion the metropolitan issued a set of regulations. The observance of enclosure was stressed, though not in such extreme terms as by the Synod of Zamość, which permitted the nuns to go out only in the case of fire, the plague, or an enemy attack, and only with the previous knowledge of the bishop at that[42]. In contrast, metropolitan Šeptyc'kyj in 1744 enjoined upon the nuns in Hrodna (and no doubt he gave similar instructions elsewhere) that they go out only in case of necessity and only by twos[43]. The same generally formulated prescription was repeated in other visitations; we shall see later that it was not interpreted narrowly.

A comparison of other regulations given to Hrodna with those of the Synod shows them to be in agreement with one another. Some further directives relate to the enclosure (the gates to be kept locked at all

---

nego y zewnętrznego, Osservantiey Pannom od IX Protoarchimandrity, podczas wizyty zostawionych, a od Nas confirmowanych doyrzał, przeiazdzek niepotrzebnych do filwarkow y krewnych Wielebnych Panien, pod exkommuniką zakazał". "Instrumentum pro visitatione", *ibid.*, fol. 55-56.

[40] Kyška's report of the visitation, with his comments, *ibid.*, fol. 28-29.

[41] *Ibid.*, fol. 268-270.

[42] "Sancta Synodus . . . statuit, ut nulli Sanctimoniali e Monasterii Septis egredi unquam liceat, nisi propter magnum incendium, vel infirmitatem leprae, aut epidemiae, vel etiam militarem incursum, quae tamen causae ab Ordinario loci probari debeant". *SPR*, p. 110.

[43] Cf. *OAZM*, 2: 91-92.

times, there is to be a bell at the gate, men are not to be allowed inside the monastery). Others stipulate the sum of the dowry and the use to be made of it. Finally, still others prescribe a one-year novitiate (implied, though not ordained explicitly by the Synod).

At a visitation of the Vinnycja monastery in 1792 besides some common points we see several regulations concerning financial matters (accurate keeping of an account book, a common treasury), as well as about monthly confession and communion, all according to the directives of the Synod. First the visitator, a diocesan priest John Čemena, gave some general recommendations on obedience, then precise directions on how to keep accounts, and finally listed the circumstances in which the nuns were to have recourse to the local hierarch[44]. This last direction, however, it was no longer possible to carry out: the local hierarch, the bishop of Lviv, and the monastery were now in different states, and the monastery was destined to be taken over soon by the Orthodox.

The Holy Synod and Monasteries

For the Orthodox monasteries of Kiev and the Left Bank complications arose with the creation of the Holy Synod and the publication of the appendix on monasticism to the Ecclesiastical Statute (*Duxovnyj reglament*) of Peter I in 1722[45]. The Statute emphasized utility and thrift in monastic life. Since Peter I saw the usefulness of monasteries chiefly as shelters for the old and the destitute, the Statute set limits on the numbers of monks and nuns and specified the age at which profession could be given, which for women was fifty to sixty years.

However, one cannot draw immediate inferences about Ukrainian monasteries from the ordinances of the Ecclesiastical Statute, as well as from further directives on the matter. An ambivalent attitude was taken with regard to the question whether all these regulations applied to Ukrainian monasteries or not, hence they were carried out only fitfully.

---

[44] Cf. SECINSKIJ, p. 266-268. The directions on how to keep accounts are detailed: "W reiestr na terminie jeneralney wizyty zostawiony, zaliniowany, s ·pomieszczeniem percepty i expensy dnia, miesianca i roku porządnie zapisywać".

[45] The addition on monks and monasteries was approved in April-May 1722. The full Russian text is found in P.V. VERXOVSKOJ, *Učreždenie Duxovnoj Kollegii i Duxovnyj Reglament* (Rostov na Donu, 1916). The title of the modern English edition is a misleading literal translation, *The Spiritual Regulation of Peter the Great*, tr. and ed. Alexander V. MULLER (Seattle, Washington Paperbacks on Russia and Asia, 1972).

Thus, on the one hand, in 1725-1726 the Holy Synod, in considering questions that touched on the minimal age requirements put to it by the metropolitan and the Kiev Lavra stated that the prescriptions of the Ecclesiastical Statute and further regulations did not apply to Ukraine[46]. On the other hand, in 1726, when the St Florus monastery of Kiev asked for permission to give profession to several women who had lived already many years in the monastery, the Synod replied that they must hold to the age requirements of the Statute[47].

Much depended on hierarchs and others responsible whether these ordinances were adhered to or not. In 1734 a number of charges were brought up before the Synod against the archimandrite of the Černihiv Dormition (Jelec'kyj) monastery. Among the accusations was one of giving profession to nuns in the St Paraskeva monastery contrary to the ukazy[48]. Metropolitan Raphael Zaborovs'kyj felt obliged to seek the Synod's consent before giving permission for the profession of a widow in the Kiev St Florus monastery in 1739[49].

Restrictions on monastic profession were especially stringent during the reign of Anna. After her death in 1740 they were mitigated, but practice in Ukraine continued to be inconsistent. In 1741 several women in their thirties received profession in the Makošyn monastery in the diocese of Černihiv without any previous correspondence with the Synod on the matter, nor did any objections from the Synod follow[50]. In the same year it was permitted explicitly to the Kiev metropolitan to admit to profession women of thirty years of age[51].

The question of who was the competent authority to decide was raised not only with regard to admission to profession. As the bishops authorized the foundation of monasteries, so they gave permission for transferrals, rebuildings, and had also the right to close them. Before the exchange of monasteries between Hamalijivka and Mutyn took place, permission was asked of metropolitan Raphael Zaborovs'kyj of Kiev, who related the matter to the Holy Synod. The Synod took three years to reach a decision, authorizing the transfer in 1733[52]. In these matters again the measure of dependence on the Holy Synod was determined at least to a certain extent by the hierarch himself. When the

---

[46] *OASS*, 5: 106-109, and 6: 382-384.
[47] *Ibid.*, 6: 69-70.
[48] *Ibid.*, 14: 535-536.
[49] *Ibid.*, 15: 111.
[50] *Ibid.*, 21:463.
[51] *PSPR,* [1st series], 10: 534.
[52] Cf. *OASS*, 10: 140-141, and *PSPR*, [1st series], 7: 37.

sisters of the St Florus monastery of Kiev in 1723 asked metropolitan Varlaam Vanatovyč for permission to rebuild their church, he referred the matter to the Holy Synod[53]. In 1742, on the other hand, archbishop Peter Smelič of Belgorod independently gave permission for a renovation of the Ascension church at the Xoroševe monastery[54]. The Holy Synod charged the metropolitan of Kiev to see to the restoration of the Barkalabava monastery in 1751[55], a task not easy to carry out, since the metropolitan and the monastery were not in the same state.

Throughout the eighteenth century, until 1786, when the integration of Ukraine into the Russian empire became complete, other examples of vacillation can be noted. This is part of a much broader question: the extent and manner in which Russian legislation regarding ecclesiastical matters was applied in Ukraine. Only when that has been studied in detail can more than vague generalities and isolated examples illustrate the particular problem of women's monasteries.

Monastery Groupings

Another factor in the regulations governing monasteries was that of monastery groupings. In principle, each monastery was independent of other monasteries and subject only to the local hierarch. But just as dependence on the local hierarch did not hold true in all instances, so it also happened that small groupings arose which embraced both men's and women's monasteries with ties of interdependence among them and usually with one monastery playing a leading role.

The origins of this development, as far as it can be traced, date from the late sixteenth century and are closely connected with the rise of the brotherhoods. An association arose very naturally among the monasteries founded or supported by a brotherhood. The brotherhoods in the large towns had their own churches and by them they would maintain a monastery for monks, who serviced the church, and often also a monastery for nuns.

It is easy to understand how a women's monastery in certain respects would depend on a monastery for monks when the two existed side by side and perhaps shared the same church. In addition, the regulations of these monasteries must have been closely similar. Slightly

---

[53] *OASS*, 3: 197.
[54] *ISOXE*, 1: 114-115.
[55] *OASS*, 31: 283.

later such associations arose also in other circumstances. For the most part we do not have any clearly defined statutes regulating these groupings and only by drawing on contemporary evidence from various sources do we learn how they functioned.

Except for the one at Lviv, brotherhood monastery groupings were all located in Lithuanian towns—Vilna, Minsk, Mahilev—embracing later within their associations other outlying towns. They were supported by the brotherhoods, though this is true only of their early history, when the brotherhoods themselves were flourishing. Later, as the brotherhoods declined, we see no trace of ties between the brotherhoods and the women's monasteries. But close affiliation persisted between the women's and the men's monasteries. In 1795 the bishop of Mahilev Athanasius Volxovskij reported dissapprovingly that the women's monastery in Mahilev was united to the men's brotherhood monastery[56], and by united he meant that it was subject to the latter.

From Vilna we have a first vague reference to such an arrangement. The monastery of the Holy Trinity came under the administration of a brotherhood during the reign of Stephen Batory (1575-1586)[57]. Already then a mention is made of nuns. According to a charter of Sigismund III from 1589 the brotherhood was to give every week, according to its ability, a donation for food to the monks and nuns at Holy Trinity[58]. This speaks only of food provisions and does not mention any ties between the men's and the women's monasteries. However, the two monasteries were side by side, with a wall between them, and the nuns never had a church of their own, but attended the services of the monks.

The development of this particular grouping came after the Union of Brest and after the founding in Vilna of the Orthodox Holy Spirit brotherhood and monasteries. These, since they drew their members from Holy Trinity, may be regarded as partial heirs of the latter. The archimandrite of the Vilna Holy Spirit monastery had jurisdiction not only over the women's monastery next to it, but also over both monasteries by the church of Sts Peter and Paul in Minsk, as well as over other Orthodox monasteries in Lithuania. The monasteries dependent on the Vilna archimandrite (sometimes called ihumen) formed the

---

[56] Cf. ŽUDRO, *Bogojavlenskij bratskij monastyr'*, p. 31.

[57] Cf. ŠČERBICKIJ, *Vilenskij Svjato-Troickij monastyr'*, p. 23-27; also the letter of Paul Sapieha to Christopher Radziwill in 1598 in which he complained of the intrusion of the brotherhood ("bractwa jakiegoś"), 1: 194.

[58] The charter of Sigismund III is printed in *AV*, 9: 140-144, and in *ČOIDR*, 1859, 3.

largest grouping of monasteries and a rather long-lived one. In 1751 a report to the Holy Synod named eleven monasteries as subject to the Vilna Holy Spirit monastery (nine men's, two women's) and listed eight others, now Uniate, as having once belonged to this group[59].

More immediately, the women's monastery of Sts Peter and Paul was in certain respects under the jurisdiction of the local ihumen, though it had its own superior, as of course did all the monasteries which belonged to such groupings. A charter granted to the Minsk brotherhood of Sts Peter and Paul in 1633 at the coronation diet stated that "the women's monastery with its land, buildings, and all its possessions is to remain under the authority of the ihumen elected by them [the monks]"[60]. This had been stipulated in its foundation grant[61], though it was not the brotherhood that had founded the monastery. That the foundress should choose to affiliate her monastery with a brotherhood monastery indicates a growth in the idea of such associations: the founders must have seen advantages deriving from such groupings. Especially after we examine associations of other origins will the advantages become more apparent.

As regards the Lviv monastery, its founding by the Stauropegian confraternity and its early ties with the St Onuphrius monastery are known. They appear clearly in the charter issued by metropolitan Michael Rahoza on 23 January 1591 in which he gives his blessing to the projects of the confraternity. In addition to the St Onuphrius monastery and hospices for the poor, these included a women's monastery[62]. So few details are known of this last, however, that it is impossible to trace how its connection with the confraternity developed and when it broke off. Since confraternity documents soon cease to mention it, the ties must have ceased quite soon, perhaps around 1646, when the monastery changed location, moving away from the neighborhood of St Onuphrius to the outskirts of Lviv.

Another basis for the grouping of monasteries was that of having been founded by the same person or family. The tendency to establish ties among such monasteries arose as among brotherhood monasteries. Soon after Constantine Ostroz'kyj founded the women's monastery by

---

[59] *OASS*, 31: 417-426.

[60] *VZR*, 2 (1863), November, 9. A Polish version of the same charter, reconfirmed by Augustus III on 10 May 1745 is printed in *AV*, 11: 101-104 (the quoted passage is on p. 103).

[61] *VZR*, 2 (1863), November, 12-13.

[62] *Pamjatniki*, 3: 66-72.

Dubno he placed it under the authority of the ihumen of Dubno[63]. The ties between the two monasteries continued after they both became Uniate. Cassian Sakovyč, who had been archimandrite of Dubno, mentions these relations in a letter written in 1639[64].

The founders in their charters decreed the mode and extent of interdependence among the monasteries; usually the ties were closer than among brotherhood monasteries. The Stetkevyč family, which founded monasteries on its property in Kutejno (men's and women's), Bujnyči (men's), and Barkalabava (women's), placed the ihumen of Kutejno over them all, as is marked in the foundation grant of each. The ihumen's authority, however, was not defined in detail: "inokyn' v nem budučyx pod spravoju i poslušenstvom mity"[65]. But his authority was generally recognized, as in a document issued in 1642 by an official of the Orša district which speaks of the two women's monasteries being under the ihumen's "vladzeju i mocnost'ju"[66]. So also the charter of Augustus II which confirmed the right of Orthodox monasteries in the grand duchy of Lithuania mentions Kutejno and Barkalabava as belonging to the Kutejno group[67].

At least in the first few decades this grouping worked out very well. The ihumen of Kutejno Joil Trucevyč looked after the needs of each and was instrumental in procuring endowments where necessary, even relinquishing his own monastery's rights to some properties[68]. Later the situation deteriorated, and, as we have already seen, two of the monasteries of this grouping fell to wrangling between themselves over property.

The other groupings on the basis of a common founder regard the Vyšnevec'kyj family. Three monasteries founded on their lands were grouped into an association by Isaiah Kopyns'kyj. The history of the foundations is set out in the chronicle of the Hustyn' monastery, though not always reliably[69]. The other two were at Lubny (the Mhar monastery

---

[63] *Arxiv JuZR*, pt. 1, 6: 94.

[64] In S. GOLUBEV, Materialy dlja istorii zapadnorusskoj cerkvi, *ČN*, 5 (1891): 225.

[65] *Akty ZR*, 5: 69 (the foundation charter of Barkalabava).

[66] *IJuM*, 24: 340.

[67] Cf. *Arxiv JuZR*, pt. I, 4: 403-405.

[68] A deed drawn up by him on 30 April 1652 says: "Misto ta intraty, kotoraja z sela Kostjanky y z sela Xolmov na monastyr Kuteenskij muzskij . . . mila doxodyty, . . . do monastyra Borkolabovskoho panenskoho pryvoročaem". *AS*, 2: 76.

[69] Published in *ČOIDR*, 1848, no. 8, by O. Bodjanskij (and also separately, Moskva, 1848).

for monks) and at Ladyn, which had Isaiah's sister Alexandra for its
first superior. During Isaiah's lifetime ties among these three
monasteries were very close, so that they planned a joint emigration to
Muscovy in 1638, though, it is true, a large portion of the members of
the Lubny monastery in the end decided not to go[70].

A second grouping of monasteries founded by the Vyšnevec'kyj
family embraced the monastery in Brahin and the neighboring men's
monastery, from the first half of the seventeenth century. The women's
monastery had no separate endowment, but one third of the monks' income was to be given over to the nuns[71]. About one hundred years later
the monastery of Mazyr was affiliated with them[72].

There exists, finally, an allusion to a grouping of monasteries on
lands of the Korec'kyj family in Volyn' under the ihumen of
Horodyšče[73].

It may be taken as evidence of a well-ordered monastic life in such
groupings if later other monasteries were affiliated with them. The
Kutejno-Barkalabava group of monasteries enjoyed such a good reputa-
tion. In 1645 the foundress of the monastery in Mozoliv requested that
nuns from the Barkalabava monastery begin the foundation. The
ihumen of Kutejno was charged with the same duties towards the new
foundation as towards Kutejno[74].

What did such associations of monasteries entail? The ihumen who
headed the grouping was to care for both the spiritual and the material
needs of the women's monastery. The foundation grant of the
Barkalabava monastery lists these duties of his: he was to see to the construction of the monastery and of the church, oversee the monastic
observance of the nuns, give profession, appoint a priest to serve the
monastery, give advice and aid in necessity[75]. He is found conducting

---

[70] Cf. *Akty JuZR*, vol. 3, no. 5 and 6; Xarlampovič, p. 52-61. The annalist of the
Hustyn' monastery, writing some thirty years later, speaks with disapproval of their flight
to Muscovy: "Sovit sebi daša nerazsmotrytelnyj i lehkoserdnyj, užasty ispolnjaxusja, ješče
že ny kym honymy tohda bjaxu, i ubojašasja straxa, idiže ne bi straxa, ... i bez
razsmotrenija voskori vdašasja puty bihstva, v čužuju zemlju moskovskuju". Letopis' o
pervozačatii i sozdanii Gustynskogo monastyrja, ed. O. Bodjanskij, *ČOIDR*, 1848, no. 8,
p. 29. The flight was occasioned by the false rumors spread by Isaiah Kopyns'kyj that
metropolitan Mohyla was inclined towards the Union.
[71] Nikolaj, p. 164. Cf. the confirmation of the original grant in 1632, when it was applied to the two monasteries without distinction, *VZR*, 2 (1863), November, 56.
[72] Nikolaj, p. 160.
[73] Cf. Petruševič, *Svodnaja letopis' 1600-1700*, p. 455.
[74] *IJuM*, 14: 514-515.
[75] *Akty ZR*, 5: 68-72.

the legal action of the women's monastery[76]. The monasteries were also to be of mutual help to one another—whether in material goods when one was in need and another had an abundance, or in sending a member to another monastery where her skills or services were needed[77].

These were the principles of the groupings. The question of how they were applied remains unanswered—such intimate sources on the life of these monasteries are entirely lacking. Only in the case of some economic matters do we see further into this arrangement. Thus, for instance, the monks on occasion took care of court matters regarding the nuns[78].

Apart from formal groupings, other kinds of ties existed among monasteries. At times they were rather casual. Thus, the Hluxiv monastery and that of the Ascension in Kiev were associated only for a time, on the basis of a common superior, Maria Magdalene Mazepa. The nuns of the Mutyn monastery, according to the wishes of its ktytor, Nastasja Markovna Skoropads'ka, were to be supplied with food provisions, clothes, and other necessities by the monks of Hamalijivka[79]. Whether the two had ties in other respects is not known. For the Xoroševe monastery we have a vague notice that in 1741-1749 it was "under the Kurjaž monastery" near Xarkiv[80].

Finally, some Orthodox monasteries in one respect or another were placed under the authority of the archimandrite of the Kiev Lavra, though this did not constitute a grouping such as those described above. Allusions formulated in general terms are found to the jurisdiction of the Lavra archimandrite over the Kiev St Florus monastery[81] and that in Popivka[82], as well as over some others.

The purposes for which such groupings were formed as well as the manner in which they functioned can next be examined. The effects of

---

[76] As, for instance, the Minsk ihumen, for the Sts Peter and Paul monastery in Minsk, in collecting a debt on its due date, see *VZR*, 2 (1863), November, 15.

[77] *Akty ZR*, 5: 70.

[78] So the monks of the Vilna Holy Spirit monastery, sent by their superior Silvester to see to some of the monastery's court business in Hrodna on 19 October 1753 reported that among other matters they had obtained a court order concerning the repayment of a debt to the Sts Peter and Paul women's monastery in Minsk, see *AS*, 11: 123.

[79] LAZAREVSKIJ, *Opisanie*, 2: 354.

[80] *ISOXE*, 1: 120.

[81] A charter of Ladislaus IV says of this monastery: "Zostajučy pod protekcieju i uradom duxovnym velebnoho v Hospodi Bozi arxymandryta Pečerskoho teperešnoho i za časom budučoho". *Akty JuZR*, 2: 97.

[82] Adam Kysil' says in his foundation grant: "Ten monastyr y te zaconnice mają byc zawsze pod rządem y posłuszenstwem wielebnych oycow archimandrytow kiiowskiei pieczarskiey ławry". *OAZM*, 1: 282.

such arrangements while these were yet in full vigor were beneficial, especially with regard to the observance of common life, which was always emphasized. Such groupings were also regarded as particularly apt to resist the advances of the Union. The close ties among the member monasteries were meant to strengthen them mutually in Orthodox constancy and to render it more difficult for individual monasteries to fall away. Embracing the Union was considered the most heinous of offenses. Should the ihumen of the chief monastery commit this apostasy, the nuns were to regard themselves as freed of his jurisdiction[83]. In the founders' charter given to the Kutejno monastery the nuns were told that at the first sign of vacillation on the part of their ihumenja they were to give the alarm, notifying all the other monasteries of their grouping[84].

All these monastic groupings, however, had real meaning only in the seventeenth century. Later even if formal ties existed, they did not have any practical consequences on the life of the individual monasteries.

In the case of Uniate women's monasteries, they were not united in one congregation as were those of the monks, nor did any special ties exist among particular monasteries. Even in such instances as the Holy Trinity monastery in Vilna and the Holy Spirit monastery in Minsk, where the nuns shared the churches with the monks, no other ties seem to have existed; certainly there is no evidence that the ihumen had anything to say with regard to the women's monastery. Although such expressions as "moniales Ordinis nostri"[85] occur, they had no practical consequences. The one exception to this is the sphere of legal action; here the Basilians often took care of matters regarding the nuns. Thus at the eighth Basilian Congregation, held in Minsk in 1652, two persons were appointed to settle an unspecified affair which concerned the Minsk Holy Trinity monastery[86]. True, the Congregations at times discussed other matters that concerned the nuns, including internal discipline[87]. Nevertheless, the Order as such had no jurisdiction over their monasteries. If action had to be taken, it was done by the hier-

---

[83] Cf. *Akty ZR*, 5: 70.

[84] *Ibid.*, 4: 523.

[85] As in a relation of Jakiv Suša in 1664, *LE*, 2: 324, and otherwise often when the nuns were mentioned.

[86] *AS*, 12: 52.

[87] At the same Minsk congregation the monks discussed disorders in the Vilna and Hrodna women's monasteries, *ibid.*, p. 50.

archs (who took part in the Congregations), who might appoint the pro-toarchimandrite or other monks to carry out a specific charge.

Relations of women's monasteries with the hierarchy or with men's monasteries were sporadic, confined at most to a few canonical matters (erection of a monastery, profession). In most matters the monasteries were left to themselves. There was no concern about them and no encouragement. Men's monasticism, both Catholic and Orthodox, following models of western religious life, became involved in providing for the needs of the Church by schools, typographies, and the like. It did not occur to anyone, however, to draw also the nuns into ecclesiastical work, though examples of women religious engaged in an active apostolate were close at hand, in the Polish-Lithuanian Commonwealth.

CHAPTER V

THE COMMUNITY

As regards the internal life of monasteries, the first item to examined is the community itself: the nuns with profession, designated by a large variety of names[1]; rarely some with the megaloschema, who were know as *sxymnyci*[2]; the novices being trained in the monastic life, usually called *poslušnyci*[3].

Novitiate and Profession

We shall begin with the entrants in a monastery. Information about the duration of a period of probation comes only from the eighteenth century; about other features of the noviceship it is non-existent.

---

[1] The term "profession" is used for "postryženie" as meaning essentially the same thing. "Tonsure", the more literal translation, conjures up an entirely different association.

With regard to the terms used for nuns (in the territories concerned and by native writers), the most common were "zakonnycy", "panny", or "panny zakonnye"; "czernicy" and "starycy" were also used, but not as widely. A term never found is "inokyni"; even in liturgical texts it had been displaced by "monaxyni" (cf. *OASS*, 50: 245-246, where the typography of the Kiev Lavra is ordered in 1770 to reinstate "inokyni" in its Psalter), which, however, is not found otherwise.

[2] As far as the profession of the great habit is concerned, no details have been transmitted—who received it, the circumstances that led to it, the life of the nuns with this profession. All we know is that a nun who had received the great habit was called "sxymnycja", that she took another name upon receiving the megaloschema, and that she could continue to hold office in the monastery. All these features are evident in the case of hetman Peter Dorošenko's mother. In *Akty JuZR*, 13: 130-133, she is mentioned as "staryca Mytrodora". Later, as sxymnycja Maria, she was superior of the Pokrov monastery in Makošyn. Cf. the article about her by Ju. Vynohrads'kyj, Marija Dorošyxa, *Istoryko-heohrafičnyj zbirnyk*, 1 (1927): 32-39.

[3] Sometimes a novice was given the habit, called "rjasa", and hence herself was called

In 1805 a certain M.Ja. Tatena entered the Lebedyn monastery. Letters to her from protoierej Ivan Levanda of Kiev, who had encouraged her, shed a great deal of light on the process of entering[4]. Though the date is late for our study, we can cite this evidence because the process remained unchanged for centuries throughout the entire Ukrainian territory, for Catholics and Orthodox alike. (In Belorussia different circumstances—the town surroundings of many monasteries in particular—led to a different practice).

Supposedly at this period the entry and profession of nuns in Orthodox monasteries required the authorization of the Synod. Protoierej Levanda reassures M. Tatena both before and after her entry that universal practice in Ukrainian monasteries does without recourse to the Synod. He says, in fact, that no one in authority is going to report this case because that would amount to reporting one's own negligence in not proceeding according to law; quite simply, the order the law prescribed had never been put into practice. Other sources bear out fully Levanda's statement. It was certainly characteristic of Ukrainian monasteries that neither permission for nor notification of entrance and profession was conveyed to bishops (or to the Synod), who often had only the vaguest notion where and how many nuns there were in their eparchies.

Acceptance into the monastery did not require much. The person concerned bought a cell (a little cabin) and settled in. This idiorrhytmic way of life too was characteristic of practically all Ukrainian monasteries. We shall see more of this when we discuss common life. Idiorrhytmic monasticism had come to be looked upon as the norm. The tone of the protoierej's letter assumes as self-evident that acquiring a cell equals entering the monastic life. But the entire society, churchmen included, looked at monasticism thus.

As concerns the duration of the novitiate, the practice of the eighteenth century also coincided with that of earlier times. The supposedly eastern tradition of a three-year novitiate was completely unknown. Legislation regulating the duration of novitiate appeared in the eighteenth century, but it had no appreciable effects on practice, which continued to follow established custom, tending to two extremes.

The Synod of Zamość did not prescribe explicitly a one-year

"rjasoforna". Examples of this are rare, but one is mentioned by Demetrius TUPTALO in his diary in 1690, *Drevnjaja rossijskaja vivliofika*, 17: 31.

[4] The letters are from 4 and 5 June 1805, Kievo-Sofijskij protoierej Ioann Vasil'evič Levanda, *TKDA*, 1878, 4: 676, 677-678.

novitiate, but such a prescription follows naturally from what it did ordain about giving the habit to a new entrant (at a minimum fifteen years
of age) and profession (at sixteen)[5]. Metropolitan Athanasius Šeptyc'kyj,
who put so much effort into carrying out the Synod's resolutions, turned
his attention also to this one, as we have already seen[6]. However, even
in his eparchy of Lviv, which he retained when he became metropolitan,
the old practice of giving the habit and profession together and, as far
as we can judge form the documented cases, very soon after a woman
entered a monastery, continued largely unchanged.

A visitation of the Slovita monastery carried out in 1763 noted in
every instance but one that the habit and profession were given together;
the period to which this information refers is about 1702 to 1755. On
the other hand, a catalog of recently deceased nuns of the Lviv
monastery drawn up perhaps in 1800 shows that while they received the
habit almost immediately upon entering the monastery, they made profession from one to six years later[7].

This other extreme, of prolonging the period of noviceship inter-
minably, was common especially in Orthodox monasteries. As already
noted in the previous chapter, the Ecclesiastical Statute of Peter I
prescribed fifty to sixty years as the age for the profession of nuns. Irrespective of the extent to which the Statute was applied in Ukraine, and
even before its issuance, there was a marked leaning for entrants in
monasteries to wait decades before receiving profession. In 1726 the
ihumenja of the Kiev St Florus monastery wrote to the Holy Synod for
permission to give profession to six women from thirty to forty-three
years of age. She reported that one had spent seven years in the
monastery, while the others had been there sixteen, twenty, and twenty-
five years[8]. From this information we learn that they had come to the
monastery at about twenty years of age.

The tendency to put off profession remained independent of official
limits and continued in spite of mitigation of the latter. In 1748 the
ihumenja of Xoroševe wrote to the bishop of Belgorod for permission
for the profession of her niece, who had spent "many years in learning
the fear of God and in obedience"[9] (granted, those "many years" can
mean almost anything). More precise is some information from Novi

---

[5] "Puella non admittatur ad habitum suscipiendum minor quindecim annis, neque ad
professionem nisi expleverit annum decimum sextum". *SPR*, p. 111.
[6] Cf. *OAZM*, 2: 91.
[7] Cf. C'OROX, p. 233-235; 237-240.
[8] *OASS*, 6: 69-70.
[9] *ISOXE*, 1: 130.

Mlyny. There in the second half of the eighteenth century profession
was taken some twenty-five to thirty years after a woman entered the
monastery[10].

As concerns the training of an entrant in a monastery, one assumes
the presence of a novice mistress in Uniate monasteries, at least in the
few well-organized ones of Lithuania. To bolster that assumption,
though, there is only one solitary signature (with three crosses) in a
court document from the Vicebsk monastery in 1750[11].

In Orthodox monasteries the traditional practice was kept up of ap-
prenticing a novice to some older nun. Again, the assumption does not
have much evidence to back it. Only from the Xoroševe monastery do
we have a few incomplete particulars. Piecing together various
statements made about this monastery, we can note only that there was
some kind of monastic training ("v obučenii straxa Božija i v
poslušanii"), that the "poslušanie" probably consisted principally in
helping the older nuns take care of their goats and cows, and that an
ascetic trial lasting seven days took place after profession[12].

Age and Social Background of Nuns

The same source that informed us about profession in Novi Mlyny
tells us also that all the twenty-seven nuns who were in that monastery
in 1777 had entered at fifteen to twenty years of age. Only in a few
other cases do we learn the ages of those entering. Our examples,
however, all provide similar data, though they come from different
regions.

In addition to the notices from Kiev and Novi Mlyny that have
already been cited above, there are a few from western Ukraine. In
Slovita in 1763 there was a certain novice Anastasia Žukovs'ka (Fevronija in religion), daughter of a parish priest. She was eighteen years old
and had entered the year before. In a catalog of fifteen nuns in the Lviv
monastery in the second half of the eighteenth century, ten had entered
at the ages of 17 to 22, and of the remaining five, one at 27, three in
their 30's, and one at 40 years of age[13]. Approximately the same holds
true for the Dubno monastery in a list of its nuns from 1818. Profession

[10] LAZAREVSKIJ, *Opisanie*, 2: 299.
[11] *IJuM*, 18: 419.
[12] *ISOXE*, 1: 130, 133-134.
[13] C'OROX, p. 234-235 (Slovita); 237-240 (Lviv).

was taken at sixteen to twenty-seven years of age[14], so if the regulations
of the Synod of Zamość were observed, the women entered at fifteen
to about twenty-six years of age.

We have already seen some examples of widows entering
monasteries.This was a widespread and old practice. The ihumenja
Mariamna of the Vicebsk monastery in 1553 had entered as a widow.
She had to summon before the episcopal court her husband's brother, a
priest, to obtain the execution of her deceased husband's will[15].

The proportion of widows, or, as it must have been, of older
women to young girls entering monasteries, however, does not seem to
have been large, though there are exceptions. Here is one such: on
1 April 1682 Demetrius Tuptalo, at that time superior of the St Nicholas
monastery in Baturyn, gave profession to three girls and two women at
the Holy Cross monastery in Baturyn[16].

There are also several cases of both husband and wife entering
monasteries. The judge of the Černihiv polk George Zaturkevyč and his
wife Euphrosine entered monasteries in 1707. He went to the St Elias
monastery in Černihiv and she perhaps to the monastery of St
Paraskeva there[17]. In 1704 Joseph Lazarevyč, a protopop of Voroniž in
the Nižyn polk, and his wife both enterd monasteries: "According to the
counsel taken with the concurrence and agreement of his wife, they in-
tend to put on the holy monastic habit and to live out their life in serving God"[18].

From the period before the seventeenth century we have a few pomjanyky which mention nuns from prominent families. With near-
certainty, however, we can eliminate all of these from any account of
women's monasteries. Such notice refer to the survival of a common
practice—an abuse, really—in these families for persons on their
deathbeds to make their monastic profession. All those names of "knjahynja inoka Teodosija" and "skymnica Evhenija Knjahynja"[19] mean

---

[14] Cf. SKRUTEN', p. 358-359, where the ages of the nuns at Dubno and the number of
years since profession are given.

[15] Cf. *Akty ZR*, 3: 46-49.

[16] An entry in his diary, in *Drevnjaja rossijskaja vivliofika*, 17: 15.

[17] MODZALEVSKIJ, *Malorossijskij rodoslovnik*, 2: 151.

[18] So Mazepa speaks of it in a universal; Lazarevyč had asked him to look after the
interests ("prynjaty v oboronu") of his son and his son-in-law. LAZAREVSKIJ, *Opisanie*, 2:
328.

[19] Examples may be found in the pomjanyk of the monastery in Derman' that
perpetuates the memory of the Ostroz'kyj family, founders and benefactors of the
monastery, *Pamjatniki*, 4: 115-118. The monastic names of members of the Sluck princely
family are in the pomjanyk which was recopied in 1684 from a considerably older original

nothing other than that in their last days these persons exchanged their worldly robes for the angelic habit and received a new name. There may have been at the most one or another person from these families that really entered a monastery.

The practice of profession on one's deathbed was already found in pre-Mongolian times, thought it was rare then. An early example is the one recorded in the Hypatian chronicle under 6686 (1178), where it is said of the widow of Vsevolod Ol'hovyč that she received the monastic habit before her death[20]. This custom seems to have been most common in the period roughly of the fourteenth to the sixteenth centuries and then gradually died out. It was the custom among certain prominent families in Ukraine to have their dead buried at the Kiev Lavra. The preliminary of a deathbed profession served no doubt to justify in some measure burial in a monastery. The professions of members of the Ostroz'kyj family, both men and women, illustrate this; the family had its own chapel at the Dormition church where its deceased members were buried.

Peter Mohyla recorded that Anna Xodkevyč Korec'ka, a founder and benefactor of monasteries and charitable institutions, received the monastic habit before she died in 1626[21]. A late example comes from about 1730 from the Černihiv eparchy. The archimandrite of the Transfiguration monastery in Novhorod Sivers'kyj sent one of his hieromonks to give the monastic profession in her home to an old woman, the mother of another monk in the same monastery, because she was ill[22]. This last example shows that the custom of deathbed profession was not confined to princely families, but had found wider acceptance.

One other example may be cited to show the social and regional extent of this custom. In the pomjanyk of Uhornyky, a small monastery of monks in southern Halyčyna, we find a "skymnycja Sofija" mentioned in 1683[23]. It is just possible that she was a nun in a monastery nearby. But since there is no mention of a monastery with her name, as there is when other monks or nuns are listed, she could have been a

---

and published by D.V. Skrinčenko, Sluckij sinodik 1684 goda, *Zapiski severo-zapadnogo otdela russkogo geografičeskogo obščestva*, 4 (1913): 185-204. The pomjanyk of the Suprasl' monastery, *AS*, 9: 454-459, records the monastic names of members of several prominent families.

[20] *PSRL*, 2: 612 (2nd ed.).

[21] *Arxiv JuZR*, pt. I, 7: 67.

[22] One is given to understand that she was on her deathbed, see *OASS*, 14: 525.

[23] Svjencickyj, *Opys rukopysiv Narodnoho Domu*, 3: 103.

laywoman, perhaps a widow, who received the schema on her deathbed.

Rarely before the end of the sixteenth century are we fortunate enough to have some particulars about the nuns. From the genealogy of the Sapieha family we learn that the widow of its founder entered the St Michael monastery in Polock some time in the second half of the fifteenth century and became its superior (she died before 1508)[24].

In the seventeenth century members of the Sapieha family, almost the last ones to be still of the "Greek rite", were nuns at the Holy Trinity monastery in Vilna. We know of at least three[25]. Vasilissa, daughter of the voevoda of Minsk Bohdan Sapieha, was its superior for about twenty-five years, from 1609 to 1633[26]. At about the same time a distant relative of hers, Euphrosine (Anne Sapieha), was also a nun there[27]. The successor of Vasilissa in the post of superior was her niece Evdoksija, daughter of Vasilissa's brother, the vice-chancellor of Lithuania Paul Sapieha. Her monastic name was Catherine[28]. In 1639 she is mentioned as the superior in a charter confirming to the Holy Trinity monastery the possession of all its properties[29]. Later she was summoned to be superior of the Holy Spirit monastery in Minsk, where she died in 1676[30].

Euphrosine Tryzna may have spent some time in the Vilna monastery before she went on to Pinsk. Somewhat later, towards the middle of the seventeenth century, another member of the Tryzna family, Anne Elizabeth, widow of Stanisław Kersnowski, was superior there[31].

---

[24] *Sapiehowie*, 1: 1, 6.

[25] Occasionally one comes across references to a Catherine Sapieha, who was supposedly a nun at the Vilna Holy Trinity monastery around 1520. Such a notice seems to derive from Ignacy Stebelsi, *Dwa wielkie światła na horyzoncie połockim* (which first came out in 1781-1783), in 2: 153 in the 1866-1867 edition. The editor of *Sapiehowie*, 1: 64, provides ample reasons for doubting even her existence, though not all his reasons are uniformly sound (as when he says, confusing matters, that the Basilian community was founded in Vilna only after the Union of Brest).

[26] She was given rights to monastic property in Braslav on 8 August 1609 (*Akty JuZR*, vol. 2, no. 33), and in 1633 she ceded them to the archimandrite of Lješč (*Akty ZR*, 5: 12-13).

[27] The few particulars we know about her are collected in *Sapiehowie*, 2: 115.

[28] The fact that several members of this important family entered the Holy Trinity monastery was heartening to the Uniates, as testified in the apologetic work *Jedność Święta Cerkwie Wschodniey y Zachodniey*, published in Vilna by the Holy Trinity brotnerhood in 1632 (cf. PETRUŠEVIČ, *Svodnaja letopis' 1600-1700*, p. 473).

[29] Published in *AS*, 10: 268-270.

[30] *Sapiehowie*, 2: 138-140, gives the biographical data concerning her.

[31] She is named ihumenja of the Vilna monastery in a document of 13 December 1645, *AV*, 15: 19.

The two Uniate monasteries of Vilna and Minsk throughout their existence attracted members of other prominent and wealthy families. Even as late as around 1770 Joanna Važyns'ka, of a wealthy gentry family, entered the Holy Trinity monastery of Vilna, of which later she became superior. From 5 January 1771 we have a document by which she attests to having received her share of the family inheritance[32].

The Vilna monastery drew members also from the pious townspeople of Vilna. Among other records there is one of a daughter of a Vilna merchant who from her early years had expressed a great desire to enter it[33]. In 1709 the daughter of a town official (burmistr) of Vilna was a nun there; she was the beneficiary of a generous inheritance[34].

The Minsk monastery of the Holy Spirit also had many well-to-do entrants. Metropolitan Sjeljava, in bequeathing to it a large sum, added the disposition that it should provide for six nuns related to him and for four from impoverished gentry ("ubogich szlacheckich") or also from townspeople[35]. But the entrants were not necessarily impoverished, as we see from a document of 1699 which describes the inheritance of one of the nuns. In addition to various sums given her over a number of years she received 3000 zloty and was left various precious objects besides[36].

Nuns in other Catholic monasteries in the grand duchy were also largely of gentry families. A niece of metropolitan Sjeljava was a nun at Polock[37], and a century later a relative of metropolitan Hrebnyc'kyj was there[38]. In the seventeenth century the St Barbara monastery in Pinsk had several superiors from prominent families. Euphrosine Tryzna, daughter of Gregory Tryzna and Regina Sapieha, showed great fortitude and zeal for the Union in the difficult times of the war in the 1650's[39]. Her successor was Joanna Vojna-Orans'ka, sister of the bishop of Pinsk and Turiv Pachomius[40]. In 1719 a nun Anastasia at the Pinsk monastery sold her portion of a village inherited from her parents[41].

---

[32] *AV*, 9: 84-86. She is named superior in a document of 1790, 8: 224-225.

[33] She died, however, before she would do so, and her inheritance, according to her father's disposition, went to the monastery, *ibid.*, p. 203-204.

[34] *Ibid.*, p. 298-300.

[35] *IJuM*, 2: 260-261.

[36] *AV*, 11: 303-306.

[37] He mentions her in his will, *IJuM*, 2: 265.

[38] The monastery's vicar in the 1700's was a Hrebnyc'ka, presumably from the same family—both she and the metropolitan came from the region of Polock, cf. *AS*, 10: 356.

[39] This appears in the letter she wrote to the bishop of Xolm Jakiv Suša on 20 November 1662 in which she describes the invasion, *LB*, 1: 97-100.

[40] Cf. the 1667 will of another brother of hers, Silvester, *AV*, 12: 592-600.

[41] *Ibid.*, 27: 122-124.

Testamentary dispositions, as in the last example, reveal a great deal both about the social provenance of the nuns and the sources of revenue of their monasteries. Numerous examples could be given; a good one comes from Orša in 1673. One of its nuns made out a legal receipt upon receiving an inheritance, a portion of the estate of her deceased sister[42]. Obviously, this was additional to what she had received from her parents upon entering. Such materials could also serve as the basis for a study of the extent to which the Ruthenian gentry passed to the Latin rite. Of special interest are documents that provide information on the family ties and background of members of the hierarchy. Besides the examples above, the legacy of the bishop of Volodymyr and Brest Ioann Potij of 1675 to Euphrosine Catherine Potij of the Navahrudek monastery, evidently his sister, can be mentioned[43].

Social and economic differentiation among the Catholic monasteries of Belorussia did exist. In Vicebsk, at the monastery of the Holy Spirit, in the first decade of the eighteenth century no nuns with dowries applied[44]. Later materials, however, refer to daughters from gentry families who received inheritances[45].

The examples noted just now indicate that the Uniate monasteries of Belorussia attracted largely members from a well-to-do milieu. The social composition of Orthodox monasteries in that territory was similar. The first superior of Barkalabava, Fotynja Kyrkor, came from a gentry family. A hundred years later, in 1760, we learn that its superior at that time was a relative of one of the town officials of Mahilev[46]. In the 1670's the superior of the Vilna Holy Spirit monastery was Elizabeth Vasylevyč, sister of the bishop of Belorussia Theodosius Vasylevyč (1669-1677), from a wealthy gentry family[47]. From a will of 1647 made by a well-off widow we learn that at the Mahilev Epiphany monastery at that time her sister was the superior, while a former servant of hers was a nun there[48].

Occasionally, as we have already seen, founders in their charters declared whom they envisaged as the entrants in their monasteries. Adam Kysil', in founding the monastery at Popivka, stated that it was

---

[42] *IJuM*, 26: 340-342.

[43] *AV*, 15: 344.

[44] This is the testimony of the superior and other nuns during a visitation in 1710: "Do Zakonu zadne się Panny z posagiem nie upraszali". Acta Kisciana, 6, fol. 29r.

[45] *IJuM*, 19: 103-106.

[46] *AV*, 11: 132-133.

[47] *Ibid.*, p. 220-222, where she lists the possessions he left at death.

[48] *IJuM*, 24: 399.

for well-born "matron y panien"[49]. In Podillja the monastery in Vinnycja, according to the founder, was to be for women and girls "of
every estate and birth". It seems to have attracted the local petty
szlachta: in 1640 one of its nuns, Elizabeth Komar, willed her property
in the vicinity of Vinnycja to her brother[50].

Thanks to detailed accounts of visitations conducted several times
between 1773 and 1779 at Mykulynci, also in Podillja, we know exactly
who were the nuns of that monastery in the period of its lingering extinction. Of nine members in 1773, one is called "nobilis condicionis"
(petty impoverished szlachta), four come from small towns (one is called
specifically "civilis conditionis"), and three are of peasant origin ("pro-
stey kądycyi"). The social condition of one nun is unspecified, but she
too probably came form a peasant family[51].

Paul of Aleppo reports of the Ascension monastery in Kiev in 1654:

> This monastery is prosperous and well-ordered: there are fifty or sixty
> nuns, all of gentle birth... The majority of these nuns are from wealthy
> and ancient Polish families; the ihumenja is related to the Polish king
> himself. Moved by attachment to this monastery, where most of them
> were educated, they return to it, receive profession, and remain there as
> nuns[52].

Though there is a little exaggeration here, we have no reason to doubt
that the archdeacon misunderstood what was told him about the nuns.
Most of them no doubt did come from leading Ruthenian families of
the Polish-Lithuanian state. Few family names of the nuns are recorded,
but from the early seventeenth century to the 1660's we come across
Sylyč, Rahoza, Soltan.

At about the same time we have Agatha Humenyc'ka as ihumenja
of Sts Florus and Laurus in Kiev. From the means at her disposal,
which enabled her to restore and build up the monastery, and from her
manner of acting it is obvious that she too came from wealthy gentry[53].

The monasteries of Cossack foundation and supported by Cossack
families also attracted entrants from these families. The recorded names,
not surprisingly, are of members of the higher ranks—of the staršyna,
of which some examples follow. Evdokija (Helen) Borozdna, whose

---

[49] *OAZM*, 1: 282.

[50] "Stanu i uroženja všeljakoho", Secinskij, p. 258, 251.

[51] *Ibid.*, p. 346-348.

[52] Pavel Aleppskij, *COIDR*, 1897, 4: 58; *PO*, 26: 697.

[53] Cf. the privilege given her by Ladislaus IV in 1636, *Akty JuZR*, 2: 97.

father was an official in the hetmanate, was a nun at Pečenyky in the period from 1725 to 1764[54]. In 1755 there is a mention of another nun from the Borozdna family, Serafyma, perhaps also at Pečenyky, since members of one family tended to favor the same monastery[55].

The monastery in Xoroševe in Slobidščyna, to judge from the names of the nuns who were there in the eighteenth century, also largely attracted members of Cossack families. Thus we find there several members of the Kvitka-Hamalija-Horlenko families (all interrelated with one another), as well as of others[56]. Anastasia Horlenko, whose father and brother were prominent supporters of Mazepa when he broke away form Russia, was a nun at Ladyn[57]. An Athanasia Hamalija was the superior in the St John (St Michael) monastery of Kiev from 1753 to 1756 and perhaps longer[58]. The monastery of Korobivka-Zolotonoša had many dealings with Cossack families, and no doubt the majority of its nuns came from them, though we also learn of some from the class of townspeople[59].

Late in the eighteenth century (1777) Serafyma Dorošenko, whose father was a Cossack official and one of whose ancestors was hetman Michael Dorošenko (d.1628), is mentioned as a nun in Novi Mlyny in Černihivščyna[60]. From 1777, in fact, we have detailed information on all the members of this monastery. They were as follows: one from "šljaxetstvo" (family of Cossack staršyna—this is Serafyma Dorošenko), one priest's daughter, ten from Cossack, and twelve from peasant families. Except for two nuns from the Smolensk gubernija, all the others were from nearby villages[61].

The most prominent Cossack nun, however, was hetman Mazepa's mother, who entered the Ascension monastery in Kiev with the name Maria Magdalene and became superior of it and of its affiliated monastery in Hluxiv. Her name apperars on monastery documents in the period 1683-1701. She used her influence to obtain grants and immunities for the Kiev monastery and to construct a new church. Ultimately all she achieved was nullified when Peter I ordered a fortress built on the elevation on which the monastery stood (facing the western

---

[54] MODZALEVSKIJ, *Malorossijskij rodoslovnik*, 1: 70.

[55] *Ibid.*, p. 69.

[56] For all of these, see *ISOXE*, 1: 129-132.

[57] MODZALEVSKIJ, *Malorossijskij rodoslovnik*, 1: 307.

[58] DUMITRAŠKO, p. 16, mentions her signature on documents within these years.

[59] As a certain Evdokija, daughter of a Kyril Mexeda of Pryluky, which name makes one think of a Greek merchant, cf. MAKSIMOVIČ, Vospominanija o Zolotonoše, p. 424.

[60] MODZALEVSKIJ, *Malorossijskij rodoslovnik*, 1: 457.

entrance to the Kiev Lavra). The Ascension monastery had to be razed, and the nuns were transferred to the St Florus monastery in Kiev[62].

At Hluxiv, a Cossack foundation, another relative of hetman Mazepa was a nun[63]. And some time in the last quarter of the eighteenth century Anna Rozumovs'ka, born in 1754, daughter of the last hetman, entered a monastery under the name of Agnes. It is not stated where, but since her sister Elizabeth, after the death of her husband, entered the St Florus monastery in Kiev in 1813, it is probable that Anna also was a nun there[64].

The sparse materials on monasteries in Halyčyna provide few notices about the nuns there. In 1627 a nun of Žovkva, together with her brother, a monk at Krexiv, sold a plot of ground[65]. One has an impression of impoverished gentry.

In fact, women's monasteries in Halyčyna never attracted wealthy entrants and were never as prosperous economically or had as many members as those in other parts of Ukraine and Belorussia. Margaret Dyškevyč in her testament speaks of the Javoriv monastery as intended for persons of the gentry and town class[66]. The catalog of nuns at the Slovita monastery in 1763 gives particulars about the background of each. They all came from villages in Halyčyna. Three of the ten nuns and the one novice were daughters of priests; the novice was the only one who had brought a dowry to the monastery[67]. In Lviv the nuns were mostly from impoverished gentry, though a few were from wealthier families, as one can judge from their dowries, which in one case amounted to 7000 Polish zloty[68].

The social background of nuns can also be detected indirectly. When the suppression of monasteries in Halyčyna was being projected in 1782 consideration had to be given to the problem of what to do with the nuns of the monasteries that were to be closed. It was at first determined to bring them all to Lviv and open a school at the monastery there. Soon it became clear, however, that none of them was capable of

---

[62] This is described by the chronicler, *Sbornik letopisej otnosjaščixsja k istorii južnoj i zapadnoj Rossij*, p. 45-46.

[63] XARLAMPOVIČ, p. 611. In 1713, because of her family connection with Mazepa, she was exiled to Russia. The Hluxiv monastery continued to attract nuns from Cossack staršyna families in the eighteenth century, cf. MODZALEVSKIJ, *Malorossijskij rodoslovnik*, 3: 720 (Theodora Ohijevs'ka).

[64] *Ibid.*, 4: 233.

[65] BARĄCZ, *Pamiatki miasta Żółkwi*, p. 51.

[66] "*Szlacheckiego iako i mieszczanskiego stanu*", C'OROX, p. 243.

[67] *Ibid.*, p. 233-235.

[68] *Ibid.*, p. 237-240.

teaching and that not a few were illiterate[69]. They all came, no doubt, from villages and the poorer classes of towns.

Foreigners in Ruthenian Monasteries

In the eighteenth century, just as there was a tendency for Latin-rite entrants among Basilian monks, so there were also entrants from the Latin-rite in Uniate women's monasteries. It is much more difficult to determine the extent of this tendency among the nuns, since there are practically speaking no sources of biographical data on individual nuns as there are or monks. There can be no doubt, however, that it was of relatively considerable proportions, especially towards the end. Among the last fifteen nuns of the Lviv monastery one, Angelina Miracka, was Polish, She was born in Warsaw and baptized in the Latin rite ("w kościele")[70].

In the Holy Trinity church of Vilna there was a marble tombstone over the grave of Constance Jelenska (d.1757), vicar of the women's monastery there, put up by her brothers, one of whom was a Latin-rite parish priest[71]. In that monastery in the early years of the nineteenth century the nun who could read a little Church Slavonic, in addition to Polish, was the exception[72].

A few things can also be said about other foreigners—Russians and Moldavians—in Ukrainian and Belorussian monasteries. Russians appear especially in the second half of the eighteenth century, chiefly in Kiev. There are, however, a few earlier cases. Among the Russians taken prisoner by "Lithuanian people" in the Period of Troubles during the Polish intervention some entered monasteries in Ukraine and Belorussia. We know of five who had become nuns in Polock, Kiev (Ascension), and Ladyn and who later chose to return to Muscovy[73]. Obviously, they were not the only ones in Ruthenan monasteries; others must have preferred to finish their days in the monasteries they had entered.

In the middle of the seventeenth century there were many nuns from Muscovy in the Kutejno monastey; even the superior, Iroida Kurakin, was Muscovite, a member of the family prominent in the tsar's

[69] CHOTKOWSKI, p. 138-140.
[70] C'OROX, p. 238.
[71] The inscription on the tombstone is reported by O.V. ŠČERBICKIJ, *Dostoprimečatel'nosti Vilenskogo Sv.-Troickogo monastyrja* (Vil'na, 1914), p. 28-29.
[72] Cf. WOŁYNIAK, p. 162.
[73] XARLAMPOVIČ, p. 75.

service[74]. How the Russian nuns came to be at Kutejno remains unanswered. Some of them were anxious to return to their native land. When Alexius appeared in Lithuania with Muscovite troops (1654), five nuns, four of them related, went to Smolensk and asked permission to go to a monastery in Moscow, which was granted them[75]. When in 1665 the withdrawal of Muscovite forces from eastern Belorussia appeared imminent, Iroida and those of her countrywomen that still remained in Kutejno asked Alexius to be permitted to go to Smolensk[76]. Their request was granted, and Alexius even appointed Iroida superior of the Ascension monastery in Smolensk[77].

A century later it was monasteries in Kiev, especially Sts Florus and Laurus, that attracted Russian entrants, including some from aristocratic families. In 1758 Natalija Dolgorukova entered there[78], and in 1771 Anna Apraksina[79]. In other monasteries too Russian entrants could be found. There is, for instance, a mention of two nuns from the Smolensk gubernia in the monastery near Novi Mlyny at this period (the notice is from 1777). They were both daughters of soldiers—"zvanija soldat-skogo"[80].

Notices about Moldavian nuns likewise come mainly from the eighteenth century, though the occasional mention of Moldavian nuns earlier indicates that to a lesser or greater degree there were always some Moldavian nuns in the monasteries of Ukraine and even of Belorussia. In 1625 we hear of one Moldavian nun coming from a Kiev monastery to Mahilev[81].

---

[74] Exactly what relation she was to other well-known members of the Kurakin family of those times has been impossible to determine, as genealogocial notes on them are very incomplete, and, moreover, no document gives Iroida's patronymic.

[75] The tsar's authorization for their transfer to Moscow is in *Akty JuZR*, 14: 209-212.

[76] Cf. ÉJNGORN, *ČOIDR*, 1893, 2: 365, footnote 476. The voevoda of Smolensk at the time was F.F. Kurakin, very likely a relation of Iroida.

[77] A charter of the tsar, dated 21 June 1670, by which the voevoda of Smolensk was ordered to supply the monastery with provisions, recounts this, *AI*, 4: 458.

[78] Natalija Dolgorukova has attracted a fair amount of attention due to the prominence of the families from which she came (Šeremetev) and into which she married, her tragic life (deportation a few days after marriage when she was only 15, many years in miserable conditions, execution of her husband), and her autobiography, the first by a woman in Russian literature. For the autobiography, further notices, and literature, see N.B. DOLGORUKAJA, *Das Journal*, Nachdruck der Ausgabe Petersburg 1913 (Slavische Propyläen, 112; München, 1972). Her tomstone in the Kiev Lavra recorded the main dates and facts of her life, cf. N. ČERNYŠEV, *Putevoditel' po Pečersku i staromu Kievu* (Kiev, 1860), p. 70.

[79] Her case is described in *OASS*, 50: 249-253. Other examples are provided by XARLAMPOVIČ, p. 631.

[80] LAZAREVSKIJ, *Opisanie*, 2: 298.

[81] Cf. *IJuM*, 8: 415. It would be interesting to know whether and in what numbers

Mainly it is in the monasteries closer to their native land—in Podil-lja and southern Kyjivščyna—that we hear of them. The monastery in Lebedyn was founded by Moldavian nuns. From the latter part of the eighteenth century we have notices of Moldavian nuns in the Uniate monastery at Mykulynci in Podillja[82]. The reports of visitators clearly show that none of the sisters in this poor and stagnating monastery were conscious of religious differences.

Statistics

The list of monasteries in Appendix I indicates the territory in which each was located. Some listing can also be done by eparchies. If one recalls the great territorial extent of most eparchies, with parishes in each running into many hundreds, the small number of monasteries will be even more striking.

An official report prepared by the synod of the Peremyšl' eparchy in 1693 lists two women's monasteries: Smil'nycja and Javoriv[83]. Sometime in the next century small monasteries existed also in Rozhirče and Sambir. But by 1761 only three women's monasteries are listed in the Peremyšl' eparchy: Javoriv, Smil'nycja, and Rozhirče[84]. If discrepancies arise, as they do when an official listing names Staryj Sambir as late as 1782, it is because these monasteries were not well known to the authorities. If on the site of an abandoned monastery some-one settled to lead a quasi-monastic life, this might lead to listing the monastery as still functioning. It seems that contemporaries were hardly better informed on the number and size of the monasteries than we are.

The neighboring Lviv eparchy, according to official statistics, had five monasteries in 1782 (they are listed as four in the Lviv eparchy prop-er, one in its Kamjanec' portion)[85]. But other sources show that three other small monasteries were still lingering on at the time.

A statement of the Theatine Jerome Moro, rector of the pontifical seminary in Lviv, at first sight contradicts these statistics. Responding in 1745 to a questionnaire of the Propaganda, he wrote: "There are

---

there were women from Ukraine in Moldavian monasteries.

[82] In a visitation report of 1775 conducted by the dean of Brajiliv Basil Rohal'-Levyc'kyj (SECINSKIJ, p. 351).

[83] "A Kievskij, de, gosudar', mitropolit Petr Mogila very xristijanskoj nyne otpal" is how it was reported to Moscow, *Akty JuZR*, 3: 8.

[84] *LE*, 4: 117.

[85] A.D. z VALJAVY, Sostojanie Eparxii, *Halyčanyn*, 2 (1863): 86.

Basilian nuns of the Ruthenian rite in almost all the cities and towns of
Poland, subject to the bishop of the diocese in which they are
situated"[86]. (Obviously, he refers to the Ruthenian lands of the Crown.)
These monasteries were certainly more numerous in 1745 than forty
years later, for reasons we shall note in a later chapter. But it is also
very probable that at least some of the Basilian nuns he found
everywhere were not living in organized monasteries.

The Catholic metropolitan eparchy in 1752 had six women's
monasteries according to an official report[87]. They are not named in the
document, but a list of them can be compiled from other sources. Five
pose no problem. They are: two in Minsk (Holy Trinity and Holy
Spirit), then Hrodna, Navahrudek, Vilna (Holy Trinity). The sixth one
is probably Brahin, which is supposed to have become Catholic that
year. It may be useful to mention, as a frame of reference, that the
same report lists 1925 parishes in the metropolitan eparchy with over
one million faithful.

The Orthodox metropolitan eparchy throughout the eighteenth century listed twelve women's monasteries[88], with a concentration of
monasteries and nuns in Kiev itself. (The number of parishes in the
eparchy was over 1100.) There were as well four monasteries in the Černihiv eparchy and one in the Perejaslav eparchy. The most complete
statistics, of 1745, show a total of 637 nuns in Orthodox monasteries in
Ukraine (hetmanate and Slobidščyna). This figure, like the others given
here, does not include novices. It is quite impossible to give precise—or
even approximative—total figures for other regions, but they were clearly nowhere near that number.

Statistics concerning the number of nuns, in general and in individual monasteries, can be gathered from various sources. In addition,
one can have an approximate idea of the number of nuns in a
monastery from such things as a description of its buildings. So as not
to burden the text with figures, dates, and footnote numbers, the
statistics and sources are given in Appendix II. Here we wish only to
comment on some of the notices and provide some additional information.

The earliest statistics available to us regard the Polock monastery.
Bishop Suša recounts in his life of St Josaphat that when St Josaphat

---

[86] CHOTKOWSKI, p. 136.

[87] *Monumenta Ucrainae historica*, 6 (Romae, 1968): 182.

[88] *Supplicationes Ecclesiae unitae Ucrainae et Bielarusjae*, ed. Athanasius G.
WELYKYJ, 3 (Romae, 1965): 106.

became archbishop of Polock the women's monastery counted 12 nuns. During his six years as pastor such was his spiritual care for the monastery that 23 other women entered it.

Another early notice comes from 1638. In that year from the monasteries grouped under the superiorship of Isaiah Kopyns'kyj a large group of monks and nuns fled to Muscovy because of false rumors concerning the "heresy", that is, willingness to embrace the Union on the part of metropolitan Peter Mohyla[89]. The contingent from Ladyn consisted of 50 nuns[90]. These may have been all, or almost all of the nuns from the Ladyn monastery, since we hear that later in the same year Mohyla assigned Athanasia Smolkovna and other nuns to Ladyn[91] (from where, unfortunately, we are not told—very probably from a Kiev monastery).

Another notice from the first half of the seventeenth century regards the Ascension monastery of Kiev. Beauplan, who lived in Ukraine 1632-1648, reported that this monastery had up to a hundred nuns[92]. Even if his information is not precise, other contemporary sources verify that the number there was quite large.

Most of the other information at this time concerns Belorussian monasteries. There was a connecting link between Kutejno and Barkalabava. Both monasteries were founded by the Stetkevyč family, and the Barkalabava foundation was begun by a group of nuns from Kutejno. Both were Orthodox throughout their existence. Joil Trucevyč, ihumen at Kutejno, recorded that there were so many nuns at the women's monastery in Kutejno that the monastery could barely hold them all. This was in the 1630's. He, therefore, brought these conditions to the attention of the Stetkevyč family, and upon his advice the latter built another monastery on their property Barkalabava. This does not say too much yet, since we do not know the size of the Kutejno monastery and how many nuns it could hold. But, whatever the size, within a ten-year period, roughly the interval between the two foundations, the monastery was filled to capacity.

Barkalabava too grew quickly. Between twenty and fifty, perhaps more nuns came from Kutejno about 1641 to start the foundation[93]. By

---

[89] *OASS*, 12: 463 (153 nuns in the Černihiv eparchy, 1733), 464-465; 14: 815, 817; 20: 592-593, 612; 22: 765.

[90] They were eventually settled in a monastery in Alatyr', *ibid.*, no. 12.

[91] Only a listing, not the text, of Mohyla's letter is in BARSOV, Opisanie, *ČOIDR*, 1884, 2: 31.

[92] BEAUPLAN, *Description de l'Ukranie* (Paris, 1861), p. 32.

[93] "Kilkadesjat", *IJuM*, 14: 139.

1652 the original land grant did not provide enough income to support all the nuns[94]. In 1655 it is recorded that there were "up to one hundred" nuns in that monastery. This figure may be an exaggeration since it is found in an alms-begging letter written to tsar Alexius on behalf of the monastery, where the hope of receiving more bountiful alms may have inspired this rounded-off number[95]. Still, it could not have been too far from the truth.

From 1650 we have information about two Uniate monasteries. Hrodna is listed as having ten nuns. All their names are given in an investigation carried out at metropolitan Sjeljava's behest[96]. In the same year Catherine Sapieha and two other nuns came from Vilna to start the Holy Spirit monastery in Minsk. Soon others joined, but we do not have exact numbers.

From the decade of the 1740's we have statistics for a few important Uniate monasteries: Vilna (Holy Trinity), Minsk (Holy Trinity and Holy Spirit), Hrodna. A superior and six other nuns are named in a draft of regulations drawn up for the Hrodna monastery by metropolitan Athanasius Šeptyc'kyj on 1 November 1744. The statistics for Vilna and Minsk come from a report sent to Rome. The figures that are given must have been relatively stable. The number of members was to a considerable extent depedent on the income of the monastery. In the case of the monasteries in Vilna and Minsk it is stated that their incomes sufficed for the actual number of members they had. The implication is that the number of members did not go beyond that figure.

The statistics for the Čyhyryn monastery, which lay in the territory of the main operations of the hajdamaky, comes from the peak year of their disorders. Twenty-four nuns signed a complaint, sent to the Russian ambassador in Warsaw N.V. Repnin, against the intrusion and consequent damages perpetrated by the Uniate official Gregory Mokryc'kyj, a violent man by all accounts. They add the names of twenty other nuns who had left the monastery when Mokryc'kyj first appeared and who had not yet returned. The Čyhyryn monastery, in an insecure borderland, thus turns out to be one of the larger ones.

There were three women's monasteries in Kiev in the second half of the eighteenth century, but we have statistical data only about one, Sts Florus and Laurus, which in 1777 had 123 nuns. For the sake of comparison we can give some figures for it thirty-four years later, in 1811.

[94] Cf. above, p. 74.
[95] "V čisle do sta", Akty JuZR, 14: 722.
[96] OAZM, 1: 291.

In July of that year a great fire devastated much of the Podil' section of Kiev, where the monastery was located. In a report on the damages caused by the fire to churches and monasteries several alternatives were considered for housing the monastery's 53 nuns and 40 poslušnyci. We might think this were all did not the author of the report, after describing minutely, twice, all the damages to the buildings, their roofs and their walls, add, as an afterthought, that twenty nuns and women boarders also perished in the fire[97].

From the diocese of Černihiv there is information on three monasteries in the year 1786, when the decree on the suppression of monasteries, in force in Russia since 1764, was applied also to Ukraine. Nižyn had eighteen nuns; it escaped suppression and was classified in the third category of monasteries. The St Paraskeva monastery in Černihiv, although it had thirty-three nuns, was closed that year. Ladyn had forty-nine nuns; it was designated to house nuns from suppressed monasteries, which raised its total to ninety-four.

In 1795 a conflict between the bishop of Mahilev Athanasius Volxovskyj and the Mahilev brotherhood served as an opportune pretext to the bishop to close the Epiphany monastery over which the brotherhood had patronage. At that time the monastery had ten nuns. The Vilna monastery of the Holy Spirit, also closed in 1795, had a building with only four cells[98]. Although there probably were more than four nuns at times, it could not have been many more. Half a century before there were three nuns (two of them blood sisters) and five novices. In 1778 mention is made only of three nuns.

We have statistical data on Uniate monasteries in territories acquired by Russia after the dismemberment of Poland, from the period of those political changes. The Holy Spirit monastery in Vicebsk had nine nuns, two novices, and four candidates. There were four monasteries in Volyn' at the end of the eighteenth century; they were all small and poor. At Polonne there were six nuns, while the monastery in Volodymyr Volyns'kyj had five in 1803[99]. In Podillja information on the size of the Mykulynci and Vinnycja monasteries comes from visitations. In Vinnycja in 1792 there were two professed nuns and two novices.

When Halyčyna, after the first partition of Poland in 1772 became a province of the Hapsburg monarchy, a first listing of monasteries was

---

[97] Kievo-Podol'skie monastyri i cerkvi sto let tomu nazad, *Kievskija eparxial'nija vedomosti*, 1912, p. 197 (4 March), p. 215 (11 March), p. 243 (18 March).

[98] AMVROSIJ, 3: 538.

[99] WOŁYNIAK, p. 252.

prepared in 1774, and two others in 1782[100]. Before this time, there are only a few meager pieces of information about them. The data officially requested in 1774 and 1782 differs widely among these three sets of statistics, even about the number of monasteries. This corroborates the impression that the monasteries were small and wretched and not much attention was paid to them. Thus no set is complete.

In 1774 seven monasteries had forty nuns. The largest was Rohatyn, with eleven, and the smallest Holoskiv, with three. Lviv had six nuns. In January 1782 ten monasteries were listed, but without the numbers for each. In March of that year only five monasteries were named. In Lviv there were eleven nuns, while four other monasteries—Javoriv, Rozhirče, Smil'nycja, and Zahvizdje—had twenty-eight all together. The nuns must have been in great part elderly. Although two went from Smil'nycja to Lviv in 1789, in 1790 only five nuns were left at Lviv—the rest had in the meantime passed away[101]. By this time it was not permitted to accept novices, so the membership could not be renewed.

The statistics gathered here show that irrespective of the period the monasteries of Kiev were the largest, followed by several in eastern Belorussia. In Left Bank Ukraine, where we have several sets of statistics for individual monasteries, we see a progressive growth in numbers, which may be connected with the settlement of and the growth of population in that territory. The monasteries of Halyčyna and Podillja, which drew their members from an impoverished population, were much smaller. Where Catholic and Orthodox monasteries existed side by side, as in western Belorussia, there was no difference in the numbers in each.

Laywomen in Monasteries

In addition to nuns, monasteries now and then housed also other women, some things about whom need to be said now. Mention has already been made of laywomen who boarded in monasteries (such as those who died in the fire at the St Florus monastery in Kiev in 1811). Very rarely in Ruthenian lands were they called *bilyci*; usually they were not designated by any special name. They were generally widows who wanted a tranquil and secure life. They bequeathed their property to a monastery, or even founded one with this purpose in mind, as happened

---

[100] CHOTKOWSKI, p. 136, 138.
[101] *Ibid.*, p. 144-145.

in Mozoliv, in exchange for being allowed to live out their days there. Regrettably, notices about them come only from the outside and reveal nothing of how such an arrangement was fitted into the life of the community. Such arrangements are not mentioned often; it would appear that they were not at all common.

Sometimes reasons other than widowhood suggested to a woman to move to a monastery. A merchant of Mahilev, arrested by the Muscovites in Smolensk when news came there in 1661 that Mahilev had been retaken by Polish forces, wrote a letter filled with business advice—what to sell and at what price—to his wife, who was at that time living with the nuns of the brotherhood monastery in Mahilev[102]. It must have seemed safer for her to be there in those uncertain times of the Muscovite-Polish war while her husband was away on a long business trip.

From the same period we see a group of nuns and one widow from Kutejno petitioning tsar Alexius to be permitted to go to the monastery of St Saba in Moscow. The widow, a relative of one of the nuns, had obviously been living with them in the Kutejno monastery[103]. To realize the range of this custom, one can also note an example from Kiev, where the presence of laywomen is observed in the Ascension monastery[104]. Later too in the face of catastrophes monasteries sheltered women, as did the Vicebsk monastery after a fire in the town in the early years of the eighteenth century[105].

In the eighteenth century the secularizing spirit of Russian state bureaucracy made its effects felt on monasteries in Kiev and Left Bank Ukraine. The case of the Russian widow Helen Ivanovna is illustrative. Her husband had served many years in the army and finally had been discharged because of numerous wounds received in service. After his death Ivanovna in 1736 sent a request to the Senate asking that in recompense for her husband's services she be admitted to the St Florus monastery in Kiev and provided there with all necessities. The Senate turned to the Holy Synod for the fulfillment of her request. The latter replied that this was impossible, due to an ukaz of Anna which forbade

---

[102] *AV*, 34: 196-197.

[103] *Akty JuZR*, 14: 209-210.

[104] *Ibid.*, 6: 94. A report of 1666 on Methodius Fylymonovyč, at that time bishop of Mscislav and Orša, notes that his son's mother-in-law lives in the Ascension monastery.

[105] Acta Kisciana, vol. 6, fol. 29r. Other examples of temporary boarding in a monastery may be found. In 1786 the wife of a certain *szlachtycz* took refuge in the Sluck monastery from his violence, cf. *AS*, 7: 295-296, the letter of bishop Victor Sadkovskyj of 10 June 1786 which describes the ensuing attack on the monastery by the husband.

all monastic professions of women[106]. The Senate then ordained that the widow Ivanovna be accepted into the St Florus monastery as a laywoman boarder, if she herself were willing. She on her part replied that she agreed, as long as she had her own room and received food from the monastery. The matter was settled at that[107].

Two things stand out in this incident. No one even dreamed of asking the monastery or the local hierarch whether they would accept the petitioner, and the entire procedure was a purely administrative one, as of settling a pension. Further, the widow's sole motive for coming to the monastery was that of material security. Whether she became a nun or not was a secondary consideration, both for her and for the authorities, as long as her livelihood was assured. Her views coincided with those of the state organs in St Petersburg, which had begun to look on monasteries solely from the viewpoint of utility to the state.

At Mahilev it was the practice to send Jewish women who expressed a desire to be baptized to the Epiphany monastery, perhaps also to others in the eparchy[108]. It many have been simply to provide them with a temporary place to stay.

Apart from women who lodged permanently in monasteries and those who sought refuge there in time of trouble, there must have been temporary visitors. One thinks especially of monasteries in Kiev, which even in the seventeenth century was a place of pilgrimage, though not yet to the same extent as later. That this is not idle speculation can be seen by examining the will of a widow, Pelahija Tyševyč, made in 1646. She herself was from Belorussia. In her will she left sums of money to a number of monasteries located in Belorussia and in Kiev, including the Kiev Ascension moastery. There, she recorded, during an illness she had experienced "humaneness" ("ljudskost") from the nuns[109]. Another example from Kiev comes from 1668. When the Nižyn home of protopop Simeon Adamovyč was plundered his daughter went to stay temporarily with her aunt, the nun Alexandra at the Kiev Jordan monastery[110].

Another category of these special groups in monasteries consisted of those who were there against their will. Church and civil authorities found monasteries useful for ends not foreseen by the founders of monasticism.

---

[106] See *PSPR*, [series I], 8: 222-223 (10 June 1734).

[107] *OASS*, 16: 399-400. This is not an isolated case. Four years later, in 1740, a similar one is described, *ibid.*, 20: 368-369.

[108] Cf. ŽUDRO, *Bogojavlenskij bratskij monastyr'*, p. 34.

[109] *IJuM*, 24: 399.

[110] ÈJNGORN, *ČOIDR*, 1894, 3: 467.

First of all, nuns who had run afoul of either ecclesiastical or civil authorities were jailed in monastery prisons—that is, they were sent to another monatery and kept there under surveillance. On the Uniate side, we have an example from 1650 of the former superior of the Hrodna monastery imprisoned in the Vilna Holy Trinity monastery for refusing to comply with an order of metropolitan Antony Sjeljava[111]. The Orthodox metropolitan of Kiev Timothy Ščerbac'kyj acted in similar fashion a century later: nuns who caused some disquiet in the St Florus monastery were sent off to various other monasteries of the eparchy for punishment[112].

Similarly, monasteries served as prisons for women sentenced for a variety of offenses. In the Ladyn monastery there were women who had been accused of adultery and witchcraft[113].

In 1762 there is a case of the (titular Uniate) archbishop of Smolensk Kesarij Stebnovs'kyj ordering that the wife of a priest be taken to the monastery in Orša and held there until further directives were given by him. His reasons are not stated[114].

Women's monasteries were used for purposes of detention in divorce cases, either pending or where the woman was sentenced. In 1786 Agrippina Mohyljans'ka, the wife of a Cossack officer, Luke Lukaševyč, was accused of attempting to poison her husband with arsenic and of witchcraft. The bishop of Černihiv Theophilus Ihnatovyč dissolved the marriage and had Agrippina imprisoned in a monastery. The Holy Synod lifted the *epitimija* in 1789, and presumably she went free then[115].

A case apart is that of Old Believers. In the early eighteenth century a campaign of persecution against them caused some to move from Muscovy to the neighboring regions of Černihivščyna. But there too they were not left in peace. In particular, efforts were made to seize and intern in Orthodox monasteries Old Believer monks and nuns[116]. Of-

---

[111] *OAZM*, 1: 292.
[112] *OASS*, 32: 402-404.
[113] *Ibid.*, 20: 195; 34: 97-101.
[114] *OAZM*, 2: 214 (no. 1809).
[115] MODZALEVSKIJ, *Malorossijskij rodoslovnik*, 3: 203.
[116] We can note here the existence of small and unpermanent monasteries of Old Believers in the Černihiv region in the first half of the eighteenth century, though some lasted longer. Zverinskij mentions a community of nuns at Dobrjanka (3: 143-144) and one at Klymiv (3: 75). The latter and others nearby are mentioned in *OASS*, 16: 31-35; there in 1735 the authorities had succeeded in discovering 33 nuns and 5 novices. LAZAREV-SKIJ, *Opisanie*, 1: 452, mentions another community in a place called Fedulina on the Zlynka river in the Starodub polk.

ficially they were considered as having returned to the Orthodox fold; nevertheless, the Synod issued reiterated commands that they should be sent only to secure ("krepkie") monasteries. The Synod decided that Hluxiv was the appropriate one for nuns, and contingents were often sent there[117].

What is lacking in most of the accounts of such monastic prisoners is a description of the conditions in which they lived and the even more interesting one of how the nuns viewed the entire matter, as well as how they dealt with these inmates. Not surprisingly, it is complaints of treatment that have been recorded. It must have been unsettling, to say the least, for the nuns to have a woman with a small child locked up in their monastery, as happened in Pysarevščyna[118]. In this case the woman had to perform various chores in the monastery and suffered humiliations from the nuns—"tvorja poslušanie i terpja ot zakonnic vsjakija ponošenija".

But this reflects our lack of any details about the more personal aspects in the monasteries: what the nuns were like, how they were formed. To know these things source material coming from the nuns themselves is needed, and this we do not have at all.

---

[117] Thus in one of its resolutions in 1723 the Synod supposedly dealth with "obrašča-juščixsja ot raskola černcax i černicax"; nevertheless, it ordered them to be sent "v krepkie monastyri", *PSPR*, [1st series], 3: 33. Other cases may be found in *OASS*, 1, pt. 2: 406-408; 7: 135.

[118] Cf. L. ORLENKO, Šljubna rozluka v Het'manščyni v XVIII st. *Ukrajina*, 1914, 4: 18-19.

CHAPTER VI

INTERNAL ORGANIZATION

The Superior

The superior at the head of the community was called generally *ihumenja*, occasionally *namisnycja*, which properly speaking means someone taking the place of the superior. There was a distinction in the use of the two terms, as we shall see. In addition, in territories with Polish linguistic influence, the most common term for superior was *starša*, used by Uniates and Orthodox alike.

The superior was either elected by her community or appointed by someone outside the monastery. On the basis of available materials it is impossible to generalize what was more frequent: that the community choose the superior or that outside authorities have the deciding voice.

Many founders' statutes, as has already been noted, explicitly give to the nuns of the monastery in question the right to elect their superior. They never proceed with details, which were doubtless self-understood (such as election by simple majority, election for life). Occasionally the first superior was appointed by the founders, as occurred in Kutejno, but it was stipulated that her successors were to be elected by the sisters. And even the appointment of the first superior, Euphrosine Kyrkor, the ustav states, followed upon the request of all the nuns[1]. The right of the nuns to elect a superior from among themselves was sometimes assured in confirmatory charters, such as in that of king John Casimir given to the Lviv monastery in 1659[2].

We have notices of elections from many Uniate monasteries[3] and

---

[1] *Akty ZR*, 4: 521.
[2] In C'OROX, p. 228.
[3] Cf. *OAZM*, 2: 459 (Hrodna); *Akty ZR*, 5: 6 (Pinsk); Acta Kisciana, vol. 6, fol. 55 (the two Minsk monasteries).

can conclude that this was the common practice in them. Apopointment of a superior when called forth by special circumstances was only a temporary measure. Thus, when the superior of the Minsk Holy Spirit monastery died, metropolitan George Vynnyc'kyj designated protoarchimandrite Leo Kyška to carry out a visitation there. Kyška appointed a superior, but specified that it was only to the time of the visitation[4]. The metropolitan in his letter accrediting the visitation says that the visitator will confirm the superior elected by a secret vote[5].

Appointment could also occur because of abuses noted in a monastery, especially during visitations. The dean of Brajiliv appointed the superior for the Mykulynci monastery in 1772 in the course of a visitation[6].

In some instances the superior of a monastery that belonged to a grouping was appointed by the ihumen of the chief monastery. Alexandra Lunkevyč was appointed superior of the Holy Spirit monastery in Vilna by the archimandrite of Holy Spirit, Jerome Volčanskyj[7]. There were only two other nuns in the monastery at the time, which perhaps explains the appointment as well as the title of namisnycja, not ihumenja. A similar case is found in Minsk. The Sts Peter and Paul monastery in 1750 had three nuns and three novices, and the superior of the Vilna Holy Spirit monastery, Silvester Dobrynja, appointed the namisnycja[8].

Benefactors who supported a monastery (ktytory) occasionally also had a say in the choice of superiors. So it was in Sluck, were it seems they confirmed superiors elected by the nuns. A list of superiors of the Sluck monastery remarks about several in the seventeenth century that they took office with the consent of members of the Radziwill family, the heirs of the Sluck princely family[9]. This is a late echo of the old practice on the part of the king and of princely families to name the superiors in monasteries located on their lands. There is a charter of Sigismund I, dated 13 December 1531, in which the king names Olexna Nemyryna ihumenja of the monastery "svjatoi Prečystoi" in Ovruč[10].

Although election of a superior was a traditional right of nuns, bishops no doubt often claimed that the choice of superiors in women's monasteries was their prerogative. Inokentij Vynnyc'kyj of Peremyšl'

---

[4] Acta Kisciana, vol. 6, fol. 38r.
[5] Ibid., fol. 55-56.
[6] SECINSKIJ, p. 346.
[7] Before 1744, when he became bishop of Mahilev, OASS, 31: 424.
[8] Ibid., p. 423-424.
[9] NIKOLAJ, p. 119.
[10] Akty ZR, 2: 218-219.

wrote in 1693: "The election of the ihumenja ought to depend on the will of the bishop"[11]. Athanasius Šeptyc'kyj of Lviv, when naming a superior for the monastery of Slovita in 1721, gives the impression as if this were the normal procedure, at least with regard to the Slovita monastery[12]. An appointment by the bishop, however, was contrary to the decision of the Synod of Zamość held the year before. The Synod had decreed:

> Elections of the ihumenja are to be carried out at the established times by secret vote. When the ihumenja is elected she is not to exercise her office until the lawfully held elections are confirmed by the local bishop[13].

Even where elections occurred, bishops were reluctant to permit a show of independence and sought to make the choice of superiors conditional on their good pleasure. While confirming the elections in the Minsk monastery, metropolitan George Vynnyc'kyj in 1710 was careful to add: "pending further directives from us"[14].

Together with his permission for the founding of the monastery in Pečenyky, archbishop Theodosius Uhlyc'kyj of Černihiv in 1693 named also the first superior, Anfysa Lypnyc'ka[15]. The person named, however, may have been the superior of Korop, from where the nuns were to move to Pečenyky.

Definite information about the ways of choosing a superior in Orthodox monasteries in the eighteenth century is lacking. The trend of administrative policies in the Church, however, aimed at ever decreasing autonomy of separate institutions. And in the nineteenth century the final choice of superiors rested with the bishops and the Synod. So the eighteenth century must have seen a gradual disappearance of monastic elections.

Once elected or appointed, the superior needed to be invested in her office. There are many references to this, though never sufficiently complete ones, so what form this investiture took is difficult to say. In Uniate monasteries it was most probably merely a confirmation by the

---

[11] *LE*, 4: 117.

[12] "Sym našym pysanijem veleb. panni Serafymi Zinkovskoj urjad staršenstva i ihumenstva, monastyrja Slovickoho z vlasty našoj pastyrskoj, konferujem, dajem i vručajem", *Vremennyk Instytuta Stavropihijskoho*, 7 (1870), 151.

[13] *SPR*, p. 112.

[14] "Do dalszey Dispositiey Naszey", Acta Kisciana, vol. 6, fol. 55.

[15] Cf. LAZAREVSKIJ, *Opisanie*, 1: 145, where he quotes from Uhlyc'kyj, but does not give the full text of the charter.

hierarch. Neither references to elections nor the decrees of the Synod of Zamość quoted above point to anything else. The sisters elected a superior, then informed their hierarch, who sent a letter confirming her in her office. One such procedure is described at the election of Dorothy Janovska as superior of the Minsk Holy Spirit monastery in August 1745. The monastery lay in the metropolitan eparchy, so the sisters turned to metropolitan Athanasius Šeptyc'kyj for confirmation, which duly followed[16].

Sometimes the election took place in the presence of the hierarch or his delegate. An example of this is found in Minsk in 1710[17].

Further formalities were observed occasionally. At the accession of a new superior, Antonina Rovinska, at the Holy Trinity in Minsk in 1748 the monastery was formally given over to her charge by the general vicar of the metropolitantate, Jason Smogorzewski. At the same time an itemized inventory of the monastery's goods and assets was drawn up[18].

In the case of Orthodox monasteries some further particulars are mentioned in the accounts that have come down to us. The founder's charter of the Sts Peter and Paul monastery in Minsk gives directives about elections. It adds that the sisters are to receive the newly elected ihumenja "as their mother and superior", with the blessing of the Orthodox metropolitan of Kiev or of the ihumen of the local monastery (Sts Peter and Paul), who had authority also over the nuns[19]. This implies at least a formal confirmation of the election before the superior actually took office.

The founder's statute of Barkalabava, speaking of the election of the superior, says that after the ihumenja is elected the sisters are to render her "obedience and her staff", then are to seek the blessing and confirmation for her in her office[20]. Perhaps one is to see in this directive an indication of some sort of ceremony among the nuns in giving the newly elected superior her marks of office, to be followed later by the rite of the blessing.

---

[16] *OAZM*, 2: 99 (no. 1406).

[17] Metropolitan George Vynnyc'kyj gave instructions concerning this to his delegate Antony Zavadzkyj, Acta Kisciana, vol. 6, fol. 55.

[18] *OAZM*, 2: 119.

[19] *VZR*, 2 (1863), November, 12: "Sestry moe zakonnye . . . majut zarazom obrat ihumenju Pannu nabožnuju . . . i za blahoslovenstvom Jeho Mlsty otca mytropolyta kyevskoho pravoslavnoho albo i za blahoslovenem otca Ihumena Monastyra tutošneho majut onuju za matku i staršuju sobe prynjaty".

[20] "Poslušenstvo i paterycu podaty", *Akty ZR*, 5: 70. Here it says to apply for the blessing to the Mežyhirs'kyj monastery of Kiev, but that is just after the possibility of closer monasteries falling away from Orthodoxy was considered.

The blessing of an ihumenja must have taken the form more or less of the bessing of an ihumen as it is found in liturgical books[21]. Being a type of consecration, it was always performed by a bishop. Direct references to it are very rare. The few cases that are known can be mentioned here.

In 1624 metropolitan Job Borec'kyj imparted this blessing to the new superior of the Sluck monastery Christine Koscjuško[22]. Peter Mohyla, when he was in Korec' in 1634, blessed Serafyma Jarmolyns'ka for the superiorship[23]. The Kvitka family diary mentions this rite at the installation of Teofanija Kvitka as ihumenja of the Xoroševe monastery by the metropolitan of Belgorod Joasaf Horlenko in 1748[24].

At least in Orthodox monasteries a superior who did not receive this blessing was, as a rule, called not ihumenja, but namisnycja, though the latter term was also used to designate the vicar in monasteries headed by an ihumenja[25]. This explains why in statistics for the Kiev and Černihiv eparchies from 1759 and 1761 twelve and five monasteries respectively are listed, but only ten and three ihumenjas[26]. In fact, in the Kiev eparchy the superior of the monastery in Bystrycja never received this blessing and was never called ihumenja.

The blessing of a superior was considered permanent in its effects, hence in principle the superior remained in office for life. The charters of founders of Orthodox monasteries list two instances in which the community could remove a superior from office: if she did not live according to the rules of common life as set out by the ancient holy

---

[21] Not easily found, however. In fact, the only liturgical book to include it that I have been able to find is the archieraticon in the Moscow edition of 1798. K. NIKOL'SKIJ, *Posobie k izučeniju ustava bogosluženija pravoslavnoj cerkvi* (7th ed., S.-Peterburg, 1907), p. 721, in discussing the rite of blessing of an ihumen merely comments at the end that the same rite was applied to women. In a long note he then describes this rite as it took place in a Russian monastery in 1845, apparently the only instance of its use that he could find. A. DMITRIEVSKIJ in his *Stavlennik* (Kiev, 1904), p. 134-136, describes the rite of blessing of an ihumenja, but has no reference to any text, no historical commentary, and nothing about the actual extent of its practice.

[22] NIKOLAJ, p. 119.

[23] Cf. *Arxiv JuZR*, pt. I, 6: 406.

[24] *ISOXE*, 1: 131.

[25] So the ihumenja of the Kiev Jordan monastery Paraskeva Tuptalo signed her will in 1710 in the presence of her namisnycja Anfija, cf. LAZAREVSKIJ, Dokumental'nyja svedenija, *KS*, 3 (1882, 3): 384. One cannot generalize from a solitary example, but there is also an example from a Uniate monastery: in the diary of the Polock Basilians under March 1770 stands the phrase "wikarya Hrebnicka (bo starszey od lat już kilku nie było)", *AS*, 10: 356.

[26] AMVROSIJ, 2: 1 xxxi.

fathers or if she showed a weakening towards apostasy, that is, towards the Union[27]. Some of the statutes provided also for other cases: if the superior proved incapable of governing the monastery, if she were arrogant and authoritarian in her dealings with the sisters[28]. The nuns were warned, however, that they must proceed to remove a superior only with the fear of God and a pure conscience, not because of private grudges, anger, rancor, jealousy, or obstinacy. The majority of votes decided.

Examples are recorded in both Uniate and Orthodox monasteries of superiors being removed from office, though not by the community itself. Metropolitan Antony Sjeljava even excommunicated the superior of the Hrodna monastery Mytrodora Kozlovyc'ka in 1650. She had been recalcitrant in answering to charges brought against her and her monastery, and the excommunication was read publicly on a Sunday[29]. In 1740 ihumenja Anysija Čujkevyč of Novi Mlyny was dismissed from office because of excessive severity[30]. Who removed her is not stated, but it seems likely that the metropolitan of Kiev exercised his authority in this matter.

At the end of the eighteenth century an official report on the Mahilev Epiphany monastery recorded that more than once in the past superiors there had been removed from office for mismanagement. In such incidents the superior was then sent to another monastery[31]. Evidently here too it was the metropolitan who dealt with the matter.

There are some, though not frequent, examples of superiors retiring from office. At the Xoroševe monastery it appears to have been a common practice[32]. During a visitation of the Slovita monastery in 1763 its superior Serafyna (Anastasia Zynkovs'ka), in office since 1721, asked that the sisters be permitted to elect someone to take her place as soon as possible ("w naypredszym czasie") so that she could resign on account of her old age. Since she was professed in 1704, she was about

---

[27] This is found in all the deeds of foundation of the monasteries belonging to the Kutejno grouping, cf. *Akty ZR*, 4: 523 (Kutejno); 5: 70 (Barkalabava); *IJuM*, 14: 515-516 (Mozoliv).

[28] *Akty ZR*, 5: 70 (for Barkalabava).

[29] *OAZM*, 1: 292. Though a reconciliation later took place, and the metropolitan offered her the vacant post of superior of the Holy Trinity monastery in Vilna, it was not a lasting one. Cf. *EM*, 2: 203, where in 1653 Sjeljava complains that the nuncio has taken the part of Kozlovyc'ka against him.

[30] LAZAREVSKIJ, *Opisanie*, 2: 298.

[31] Cf. ŽUDRO, *Bogojavlenskij bratskij monastyr'*, p. 34.

[32] Cf. the list of superiors in *ISOXE*, 1: 130-131.

seventy-five years old. The visitator on his part reported that she was ex-amplary both in her conduct and in the discharge of her duties[33].

But the election of a superior for a limited term too was not unknown. In her testament of 1644 Margaret Dyškevyč, foundress and superior of the Javoriv monastery, stipulated that after her death elec-tions of a superior should take place every year ("na każdy rok"). The elections were to take place after the "usual devotion", probably the Divine Liturgy, and were to be preceded by an accounting of the income and expenditures under the previous superior[34].

The Synod of Zamość rather vaguely stated that elections should take place "at the established times"[35], which could mean either at set intervals or within a certain period after the death of a superior. There is nothing to indicate what the practice was; it need not have been everywhere uniform. The example of the Slovita superior cited above in-dicates a life term. On the other hand, in a list of sisters at the Dubno monastery in 1818 we find several named as former superiors[36]. From this it can perhaps be inferred that in Dubno the office was only for a limited term (unless it is a matter of successive resignations).

Quite naturally, more information has come down about superiors than about other nuns. There are some instances of several superiors from the same family succeeding each other, sometimes at intervals. We have already seen that at the Holy Trinity monastery in Vilna Catherine Sapieha succeeded her aunt Vasilissa. In the Hrodna monastery the first superior, circa 1635-1644, was Justyna Syruciv, then in 1675 a Fevronija Syruciv became the superior[37].

We find related superiors also in monasteries with close ties to one another. The first superior of Kutejno was Euphrosine Kyrkor[38]. Ten years later, when sisters from that monastery went to begin the Barkalabava monastery the first superior there was Fotynja Kyrkor[39]. From 1679 there is a notice of three blood sisters as superiors of three different monasteries: Euphrosine Xlevnyc'ka in Kutejno, Teofila in

---

[33] The visitation report is in C'OROX, p. 233.

[34] "Na każdy rok po zeysciu moim z tego świata, obieranie Starszej albo Hegumenicy po Nabozenstwie zwczaynym y wysłuchaniem Rachunkow wedle przychodow y rozchodow przeszłey Hegumenicy aby odprawowały", ibid., p. 244.

[35] "Electiones Abbatissarum statutis temporibus fiant per vota secreta". SPR, p. 112.

[36] The superior in 1818 had been in office already 15 years. In the monastery there were two former superiors and a nun who had been superior in Polonne, Skruten', p. 358-359.

[37] WOŁYNIAK, p. 68.

[38] Akty ZR, 4: 521.

[39] Ibid., 5: 72.

Baturyn, Polyfronija in Mahilev at the monastery of St Nicholas[40].
Here, incidentally, we have an example of the church ties and influences
that existed between eastern Belorussia and Černihivščyna. At Xoroševe
in the eighteenth century two sisters of the Kvitka family succeeded each
other as superiors[41].

Administration of Monasteries

Only a few things can be said about the actual extent of the
authority of the superiors. Metropolitan Kyška, in his instructions to the
Minsk Holy Spirit monastery in 1724 ruled that the superior should have
councillors—how many is not said—without the advice of which she
may not do anything[42]. In many documents coming from Uniate
monasteries in Belorussia there is found a formula more or less as
follows: "I, N.N., superior of..., in my name and in the name of the
entire monastery, with the consent and permission of the reverend
nuns...", or, more simply, "I, N.N., superior of..., and I, N.N., vicar
[and perhaps other names] and the entire monastery..."[43].
The difficulty with such legal phrases is that one does not know
whether they were mere formulas or give evidence of real consultation.
The same may be said of signatures to documents, where the superior's
name is often followed by that of her vicar alone[44], or her vicar and
councillors. From such signatures one cannot really draw conclusions
about the number of councillors—not all were necessarily present, they
were not always designated as such, and the number varies at one[45],
two[46], and three[47]. In the Holy Trinity monastery of Vilna, at least, the
number remained stable at three. Presumably all these were elected. On
one document of 1738 we have the signatures of the superior and the
secretary, at the Minsk Holy Spirit monastery[48]—a unique mention of
the office of secretary, which may have existed elsewhere.

---

[40] *IJuM*, 26: 355. A fourth sister was a simple nun in Kutejno.
[41] *ISOXE*, 1: 130-131. Another example may be had at the Sluck monastery, cf. the partial list of superiors in NIKOLAJ, p. 119.
[42] Acta Kisciana, vol. 6, fol. 240.
[43] *AV*, 9: 290; *IJuM*, 19: 103.
[44] *AV*, 9: 291 (Vilna, Holy Trinity, 1701).
[45] *Ibid.*, p. 86 (Vilna, Holy Trinity, 1771).
[46] *Ibid.*, 11: 189 (Vilna, Holy Trinity, 1669); 388 (1750).
[47] *Ibid.*, 9: 303 (Vilna, Holy Trinity, 1709); 329 (1740).
[48] *Ibid.*, 11: 485.

Uniate monasteries in Ukraine, so much poorer and hence more abandoned under all other respects—the direct consequences of economic misery on other aspects can hardly be overstressed—do not seem to have observed such administrative niceties. At Dubno the office of vicar was known, but elsewhere in visitations and other reports only the office of superior is mentioned[49].

The practice of Orthodox monasteries, taken as a whole, was similar to that of Catholic ones. At Vinnycja to receive and administer the annual sum left to the nuns their founder, Michael Kropyvnyc'kyj, required three persons—the superior and two other sisters. In the latter capacity two different sisters were to take their turn each year[50]. The testaments of two foundresses and superiors, from Javoriv and Minsk, are very similar in spirit and in many particulars. They both prescribe that the superior should carry out her charge with the advice of all the sisters[51].

The testament of Eugenia Šembelev of Minsk gives other intimate glimpses into the daily life of the sisters. Among other things it provides that every matter should be settled by the superior with the advice and counsel of all the sisters, not excluding any of them, from the oldest to the youngest; that a chest with the monastery's documents and money be kept in the superior's room, but the keys to its three locks should be held by three different sisters, The sisters charged with the monastery's valuables may have held formal office in the monastery. Metropolitan Peter Mohyla, during a visit to this monastery in 1635, ordained that there should be a vicar to assist the superior[52].

In other Orthodox monasteries too the superior had a group of sisters who advised her in important matters. References to such councillors come from various regions and periods and show it to have been a common institution. So in the Kiev monastery of the Ascension in 1669 the superior, disposing of her personal property, says she is doing so on the advice of her councillors, "sovitom staršyx moix i sobornyx"[53]. This gives us also the name the councillors went by, here and elsewhere: soborny [starycy]. From Kutejno we have a mention of "soborny starycy Mytrodora i Taita"[54]. In statistics on monasteris of the eparchies of Kiev (1759) and Černihiv and Perejaslav (1761) it ap-

---

[49] SKRUTEN', p. 357. Cf. C'OROX, p. 233-235 (for Slovita in 1763).

[50] SECINSKIJ, p. 259-260.

[51] For Javoriv, cf. C'OROX, p. 244; for Minsk, *VZR*, 2 (1863), November, 12, 14.

[52] Cf. NIKOLAJ, p. 93.

[53] *Akty JuZR*, 8: 150.

[54] *Ibid.*, 14: 207. The same term is found also in Ladyn in 1638, *ibid.*, 3: 7.

pears that in most monasteries there were at least the two other offices
of vicar and cellarer (one person) and econome[55].

Monasteries that were fairly large, as were those of the Ascension
and of Sts Florus and Laurus in Kiev, had a full range of monastery offices. If the superior was an ihumenja, there was regularly a vicar
(*namisnycja*). Besides councillors, an *ustavščica* or *ustavnycja* is noted.
The *ustavnycja*, properly speaking, was to see to the correct and orderly
celebration of the Office. But her duties were often of wider scope, as
we note in the example of the St John monastery, whose ustavnycja in
the 1750's is seen presenting the monastery's affairs before civil officials[56]. Two other stable offices in these monasteries were those of
econome and *ekklesiarša* (overseer of the churches and church services).

Common Life

There is little material on the basis of which one can form a judg-
ment of the internal life of monasteries before the end of the sixteenth
century, but what there is points to an absence of common life. With a
resurgence of monasticism that began at the close of the sixteenth century more attention began to be given to this aspect. In the seventeenth-
eighteenth centuries taken as a whole the impulse to common life came
primarily form the outside, even through such indirect encouragement as
in the will of Peter Mohyla, in which he left a sum to be distributed
among men's and women's monasteries that observed common life[57].
Promoters of common life, however, were especially the founders of
monasteries.

Particular mention should be made of Kutejno and Barkalabava,
whose founders insist on this point[58]. The influence of these two
monasteries can be traced further. In 1675 Marianna Suxdol'ska founded a monastery on her property at Mozoliv with the provision that it
observe common life "according to the example of the regulations and
order of the monastery at Barkalabava"[59]. Indirectly other monasteries
as well may have been influenced by it.

---

[55] Amvrosij, 2: lxxxi.

[56] A.A. [Aleksej Aleksandrovič Andrievskij], *Istoričeskie materialy*, 1 (Kiev, 1882):
49.

[57] *Pamjatniki*, 2, pt. 1: 168.

[58] The term "obščežytel'nyj" is used repeatedly in the foundation grants, cf. *Akty
ZR*, 4: 520-524, for Kutejno; 5: 68-72, for Barkalabava.

[59] "Prykładom ustawu y poriadku tohoż monastyra Borkołabowskoho", *IJuM*, 14:
514.

Although in the foundation grant of the Dubno monastery in April 1592 prince Constantine Ostroz'kyj did not mention common life, in December of the same year he issued another charter, making this women's monastery dependent on the monastery of the Transfiguration in Dubno, the ihumen of which was to see to the observance of common life in both[60]. Michael Kropyvnyc'kyj, in founding the Vinnycja monastery in 1635, also made common life a requirement[61].

In general, one can observe that a rule of common life was kept in monasteries that were grouped into little federations. Slightly earlier than the Kutejno grouping the monastery at Ladyn is described as observing common life[62]. For the Sts Peter and Paul monastery of Minsk common life was specified in its foundation grant, and the nuns, in the eventuality of a "great persecution" forcing them to disperse, were to divide the money earned by their handwork absolutely equally among themselves[63].

This is not to say that only such monasteries observed common life. The conditions and spirit prevailing at the monastery in Javoriv, which stood quite alone, are reflected in the testament of the superior Margaret Dyškevyč: the superior was to see that common life was observed both as to clothing and as to food, and all the sisters were bound to keep it diligently[64].

Even in the eighteenth century, though foundations were fewer then, the tendency remained to establish communities with common life, as when Nastasja Markovna took Hamalijivka into her hand[65].

The Synod of Zamość in 1720 not only ordained the introduction of common life into monasteries (and the very turn of phrase "vitae communis observantia introducatur" shows it to have been a novelty), but gave several specific directives about it as well[66].

These were, nevertheless, merely directives; it is necessary to see how common life was observed. Observed it was, no doubt, in many cases, but there is evidence also of a constant pull in the opposite direction[67].

---

[60] *Arxiv JuZR*, pt. I, 6: 90, 94.

[61] SECINSKIJ, p. 259.

[62] *Akty JuZR*, 3: 24.

[63] *VZR*, 2 (1863), November, 15.

[64] "Starsza aby . . . wszelki pilni dozor okolo nich wszystkich opatrowała, iako wspólnym zycia zachowac się zwykło, tak z strony odzieży iako i pokarmow trapeznych. . . . Siostrzyczki też . . . aby obszczego życia iako się to nazywa pilnie zachowały". C'OROX, p. 244.

[65] LAZAREVSKIJ, *Opisanie*, 2: 351.

[66] *SPR*, p. 111, 140, 141.

[67] This is borne out by later developments as well. In the second half of the nineteenth

Quite often even the structure of monasteries proclaims them not to have observed common life. The dwellings in the majority of monasteries were not cells in one larger building, but separate cottages. This in itself does not necessarily connote a lack of common life. A description of the Slovita monastery form 1763 reports that it consisted of eight small and dilapidated cottages, each one inhabited by one or two nuns, but there was also a common refectory, bakery, and storerooms[68].

More often, however, such a monastery was so arranged that there were no common stores, each nun had to fend for herself (though there were degrees with regard to this), and even the cells were considered as the personal property of the individual nuns. Several, if not all of the monasteries of Kiev were so arranged. In the early years of the women's monastery by the large and famous St Michael *Zolotoverxyj* in Kiev metropolitan Job Borec'kyj, who resided in that monastery, in his testament left a new cell to his daughter Evpraksija and his niece Mynodora, nuns in the women's monastery[69]. Obviously, it was a small cabin.

When the need arose, such cells were moved to a new location. When the nuns transferred in 1709 to another locality they took with them not only all movable property, but also took apart their cells, which they then sold to people[70]. The cells of the Jordan monastery too were the personal property of individual nuns, as appears clearly in the last will of its superior, Paraskeva Tuptalo, written in June 1710. She disposed actually of two cells, a new one and the old one in which she had lived and was dying[71].

Some decades later the layout of the St Florus monastery in Kiev is seen to be similar. When a wandering nun from Moscow, Melania, appeared and asked to be admitted, the ihumenja replied that Melania would first have to build herself a cell from her own funds[72]. At the

---

century the Holy Synod attempted to introduce common life into at least some of the state-supported monasteries. A telling example of the kind of objections raised and of the resistance shown appears in the case of the Mahilev monastery of the Epiphany, where it never did materialize, see ŽUDRO, *Bogojavlenskij bratskij monastyr'*, p. 39-40.

[68] Cf. C'OROX, p. 71-72, and illustrations on p. 70-71.

[69] Job Borec'kyj's will was published by S. GOLUBEV in Materialy dlja istorii zapadno-russkoj pravoslavnoj cerkvi (XVI i XVII stol.), *TKDA*, 1878, 4: 395-399.

[70] Cf. P.L-v, Istoričeskija zametki o Kieve, p. 240.

[71] The will is printed by LAZAREVSKIJ, Dokumental'nyja svedenija, *KS*, 3 (1882, 3): 383-384.

[72] Cf. *OASS*, 8: 470. The response, though, may have been the only means to avoid accepting an undesirable member, who had permission from the Synod to apply there.

closing of the St John the Evangelist monastery of Kiev in 1789, when the nuns were being transferred to Krasnohora, the metropolitan of Kiev pointed out that no state funds would need to be spent for the transfer. The cells at the Kiev monastery were the personal property of each nun, who could sell it to whomsoever she liked and use the money from the sale for traveling expenses[73]. The Pečenyky monastery near Starobud also was a settlement of separate cabins[74].

The monastery at Mykulynci in the eighteenth century was a tiny hamlet of huts, put up presumably by the nuns themselves, and when someone joined them she bought one of those huts for her use[75]. A sense of community life was very little developed here. An elderly nun, when the discomforts of living in such a hut would become too much for her, would go to the nearby village to live for a time with the local people and would return to the monastery upon feeling better.

At about the same time, when the monastery of Xoroševo burned down, some of its nuns, unable to rebuild their cells from their own funds, left for other monasteries[76]. A glance at the items in a list of damages sustained by individual nuns of the Čyhyryn monastery in 1767 is proof sufficient that each nun fended for herself as best she could. The property of each nun is listed separately. Maintenance of a monastery church was a communal responsibility. In this case we are told that the the church was maintained by alms collected for that specific purpose[77].

The rejection of common life was carried to extremes at times, and we have nuns living totally apart from any community, without ties to any monastery. One factor that contributed to this was the habit, to which eastern monks and nuns were so prone, of wandering around from place to place. This could not but weaken the bonds between an individual and a monastery and found its extension in the person concerned settling away from all monasteries. Numerous residents of Mahilev testified in the early seventeenth century that a certain nun from a Kiev monastery had appeared in Mahilev and there lodged with a townswoman[78]. Here and there we find other examples: in 1729 the

---

[73] *PSPR*, Catherine II, 3: 290.

[74] A widower priest who had become a monk in Starodub arranged to have a cottage from that monastery moved to Pečenyky, where his daughter was a nun, *OASS*, 22: 461-462.

[75] Secinskij, p. 347.

[76] *ISOXE*, 1: 129.

[77] Cf. *Arxiv JuZR*, pt. I, 3: 226-242.

[78] Cf. *IJuM*, 8: 415.

owner of a village in the Starodub polk who had become a nun was living at home with her children[79].

A different and unique case in the mid-seventeenth century is that
of Sophia Anne Esman. She became a nun—not in any monastery, but
with the intention of leading a solitary life in Žyrovyci. Žyrovyci
possessed a renowned icon of the Mother of God and attracted
numerous pilgrims; to serve them there was a large community of
Basilian monks. The monks favored Sophia Esman's choice. Some kind
of dwelling was to be built for her near the church of Žyrovyci; in the
meantime she lived on her property in the same district, in a small
house, one part of which was fully outfitted as a chapel. Sophia Esman,
however, fell sick and passed away before she had a chance to move to
Žyrovyci. The monks call her a "nun of the rule of St Basil", and it is
obvious that she had made a monastic profession[80].

Provisions that touch on common life—or rather on the lack of
common life—are difficult to judge because we do not know how they
were carried out in the day-to-day life of the monasteries. Nevertheless,
analyzing them we obtain some light on this aspect of monastic life.

When at times it is stated that so-and-so-much of a certain food
supply should be given for each nun, this is not to be interpreted that it
was given out to individual nuns, but that care was taken that the provisions be sufficient for all. This is seen in the project for the support of
the Kutejno monastery submitted to the Holy Synod in 1743. There
money and grain is computed individually per sister (it is seen, incidentally, to be distributed equally, except for a larger portion for the
ihumenja), but the list of monastery charges in that same computation
could be arranged only in a monastery of common life[81].

Details in other instances point to a lack of common life. A Vilna
merchant specified in his will in 1691 that his daughter, a nun at the
monastery of the Holy Spirit there, should receive every year 150 zloty
and be provided with clothes[82]. And Silvester Volčaskyj, administrator
of the Belorussian diocese, in his will of 2 December 1686 specified that
the 60 zloty he was leaving to the St Nicholas monastery in Mahilev
should be divided equally among the nuns there[83].

---

[79] *UA*, 1: 37-38: "Vladeet toeju derevneju Nerinovkuju žena ego nnešnaja monaxinja
v domu živučaja Ekaterina z detmi".

[80] Everything we know about this interesting case comes from court documents; after
her death in 1662 her relatives contested, by force and by law, her bequests in favor of the
Basilians of Žyrovyci. See *AV*, 15: 68-73, 78-80, 90-92, 134-135.

[81] *OASS*, 23: 35-38.

[82] This will was printed twice in the same volume, *AV*, 9: 505-506 and 518-522.

[83] "Pannom zakonnym Mykol'skym, na molytvu, v rovnyj podil mežy sestry, zolotyx

These were Orthodox monasteries. Turning to Uniate ones, we can begin by studying the will of metropolitan Antony Sjeljava, written on 5 May 1651, four years before his death. In leaving a large sum—20.000 Polish zloty—for the Holy Spirit monastery in Minsk he gave the following directions concerning the use to which the interest on it was to be put (the original sum was to remain intact). The interest from 12.000 was to go for six nuns from his family, from another 4000 for four other nuns (impoverished gentry or townswomen), and from the remaining 4000 for the general needs of the monastery. Should there not be six nuns from among his relatives, then in lieu of each one of them two poor girls should be accepted in the monastery and benefit from his fund. These sums the superior should use for clothing and food for the specified nuns[84]. A little further on he made a similar bequest in favor of his niece, a nun in the Polock monastery. The amounts named in the will are unequal. Furthermore, the question arises whether there was even a common table, if the food for individual nuns was paid for from money accruing to them.

The Synod of Zamość, with all its good intentions, did not produce any great changes. It legislated on sufficient common funds in monasteries, on accepting only as many entrants as a monastery could support, and issued various directives on common life. But Jerome Moro, rector of the Ruthenian and Armenian seminary of Lviv, in a report written in 1746 noted that only two Uniate women's monasteries observed perfectly the enclosure and common life[85], and added that the monasteries had no funds for the support of the sisters. All these items are interconnected: without a common monastery fund there could be no common provision for the sisters, hence no common life, and the sisters, left to provide each one for herself as best she could, were compelled to go out at least to sell their handicrafts. In 1763 the visitator of the Slovita monastery noted that each sister lived from the work of her hands—"z pracy rąk sustentuie się"—even those close to ninety years of age[86] and even though this monastery was so arranged as to provide for common life, as described above.

šestdesjat", *IJuM*, 10: 421. Similar sums were left to other women's monasteries without this added directive.

[84] *Ibid.*, 2: 260-261.

[85] *Acta S.C. de Propaganda Fide*, 4 (Romae, 1955): 49. It is hard to say which two monasteries the author had in mind, perhaps Vilna Holy Trinity and Minsk Holy Spirit, and perhaps there were more, but substantially he is right: the overwhelming majority of them observed neither.

[86] C'OROX, p. 233-234.

Dowries in practice were often applied to individual nuns rather than to the monastery fund. In 1761 the parents of an entrant in the Vicebsk Holy Spirit monastery speak of the dowry as sufficing for her board and comfort and they also obligate themselves to provide their daughter with clothes as long as they live[87]. Two years later further specifications are noted: besides the dowry another equal sum of 200 talers is marked for their daughter, by this time a professed nun. During her lifetime she is to use only the interest on the sum; it is specifically stated that the superior and the monastery are not to concern themselves with this money, but only that particular nun may do with it what she likes. The person concerned was not of good health, and this money must have been meant to provide her with medicines, among other things. After her death the entire sum was to go to the monastery[88].

Closely connected is the matter of individual disposal of money and property, contrary to the ideal of common life and monastic poverty, but very much a part of reality. Here again we can begin with an early example. From much later documents we learn of a testamentary disposition of a nun Pelahija, made about 1525 in favor of the Kiev Lavra[89]. However, she may have been one of those who never really entered a monastery, but made profession during her last illness and then also made her will.

A similar case is that of a certain nun Paraskeva Kupčyns'ka who sold some property of hers in Kiev to the brotherhood monastery in 1621[90]. Her monastery is not mentioned; perhaps she lived alone. Thus in both examples someone only nominally a nun was disposing of her property.

Two further examples are different. The locality is again Kiev, but it is a matter of two ihumenjas disposing of their personal property. In 1669 the ihumenja of the Ascension monastery in Kiev gave her property, which included four villages, to the Lavra. Her request to tsar Alexius to confirm her gift reveals that only her inability to defend her rights to the land prompted her to this act, this being the ruinous period of strife among various contenders to the hetmanate.

---

[87] *IJuM*, 19: 103-106.

[88] *Ibid.*, p. 125-127. Other cases of dowries providing for medications occur, so at the Vilna monastery of the Holy Trinity in 1741, *AV*, 11: 493.

[89] Cf. *OAZM*, 1: 108 (no. 243). Other documents refer to the same property, but they add nothing to our knowledge about Pelahija. The dispute about the property, though, was still being dragged out in 1766, cf. 2: 236-237 (no. 1901).

[90] Cf. PAMJATNIKI, 2: 292-293.

> Since at the present time I live in Kiev more than 40 miles from those in-
> herited properties and cannot manage to assist them and to defend them
> from injustices and military skirmishes and to administer them, for that
> reason I have given over my inherited possessions with everything on them
> to this holy Lavra[91].

No doubt she gave it to the Lavra and not to her own monastery
because she knew that the former would be in a much better position to
assert its ownership. In another note she reported that she was acting
with the advice of other sisters.

The will of Paraskeva Tuptalo, ihumenja of the Jordan monastery
in Kiev is interesting in its details. She disposed of inherited family property, her own goods and money, and recorded her debts. To her own
monastery she left a relatively small sum; more was given to the nearby
men's monastery of St Cyril of which her family were ktytors[92].

A few Uniate monasteries observed the precept that a novice could
freely dispose of her property, but upon her profession everything she
still owned became the property of the monastery. We find this stated
explicitly in a document of 1794 from Vilna. Scholastica Vasylevska
made a gift of her inheritance to the Holy Trinity monastery "while I
am still free to do it before profession"[93]. The same principle had been
in vigor in that monastery for a long time. A document of 1709 states
that a nun's portion of an inheritance had been in the care of her guardian, but "after Barbara Minkiewicz entered religious life it has belonged to our convent in Vilna"[94].

In documents concerned with this inheritance it is stressed that
eveything proceeded with the permission of superiors and according to
rule[95]. Common life might seem to prevail in this monastery. But even
here contradictions have been found.

In the Vilna Holy Trinity monastery there was a nun Anna
Ivanovyč, several of whose relatives were Basilian monks. She was not
one to overlook her rights, and when one of her brothers who had been
superior at Xoms'k died, she demanded the inheritance he had left
her—various objects plus 1000 zloty. The matter was discussed at the

---

[91] *Akty JuZR*, 8: 150.
[92] LAZAREVSKIJ, Dokumental'nyja svedenija, p. 383-384.
[93] *AV*, 9: 129.
[94] *Ibid.*, p. 302.
[95] *Ibid.*, p. 299: "Maiąc na to od w Bogu przewielebney imci panny Konstancyey Sud-
nickiey—przełożoney naszey licentią i osobliwe pozwolenie iako nasza powinność obedien-
tia y posłuszeństwo każe według reguły zakonney". On p. 302 it is stated that the sum was
given over "do rąk naszych wyż namienioney starszey y całemu konventowi naszemu".

Basilian Congregation in Bycen' in 1698, and though the fate of the 1000 zloty is unknown, she received at least the other items[96].

Five years later at the same monastery a nun Alexandra Ivanovyč asked for the restitution of some items—a French carriage, a pair of horses, and some material—given to her by her brother Alexander Borysovyč, superior at Ušač, before his death. This too was discussed at a Basilian Congregation, where it was decided that although the monks did not have the right to make wills, since Borysovyč's sister was a nun of the same Order, the items should be given over to her[97].

In both of these examples the nuns acted on their own, not on their monastery's behalf. The involvement of nuns in financial matters is attested to also by the fact that money was deposited at times with individual nuns, not with the monastery. Leo Kyška reported one such case at Hrodna in 1710[98].

Various other cases could be brought up, such as bequests made by nuns. In 1685 the Vilna Holy Trinity monks were given a building in Vilna by a certain "p. Rzepniecka" and her daughter Magdalene, "a nun of the order of St Basil the Great"[99].

Monasticism, from its beginnings in Rus', as Golubinskij has already pointed out[100], did not observe common life. This in fact became the rule in the centuries of decadence of ecclesiastical life. Regulations more in keeping with monastic observance, since they stood alone, unsupported by any means which would deepen monastic spirit, were not very effective in bringing about a change.

[96] *AS*, 12: 139.

[97] *Ibid.*, p. 145-146.

[98] Acta Kisciana, vol. 6, fol. 35r.

[99] The original document of their bequest is noted in a Memoryał drawn up by a monk of Vilna in 1701, *AS*, 10: 123.

[100] GOLUBINSKIJ, 1, pt. 2: 633-634.

Chapter VII

THE LIFE OF THE NUNS

It is hardly possible to draw a full picture of the internal life of monasteries. More than for any other aspect one can complain here of a lack of sources. That conditions varied greatly is equally limiting. The size of a monastery, its economic fortunes, the social background of the nuns—all this had a bearing on the daily life in a particular monastery. In certain instances one phrase almost defines a whole way of life—yet of its relations to other aspects we know nothing. In the introduction of a legal document we are told that all the nuns of the Vilna Holy Trinity monastery came together at the ringing of the bell, "as is the custom in our monastery", to witness its signing[1]: a flash upon a well-ordered life, yet for what other occasions did the bell call the sisters and at what times was it rung?

What the nuns did can be divided broadly into two categories: prayer and other activities. Before turning to the topic of monastic prayer, however, it is necessary to form some kind of estimate about the literacy of the nuns. This can be done on the basis of the rare direct information, as well as by noting such things as lists of books or mention of separate books in monasteries, signatures of the nuns, and a few other details of monastic life.

Literacy

Precise data is late, but it offers the most secure basis for estimating literacy in monasteries. In 1767 the nuns in Čyhyryn lodged a

---

[1] "My wszystkie zakonnice . . . na znak dzwonka podług zwyczaiu klasztoru naszego zgromadzenia", *AV*, 9: 302.

complaint with the Orthodox metropolitan of Kiev Arsenij
Mohyljans'kyj. The complaint bears four signatures (that of the superior
and of three other nuns); twenty-one other nuns had their names signed
in by the monastery chaplain Ivan Tatarčenko[2].

The information from the monastery of Novi Mlyny in 1777 is even
more detailed. There, of twenty-six nuns, nine were literate, five literate
to some measure, ten illiterate, and for two no information is given. The
superior, too, surprisingly, was illiterate. Those entering were taught in
the monastery to read and write—but evidently not all. Instruction did
not advance very far: enough to read the psalter and the časoslov (the
traditional basic instruction, given also to children) and to keep accounts
(for those who might oversee the monastery's property and affairs)[3].

Documents of monasteries in the grand duchy of Lithuania have
been published in relative plenty. Generally the signatures of the nuns
are noted to be in their own hand. Exceptions are infrequent. The foundress and first superior of the Sts Peter and Paul monastery in Minsk admitted in her testament that she could not write[4]. In 1750 a nun at the
Vicebsk monastery of the Holy Spirit—she was the novice
mistress—signed herself with three crosses[5].

Signatures to documents provide further interesting details on the
extent of literacy. There is, for instance, a document from 1759 concerning a legal agreement between the Bujnyči and the Barkalabava
monasteries, signed by two persons from each. The document is in
Polish, as are also the signatures, except for that of the second nun
from Barkalabava, who signed herself in Cyrillic[6]. Her literacy evidently
extended only to Ruthenian.

Materials of monasteries in other regions are far less abundant, so
one is less justified in drawing from them any conclusions about the extent of literacy and can note only some individual cases. The fact that
the superior of the Černihiv monastery asked the polk secretary to sign
some monastery documents in her stead can be assumed to indicate that
she herself was illiterate[7]. Paraskeva Tuptalo, ihumenja of the Jordan

---

[2] *Arxiv JuZR*, pt. I, 3: 242.

[3] This information is given by LAZAREVSKIJ, *Opisanie*, 2: 298-299, from a manuscript
which was in his possession and which contained lists of and information about members
of Ukrainian monasteries as part of a report submitted to the Kiev consistory in 1777. One
can only regret that it was never published integrally.

[4] *VZR*, 2 (1863), November, 15.

[5] *IJuM*, 18: 419.

[6] *AS*, 2: 130.

[7] VASILENKO, 3: 466. No date is given when these documents—copies of
charters—were made, but it was after 1729 (the date of the last one).

monastery in Kiev, says in her will that she is signing with a cross since she cannot write[8]. But of the last superior of this monastery, in the 1780's, it was noted that she was literate in Cyrillic—"russkoj gramote obučena"[9].

Concerning the monasteries in Halyčyna, information from the period of suppressions can serve to give an idea of earlier times as well. Of the few surviving nuns at the beginning of the nineteenth century some knew how to read, but not how to write[10]. The rest presumably knew neither.

The books that the sisters had for reading were few. Their number can be gathered from the rare complete inventories. What these books were can also be retraced from all kinds of chance notices (not that these occur frequently).

The sisters of the Ladyn monastery in 1638 drew up a complete list of their movable possessions, among which figures a list of books. The monastery was large (about fifty nuns) and well-off economically. The list of books for reading is as follows: an "učitel'noe evangelie" (a book of sermons following the liturgical year), a manuscript Acts of the Apostles, five "small books", about ten "various books", Barlaam and Joasaph ("kniga Jasafa careviča pečatanaja novaja"), a Hexaemeron (Moscow edition), two books of Macarius of Egypt, a *Cvitnyk*, a Polish Lives of the Saints, a manuscript copy of John Climacus[11]. The sisters had taken thse books with them when they decided to emigrate to Muscovy, but they were robbed of all their possessions, including the books, along the way. Hence the list: to seek a proper reimbursement.

Another list, this time of old books found in the same Ladyn monastery in 1825 reported the following: an "učitel'noe evangelie" of 1616, *Ključ razuminija* of Joanikij Galjatovs'kyj (Lviv 1665), *Truby na dny naročytyja* (a collection of sermons of Lazar Baranovyč printed at the Kiev Lavra in 1674), *Ohorodok Marii Bohorodycy* (a collection of sermons by the hieromonk Antony Radyvylovs'kyj printed at the Kiev Lavra in 1676)[12].

---

[8] LAZAREVSKIJ, Dokumental'nyja svedenija, *KS*, 3 (1882, 3): 384.

[9] F.A. TERNOVSKIJ, Izlišnie malorossijskie monaxi konca XVIII st., kakix oni byli kačestv i kak doživali svoj vek, *KS*, 2 (1882, 2): 329-337.

[10] CHOTKOWSKI, p. 148.

[11] *Akty JuZR*, 3: 23-24. The *Cvitnyk* is the *Limonar syrič cvitnyk*, a translation of *The Spiritual Meadow* of John Moschus, published in Kiev in 1628 by Job BOREC'KYJ. Earlier Slavic translations of this work were called *Sinajskij paterik*.

[12] The list is given as an appendix to Letopis' o pervozačatii i sozdanii Gustynskogo monastyrja, *ČOIDR*, 1848, no. 8, p. 70.

These two lists give a good idea of the extent of reading material available. In other monasteries mention is made of the same books. Barlaam and Joasaph is seen again at Barkalabava[13]. The monastery in Bibrka received in gift the Stauropegian edition of 1666 of *Tablyca nevydymaja serdca človečaho* (the Epistles with commentary)[14]. Besides Macarius and Climacus references are found also to the "ancient holy fathers" in general, as at Sluck, where manuscript copies both of Climacus and of a Lives of the holy fathers are mentioned[15].

The question arises how much even these few books were read. It is an ancient monastic practice to have reading in the refectory during meals. But outside of a mention of this by the Synod of Zamość, repeated by metropolitan Kyška in a visitation, no references to this practice in Uniate monasteries have been found.

The intention of the Synod of Zamość was that the visitator should find out "what kind of devout and of profane books the nuns read and whether there is reading of a spiritual book during meals"[16]. The second reference is interesting: the metropolitan set it down as a rule that each sister without exception should take her turn in reading in the refectory[17]. Evidently in the Minsk Holy Spirit monastery, to which this refers, all knew how to read. For the rest, one could onclude either that the practice was so common as not to deserve comment, or, obversely, that it was such a rarity as to be practically unknown.

This does not mean that reading in the refectory was entirely neglected. One description of this practice comes from the community of "Cossack nuns", as Paul of Aleppo calls them, who had been resettled from Ruthenian monasteries in the Novodevičij monastery outside Moscow. As the monastery was entirely given over to them, they continued with the practices they had followed at home. Archdeacon Paul was present at a meal in their refectory after a service celebrated by patriarch Macarius. He describes the meal. After the service in church the nuns

> singing as they went, preceded the patriarch into the refectory, where we sat down in the customary order. The ihumenja, cellarer, econome, and

---

[13] Xarlampovič, p. 279.

[14] Svjencickyj, p. 10.

[15] Snitko, Opisanie dokumentov, p. 153. The other books for reading were *Knyha Kalyksta*, *Ohorodok* by Radyvylovs'kyj, and *Ključ razuminija*, and a manuscript copy of prolohy (short lives of saints).

[16] *SPR*, p. 142.

[17] Acta Kisciana, vol. 6, fol. 268-270.

the older nuns sat down according to their rank... [Here follows a description of the food]. One of the nuns began to read what was prescribed in a soft, pleasant voice, in a manner so well-ordered that it was amazing, better than among men. We arose from the table full of amazement at them and the neatness and orderliness there[18].

Monastery Churches

A whole series of monasteries either did not have their own churches at all or else had oratories where only occasionally services were held. The nuns attended services in common with others—most often with monks in the monastery churches of the latter. This arrangement existed at Vilna (Holy Trinity), Minsk (Holy Spirit), Mahilev (Epiphany), Polock, Kiev (St Michael), and probably at some others. As has been mentioned, it was a natural arrangement in monasteries founded next to brotherhood churches. At Polock the women's monastery was by the cathedral, where the nuns used to attend services.

We have descriptions of some external points of such an arrangement[19], but nothing about the principal one: how did the nuns participate in the Divine Liturgy or the Office under such an arrangement. At the Holy Spirit monastery in Minsk the nuns had a small oratory of their own, but attended most services in the large church of the monks. It fell to their charge to take care of the church—not only to see to its cleanliness, but to take care of other matters connected with the services and with the furnishings of the church. Varlaam Kozinskyj, archimandrite of Minsk, in his will of 1660 in which he made various provisions for the church, charged not his monks, but the ihumenja of the women's monastery with carrying them out. She was to have the cover of the church's icon resilvered, a lamp made to burn before it, take care of and give out on proper occasions the splendid vestments he was leaving to this church. From another legacy of his we learn that the sisters gave out the wine for the liturgies in the Holy Spirit church[20].

A similar arrangement can be found in Orthodox monasteries. The nuns of the Epiphany monastery in Mahilev attended all the services with

---

[18] Pavel ALEPPSKIJ, *ČOIDR*, 1898, 4: 152.

[19] The nuns of the Vilna Holy Trinity monastery at the end of the seventeenth century had an opening made for a side door in the Holy Trinity church to give them a more direct passage through their garden into the church, "for greater convenience in inclement weather", they say. Cf. *AS*, 12: 139; ŠČERBICKIJ, *Dostoprimečatel'nosti*, p. 22-23.

[20] *AV*, 11: 154-155, 157.

the monks in their common church. Their care of it included guarding
the precious icon covers from theft during vespers and matins[21]. Not
always did such an arrangement work out well, and we hear of the nuns
at the the monastery next to St Michael of Kiev complaining of it[22].

The fact that a women's monastery had a church of its own with
services there did not exclude the possibility that at least occasionally the
nuns attended services elsewhere. When patriarch Macarius of Antioch
celebrated the liturgy in the Kiev Lavra on the feast of Sts Peter and
Paul it was attended by the nuns of the neighboring Ascension
monastery[23]. This may have been a general practice on great feasts and
other special occasions.

While the town monasteries of Belorussia often shared a church
with monks, most monasteries in Ukraine had not one, but at least two
churches. During the severe winters the long offices could not be
celebrated in an unheated church building, so there was often another
church connected with the refectory and kitchen, called the "warm
church".

Apart from this practical reason, the construction of a number of
churches, beyond strict need, was an expression of traditional piety. The
location of most Ukrainian monasteries, not hemmed in by other
buildings, but with an enclosure of some extent, encouraged this tendency. Few constructions survive. Until the end of the seventeenth century
all these churches were built of wood, and even later wood was the common material. Sooner or later, then, they were the prey of fire. More
lasting constructions have not enjoyed a better fate.

In some instances one of the churches of a monastery served as a
parish church for the nearby community. This has already been noted
for Xoroševo. The secondary church of St Nicholas at Ladyn likewise
served as the parish church for the village of Ladyn[24]. Other examples in
the territories colonized in the seventeenth century could probably be
found.

When a monastery church possessed a specially venerated icon,
especially of the Mother of God, it attracted at least local *bohomol'ci*
and became to some degree a focus of piety. That few examples are
documented is due to the relative scarcity of materials on women's

---

[21] Żudro, *Bogojavlenskij bratskij monastyr'*, p. 31, 33, 34.
[22] Cf. P.L-v, Istoričeskie zametki o Kieve, p. 238-239, where the complaint is described
in general terms.
[23] Pavel Aleppskij, *ČOIDR*, 1897, 4: 61.
[24] Letopis' Gustynskogo monastyrja, *ČOIDR*, 1848, 8: 69.

monasteries and to the closing of a great number of them before the nineteenth century. The special veneration accorded particular icons, often regarded as miraculous, was prominent in Ruthenian religious culture. The number of such icons was large, though of course many of them enjoyed only local fame.

Icons popularly considered miraculous were found in Lebedyn[25] and Korobivka[26]. In Korobivka even long after the monastery was closed services were kept up in its church because people continued to flock there to pray in front of its icon of the Mother of God.

One source of information are old songbooks. One such, compiled in 1727 in Halyčyna, contains a song in honor of an icon at the Ascension monastery in Kiev[27]. That Kiev, and especially the Kiev Lavra, to which the Ascension monastery was very close, attracted pilgrims from all parts of Ukraine explains the rather far range in place and time of the song (the monastery had been closed for over a decade already).

Prayer

To contemporaries the form and manner of monastic prayer was so obvious that it never occurred to them to set down a description of it. In consequence, we have only extremely fragmentary notices about prayer and services in monasteries. Exception is made by a few fuller descriptions left by foreigners, who were struck by either surprising differences or similarities to what they themselves were accustomed.

The outstanding monastic prayer is the Divine Office. We can speak only of its major parts, vespers and matins. The other hours of the Office are never mentioned. If they were recited at all, it must have been done for the most part privately in one's cell, though there is also recorded the practice of reading the hours during a celebrant's preparation for the Divine Liturgy[28].

The celebration of the Divine Office was a task of the community, not an obligation of the individual nuns. In fact, obligation is not a good term to use; the concept of a binding regulation, applying to each

---

[25] POXILEVIČ, *Skazanija o naselennyx mestax Kievskoj gubernii*, p. 666.

[26] MAKSIMOVIČ, Vospominanija, p. 422.

[27] The song was published by M. HRUŠEVS'KYJ, S'pivannyk z počatku XVIII v., *Zapysky Naukovoho Tovarystva im. Ševčenka*, 17 (1897, 3): 49.

[28] This is noted in the Novodevičij monastery when patriarch Macarius was being vested in the narthex, *ibid.*, 1898, 4: 152.

nun, was quite foreign and is totally absent. As various other tasks were
assigned to the members of the community, so was that of singing the
Divine Office. Obviously, this does not apply to monasteries with only a
handful of nuns, who, moreover, lived each one for herself. There the
recitation of the Divine Office was probably an entirely individual affair.

In the larger monasteries the Divine Office may have involved a
considerable proportion of the sisters, but by no means all. The old and
the ailing were excluded, as well as those whose charges claimed a large
amount of their time. The nuns assigned to the Divine Office were
divided into two choirs (*krylosy*), hence called krylošanky, a term very
widely used, as it is noted in monasteries in different regions. Statistics
of the Kiev Orthodox eparchy monasteries state how many nuns were
"krylošanky". In small monasteries this was all the professed nuns; in
large ones in the eighteenth century only a small proportion were formally so designated (in 1743-1745, 16 krylošanky in Sts Florus and
Laurus, 10 in Jordan, 6 in St John). In a listing of various chores
assigned to the sisters at Novi Mlyny, one of the charges is called
"krylošanskoe"[29]. Petruševyč records the same term in use at the
monastery in Kaminka Strumylova[30]. And of a nun in Slovita in 1763 it
is said that she "belongs to the krylos"[31].

In founders' statutes are found some very general directives concerning the praying of the Divine Office, all on the pattern that the rites
and ceremonies of the Church should be preserved. As an example we
can quote from the one for Kutejno from 1631: "May the glorification
(slavoslovie) of God, in the manner the rule, order, and ceremonies of
the Church teach, never cease in this monastery of our foundation to
the end of the world"[32].

A more promising source of information is notices of books in
monasteries. The inventory of the Ladyn monastery already referred to
gives also a full list of its liturgical books in 1638: one trefolij (a collection of services for feasts), one oktoix, two časoslovs (one of them
described as "new"), a manuscript ustav, three manuscript sobornyky
(collections of services), three hirmologia, a Lenten and an Easter triodion (these last two noted as of Moscow edition)[33].

---

[29] LAZAREVSKIJ, *Opisanie*, 2: 299.
[30] PETRUŠEVIČ, *Svodnaja letopis' 1600-1700*, p. 161.
[31] C'OROX, p. 234.
[32] *Akty ZR*, 4: 522.
[33] *Akty JuZR*, 3: 24. These books were what the sisters took with them to Muscovy.
It may be of some interest to note that in a description of the Ladyn monastery made in

The Ladyn monastery possessed several copies of at least some books. Most monasteries had only one copy of each book needed. A complete set of all the books was expensive. The twelve volumes of the menaion were often replaced by collections of general services.

The Sluck monastery in 1724 had one full set of menaia, a trefolij and an oktoix of a Lviv edition, the two triodia, an octavo časoslov, a folio časoslov of a Moscow edition, and an akafistnyk[34]. The following books were found at Mykulynci, a small Uniate monastery, in 1773: a Lenten triodion (Počajiv edition), an Easter triodion, a small oktoix, and a psalter (all Moscow editions), and a trefolij[35]. One final example: two nuns from Bibrka bought a triodion (Lviv edition of 1699) for their monastery[36]; its description in a catalog as "clean" leaves one to wonder if it was ever used.

From such lists it can be inferred that in the celebration of the Divine Office the various books needed were distributed among a few sisters who alone read or chanted the parts contained in them. Others might have participated in those parts that could be learned by heart—the psalms and the responses.

It may be that in a very few cases the Divine Office was prayed not by the nuns themselves, but by hired cantors. Such a supposition is the only explanation that comes to mind why a monastery—Ladyn in 1638—would have seven cantors[37]. However, such an arrangement could not have been common. In 1726 the ihumenja of the St Florus monastery in Kiev asked the Holy Synod to waive the minimal age requirements for profession of nuns in her monastery. She complained that in the course of several years a number of the sisters had died, while others were too old to sing in the krylosy. Divine services were in consequence neglected, since Ukrainian monasteries did not have the custom of hiring cantors as did those in Russia[38]. Indeed, outside of the one case cited above, there is no other reference to cantors serving a monastery. There is, on the contrary, other evidence that the nuns sang

---

1825 it was reported that the monastery possessed all the necessary service books in sufficient numbers and in addition the following old books no longer in use: Gospels (Moscow 1657), Gospels (Kiev Lavra 1697), Epistles (Lviv 1639), potrebnik (Moscow 1636), oktoix (Lviv 1644), trefolij (Lviv 1637), Letopis' o pervozačatii i sozdanii Gustynskogo monastyrja, p. 69-70.

[34] SNITKO, Opisanie dokumentov, p. 153.

[35] SECINSKIJ, p. 346.

[36] SVJENCICKYJ, p. 30.

[37] Akty JuZR, 3: 24. They left Ladyn for Muscovy together with the nuns.

[38] OASS, 6: 69-70. As it tends to happen in petitions, there is some exaggeration here; the monastery was rather large and could not have lacked nuns to sing the Office.

the Divine Office and took some pains at doing it well, as we shall see.

There were, then, various practices: some monasteries with a minimum of Divine Office and neglect to some degree or other, others with only a few nuns actively participating, still others where a good proportion of the members of a monastery sang it with skill and devotion. Size was not necessarily a determining factor. From a casual reference we learn that at the monastery of Čerčyci in Volyn', which one cannot imagine ever being large, the sisters with their chaplain celebrated the Office, which the local people attended. In 1625 the nuns lodged a complaint in the Luc'k tribunal in which they specify the time of an armed raid by a neighbor (a commonplace in the Polish-Lithuanian state) thus: "Yesterday, Sunday morning, the 4th of May, when we were celebrating matins and our devotions with the priest and with other people..."[39].

Although references to the Divine Liturgy are rare, they seem to indicate that on the whole it was celebrated daily in monasteries. The founder's statute for the Kutejno monastery obligated the ihumen of the Kutejno men's monastery to send one of his hieromonks every day to celebrate the Liturgy for the nuns; on Sundays and feasts a deacon and a *ponomar* (person to light candles, and in general to serve at the Liturgy) were also to be sent. Should the ihumen ever fail to do this, whether on a festive or on an ordinary day, the monks were to be removed completely from conducting any services at the women's monastery. The ihumenja then was to seek out another priest, with the approval of the metropolitan of Kiev "so that the daily Divine Liturgy might never cease to be celebrated in the Lord's church of the Dormition of the Mother of God for us sinners, for all our household, and for the entire Orthodox Christian world"[40].

According to the Synod of Zamość the visitator of women's monasteries was to note whether a daily Liturgy was celebrated in them[41]. One finds some confirmation that it was, as in Orša[42]. Even a small monastery, such as Vinnycja was towards the end of the eighteenth century, had a daily Liturgy[43].

At least some monasteries gave great attention and care to a worthy celebration of the Divine Liturgy and Office. The singing of the

---

[39] *Arxiv JuZR*, pt. I, 6: 555.
[40] *Akty ZR*, 4: 523.
[41] *SPR*, p. 142.
[42] WOŁYNIAK, p. 79.
[43] According to the testimony of the local people, SECINSKIJ, p. 345.

"Cossack nuns" at the Ascension monastery in Kiev moved Paul of Aleppo to high-flowing praises. At the Liturgy patriarch Macarius celebrated in the monastery church

> the nuns sang and recited prayers with a pleasant tone and soft voices which melt the heart and bring forth tears; the singing was so moving that it penetrated the soul, much better than the singing of men. We were enraptured by the pleasant voices and the singing[44].

The cultivation of liturgical singing must have been widespread in the Ruthenian Church. Paul's travel diary records the services of other Ruthenian nuns, this time mostly from Belorussia, in the same enthusiastic tones. When patriarch Macarius arrived at the Novodevičij monastery

> the nuns all came out to meet us and went in front of us, singing in tones that enchant the heart, until we entered the church. The patriarch, according to custom, venerated the icons, during which time the nuns sang "Dostojno jest'". How marvelous! how harmonious and sweet is their manner of singing[45].

These nuns had been transferred to Muscovy in 1654 by tsar Alexius.

> He [Alexius] had the Muscovite nuns move out from the large women's monastery [Novodevičij] and assigned them places in other monasteries in his capital, while there he settled all the Cossack nuns, as belonging to one nationality. He did this because of his, as well as the tsarina's and the patriarch's great love for them and from a passion for their singing and services, which drive away all griefs from one's heart[46].

Paul provides some further interesting details about services in the Kiev monastery. The nuns, as was usual, were divided into two choirs; though on the occasion of his visit, since patriarch Macarius and his suite were installed on the left, the nuns squeezed together on the right. Some parts were sung antiphonally, others together by all the nuns and

---

[44] Pavel ALEPPSKIJ, *ČOIDR*, 1897, 4: 58; *Patrologia Orientalis*, 26 (Paris, 1945): 698.

[45] Pavel ALEPPSKIJ, *ČOIDR*, 1898, 4: 152.

[46] *Ibid.*, p. 51. He also reports there, repeating what the nuns told him, that Maria Lupul Radziwill had often attended their services in Lithuania. Since she willed money to the women's monasteries in Vilna, Minsk, and Sluck, it is there that she must have visited them, and it is from these monasteries that at least some of the nuns in Novodevičij had come.

the girls who were their pupils. The epistle was read by one of the nuns. At the "Dostojno jest'" the nuns came out into the middle between the two choirs and sang it kneeling. They all received Holy Communion[47].

The last point raises another question, about the frequency of confession and Holy Communion in monasteries. As concerns these nuns of the Ascension monastery, the following day, which was the feast of Sts Peter and Paul, Paul of Aleppo saw them again in the Assumption church of the Lavra for a liturgy celebrated by the patriarch, and again they received Holy Communion[48].

Other information on this point is very hard to come by. The Synod of Zamość did ordain that nuns should receive Holy Communion once a month[49], but we do not know with what exactness this was carried out. At Mykulynci the priest serving the monastery, who was also a parish priest, was given to drink, so the visitator in 1773 appointed another priest, the pastor of another village, to be the nuns' confessor, twice a year, at Easter and during retreat[50].

Specific requests on the part of donors concerning certain prayers inform us not only about monastery usages, but also about types and forms of popular devotion in a given period and place. In 1763 the nuns of the Holy Spirit monastery in Vicebsk assumed the obligation of singing every Monday a Mass with a panaxyda (a short service for the dead), litanies to the Blessed Virgin, and the Angelus with the ringing of bells for the repose of the souls of the benefactor's parents[51]. At the Vilna Holy Trinity monastery the superior, in the name of all the sisters, accepted the obligation in 1770 to recite "as many prayers and rosaries as possible" for a bequest of 400 zloty[52].

Chaplains

This in turn brings up the matter of the priests that served as chaplains and confessors in monasteries. First it is necessary to say a few words about terminology, as found in the sources. "Duxovnyj otec" or "duxovnyk" could be translated literally as "spiritual father".

---

[47] Pavel ALEPPSKIJ, ČOIDR, 1897, 4: 58-59; PO, 26: 698.
[48] Pavel ALEPPSKIJ, ČOIDR, 1897, 4: 62; PO, 26: 704.
[49] SPR, p. 142.
[50] Cf. SECINSKIJ, p. 348-349.
[51] IJuM, 19: 117-118.
[52] AV, 12: 261-263.

These terms, however, signified not what is now understood by them, but rather the priest who celebrated the services in the monastery and who occasionally had some say in the administration of the monastery.

The term "ihumen", with reference to women's monasteries, could mean the head of the monastic grouping to which a community belonged, but it could also be used synonymously with "duxovnyj otec". Both terms are used interchangeably in this passage written in 1638: "Ihumen Methodius of the Ladyn women's monastery of the Intercession of the Mother of God, and with him the ihumenja of the monastery Elizabeth Letynska with the sisters...; and he, ihumen Methodius, is the spiritual father [duxovnyj otec] of all the nuns"[53].

The term ihumen has the same meaning in the following entry from 1608: a woman is making a donation "to the nuns, popularly known as Czernicy, with their superior, otherwise called Ihumen, at the church of the Blessed Virgin Mary of the Greek rite situated in the town Bil'če"[54].

A third example comes from Volyn', showing how widespread this meaning of the word was in that period. The priest serving the monastery in Četvertnja was called ihumen of Uhornyky; he bore also the title of ihumen of the Četvertnja women's monastery[55].

Finally, we can cite a document in Polish regarding the hieromonk at the Slovita monastery in 1626. He too is called "Duchowny Oyciec" and "Starszy" (which corresponds to "ihumen"). He had rather wide authority over the monastery. Besides celebrating the services and giving spiritual instruction to the nuns he was to name the superior, accept new members, and all matters concerning the property of the monastery, although in the care of a layman, were to be settled only with his consent[56].

In the case of Orthodox monasteries that belonged to a grouping the superior of the chief monastery appointed the chaplains. Thus, the ihumen of Kutejno appointed the priest for the women's monasteries of Kutejno, Barkalabava, and Mozoliv[57]. In all three instances, this was according to the dispositions of the founders. The priests could be either hieromonks from the other monasteries in the grouping or they could be of the secular clergy. Where the priest could not come over daily (as at Kutejno), he was to have his own living quarters by the church, outside the monastery enclosure, and was to be supplied with food and clothing

---

[53] *Akty JuZR*, 3: 7.
[54] KOSSAK, p. 204.
[55] *Arxiv JuZR*, pt. I, 6: 473, note.
[56] See C'OROX, p. 236-237.
[57] *Akty ZR*, 4: 523; 5: 69; IJuM, 14: 513.

from the monastery's stores. If the ties with Kutejno were broken, the sisters could obtain a hieromonk from any Orthodox monastery[58].

Who appointed or invited priests in monasteries not belonging to a grouping is difficult to say. Only a few early examples are known, each one different. At Javoriv the foundress-superior named the ihumen of Hrušiv to be the monastery's spiritual father—"overseer and confessor", she says[59]. The superiors of other monasteries no doubt also arranged for the priests in their monasteries. Founders at founding had a voice in the appointment of chaplains and confessors for the nuns. The minutes of the sixth Basilian congregation held in Vilna in 1636 record about Wiazowiczowa, who had aided Basilian monasteries and founded the Minsk Holy Trinity monastery for nuns: "This same benefactress of ours put in a request for a chaplain who would hear the confessions of the nuns at the recently made foundation of hers in Minsk; since we saw in this a justified wish on her part, we readily permitted it"[60].

Although here the order named the confessor, it did so only on the initiative of the foundress. When the chaplain was appointed by a church authority the ktytor confirmed this appointment. In 1626 the bishop of Lviv named a hieromonk Gregory as chaplain of the Slovita monastery. The ktytor of this Orthodox monastery was a Latin Catholic, Stanisław Mniszek, but it was he who confirmed the hieromonk in his post[61].

At Dubno the founder Ostroz'kyj provided an annual sum for the support of its chaplain, who was to be one of the monks of the Dubno Transfiguration monastery[62].

In Uniate monasteries the priest serving them was often a Basilian monk. At the sixth Basilian Congregation held in Vilna in 1636 the question was brought up whether confessors of nuns were to be ex officio members of the chapter[63]. This may seem to indicate that all the Uniate women's monasteries at that time had officially appointed Basilian monks as confessors. It is not necessarily so.

A biographical notice records that the Basilian hieromonk Peter

[58] In time, the chaplains at the Kutejno monastery came to be chosen from the secular clergy, cf. OASS, 23: 35-36 (a report of 1743).

[59] C'OROX, p. 244-245.

[60] AS, 12: 40-41.

[61] Mniszek's confirmatory document is printed in C'OROX, p. 236-237. He was in general quite generous to the monastery.

[62] Cf. SKRUTEN', p. 358.

[63] AS, 12: 39.

Mymonskyj was the confessor at the women's monastery in Navahrudek[64]. A resolution of the Basilian chapter in Bila in 1709, referring specifically to the Holy Trinity monastery of Vilna, stated that the nuns should be provided with a knowledgeable confessor—without any obligation to provide him with material for his habit[65]. In 1720 the Synod of Zamość ruled that it should be the local bishop who should "approve and choose" the confessor, implying that up until then the Basilian Order had chosen him[66].

The above examples speak only of confessors; where the nuns had a church of their own someone must also have been assigned to celebrate the liturgy there. In Orša, where the women's monastey was located just outside the town, the priest came daily from the Basilian monastery in that town[67]. The priest serving a monastery was not necessarily a monk, however; he could be from the white clergy, living with his family in a small house near the monastery, with some land at his own disposal. Towards the end of the eighteenth century the priest at the Vinnycja monastery was a Uniate secular priest who had been ordained in Moldavia, but later was reconciled to the Catholic Church. He lived with his wife and son by the monastery church in a small cottage with a vegetable garden attached[68]. At Slovita the chaplain had a house by the belltower and for his support he had vegetable gardens, orchards, fields, and pastures[69].

Some monastery churches served parishes at times. In Slobidščyna, where the monasteries arose about the same time as the settlements themselves, it was only natural that one church should serve both the monastery and the local population. The practice continued even when other churches were built. In Xoroševo the monastery church continued until 1786 to serve as the parish church for the Ukrainian population ("čerkasy"), while the Russians, mostly state employees, had a separate parish church[70]. In Ostrogožsk too the monastery church served a parish. The church and the priest were supported by the parishioners, who rebuilt the church in stone and added a belltower in the second half of the eighteenth century[71].

---

[64] Žyttjepysy Vasylijan, *AOSBM*, 2, no. 3-4 (1927): 391; see also *AS*, 12: 47.
[65] *AS*, 12: 161. The confessor was to be "czuły y dowcipny"—a phrase that defies translation.
[66] *SPR*, p. 112.
[67] Wołyniak, p. 79.
[68] Secinskij, p. 267.
[69] C'orox, p. 72.
[70] *ISOXE*, 2: 99-100, gives materials describing the arrangement.
[71] *Geografičeskoe opisanie rossijskogo gosudarstva*, 4: 948.

While there is every indication that in Xoroševo such an arrangement was to the satisfaction of all concerned, elsewhere it did not work out so well. In Minsk the parishioners of the Holy Trinity church complained to the metropolitan about the nuns, who had removed the parish priest and dismissed the cantor. The nuns had stated that their chaplain could perform whatever services were needed, but he for his part did this very irregularly[72]. The little chapel at the Mykulynci monastery also served as a parish church for a short while, but it was done without proper authorization, the nearby population was unhappy with the arrangement, and the visitator in 1773 put a decisive end to it[73]. Some monasteries, conversely, were founded next to parish churches, such as the one in Volodymyr Volyns'kyj, and did not acquire a church of their own.

The eastern rule concerning the rite of postryženie was that it be performed not merely by a monk, but by a superior and, moreover, that only one person be professed a monk or a nun in any one ceremony[74]. The first condition was generally, though not always, observed, there being cases where not only simple monks (hieromonks), but secular priests gave profession, but the second one was largely disregarded, or, to put it more accurately, totally unknown.

Not even allusions to the second condition exist, and actual practice gives us examples solely to the contrary. When Demetrius Tuptalo, then ihumen of the Baturyn St Nicholas monastery, described the profession he gave to five women at the Holy Cross monastery in 1682, he did not give the impression that such a procedure was unusual[75]. The practice among Ruthenian monks was the same.

As at Baturyn the ihumen carried out the rite of profession, so also at other monasteries. In the Kutejno group of monasteries the ihumen of the Kutejno monastery was to give profession at the women's monasteries, according to the founders' grant[76]. To judge from known examples, the archimandrite of Xarkiv used to give profession at the Xoroševo monastery in the eighteenth century[77]. At Mykulynci in the eighteenth century some of the nuns received profession (the terminology used is "the small and the great habit") from Basilian monks,

---

[72] OAZM, 2: 576-577.

[73] We learn all this from his report, SECINSKIJ, p. 345.

[74] Cf. Konstantin NIKOL'SKIJ, Posobie k izučeniju ustava bogosluženija pravoslavnoj cerkvi, p. 741-742.

[75] Drevnjaja rossijskaja vivliofika, 17: 15 (2nd ed.).

[76] Cf. Akty ZR, 5: 69.

[77] Cf. ISOXE, 1: 130.

while others went to Moldavia for it[78]. Similar confusion existed at Ryp-janka. Kossak says that the sisters used to go to Moldavia for profession, but to receive the great habit they would go to the Basilian monastery in Krylos[79]. Here we meet with a rare reference to the megaloschema. It is difficult to imagine, though, that it was assumed in any but rare and exceptional cases. And in a register of the nuns of the Slovita monastery in 1763 it is noted of one that she made profession before a secular priest[80].

Occupations of the Nuns

The work of the nuns was connected primarily with household needs and with providing the monastery—or, if the monastery did not have common life, each individual nun—with what it needed. In monastery work, even within the enclosure the nuns often had hired help. In 1638, when the nuns of Ladyn fled to Muscovy, eight of their servants went with them[81]. When the superior and three nuns of the Kiev St Michael monastery traveled to Moscow in 1688 they had twenty servants with them[82]. In 1795 it is reported that the nuns of the Epiphany monastery of Mahilev had girls and women to serve them, and also had two workers[83]. It was a generally known practice to have someone wait on and take care of elderly nuns: we see it in Kiev (Jordan monastery) in 1710[84] and in Dubno in 1818[85].

Some of the chores of the nuns are the kind one would imagine. The nuns of the St Michael monastery of Kiev worked in the monastery's vegetable garden and field[86]. In the Xoroševo monastery, where the nuns lived in separate little houses, each one had her goats, or even cows, that she took care of[87].

---

[78] SECINSKIJ, p. 346-348.

[79] KOSSAK, p. 209.

[80] Cf. C'OROX, p. 234:"Wielebna Kornelia . . . Professyą uczyniła in manibus Nayprzew. Xdza Hypacego Bilińskiego, pod ten czas Offła. Lwowsk.".

[81] Akty JuZR, 3: 24.

[82] P.L-v, Istoričeskija zametki o Kieve, p. 239.

[83] ŽUDRO, Bogojavlenskij bratskij monastyr', p. 31.

[84] Cf. LAZAREVSKIJ, Dokumental'nyja svedenija, p. 384. (Paraskeva Tuptalo speaks of "kelejny moi").

[85] "Służący klasztorni naięci: Parobek, kucharka i iey dziewczyna pomocnica i służebnic 4 u Zakonnic 4 Staruszek". SKRUTEN', p. 359.

[86] P.L-v, Istoričeskija zametki o Kieve, p. 239.

[87] Cf. ISOXE, 1: 133.

A project to limit the number of nuns in the Kutejno monastery permanently to seventy gives a detailed list of all the charges to which the nuns were assigned. At the time it was drawn up there were just a few more than that number. Among the assigned charges was that of singing in the krylosy, the duty of 24 nuns. The list of the other charges, which gives a good idea of the day-to-day running of the monastery, is as follows: ihumenja, vicar, 2 ponomarky (who took care of the church), 1 baker of prosfory, 2 bellringers, 2 "stoličny" (their charge was connected with food provisios), 4 cooks, 2 refectorians, 4 bread bakers, 2 to cut and distribute the bread, 2 portresses, 4 in charge of the monastery's horses, 3 charged with the vegetable garden, 2 cellarers, 1 to take care of the monastery's tools and implements, 1 to oversee the buildings, 2 infirmarians. Ten other nuns had no charge assigned to them because of old age or infirmity. Novices are not listed; whatever novices there were assisted with the various chores[88].

A short listing of similar chores is from Novi Mlyny in 1777. The sisters were assigned to the kitchen, the bakery, to oversee the monastery's economy (šafarnja), to take care of the church, and to oversee mills and other monastery property[89].

Although Kutejno also had land, worked by fifteen serfs, the nuns themselves did not oversee it. Elsewhere the nuns were involved in this, unless they leased the land to others, as was the common practice in Lithuania. Looking after their properties, especially in Left Bank Ukraine, often took individual nuns far from the monastery, perhaps for longer periods of time.

The references to manuscript liturgical books, as well as to other manuscript books, lead one to think that some of the copying was done by the nuns themselves. This could have been done especially in the larger monasteries with common life, where such work could be organized, the sisters not having to provide each one for her own livelihood. The monastery of Smolensk preserved a hirmologion copied out at the Kutejno monastery in 1648 and taken to Smolensk by the group of Kutejno nuns who went there about twenty years later[90].

Although it may seem strange to speak about the copying of books by hand at such late date, eastern Europe provides more than one example of what would be an anachronism in the West. In Ruthenian lands the copying of manuscripts continued into the nineteenth century. Not

[88] *OASS*, 23: 35-38.
[89] LAZAREVSKIJ, *Opisanie*, 2: 299.
[90] Cf. *Istoriko-statističeskoe opisanie Smolenskoj eparxii*, p. 229.

all books needed for church use were printed in sufficient quantities, perhaps. In addition, they were costly and, as inscriptions in church books testify, they were acquired primarily by way of donation from pious and generous benefactors. If one had the skill, it was cheaper to recopy an old book than to buy a new printed one. Finally, some books necessary for services saw print only at a very late date: the first printed Ruthenian hirmologion was issued in Lviv in 1700.

Very often the nuns did handwork—sewing and embroidery—and sold it to help support themselves. The nuns of Kiev were noted for the fine embroidery they did. Beauplan mentions this in the first half of the seventeenth century[91].

Items for church use were the chief but not the sole product of the nuns. The polkovnyk of Braclav Daniel Nečaj, killed in battle in 1651, possessed a banner of velvet, embroidered with pure gold by Kiev nuns[92]. This could hardly have been the only one such made; the notice, incidentally, points to ties, family and other, between the monastery and Cossack staršyna. Three decades later the nuns of the Kiev Ascension monastery stated that they supported themselves exclusively by their handwork[93]. That their handwork was indeed very fine we know both from contemporary sources and from the objects that have survived. In 1687 ihumenja Maria Magdalene Mazepa brought to Moscow as gifts ''cloths'' sewn with gold, probably by herself[94].

The girls who entered the monastery of Novi Mlyny were taught, together with reading and writing, also sewing and spinning[95]. The nuns in Lviv spun and bleached thread, then sold it not only in Lviv, but even in Warsaw, going with it there themselves[96]. The making of thread and cloth was the chief means of support for the monasteries in Halyčyna and Podillja, but it was neither economically satisfactory nor conducive to monastic observance.

Even less profitable and appropriate was the practice of working as hired help in the fields during the harvests, but it must have been an economic necessity. The rector of the Armenian and Ruthenian seminary

---

[91] BEAUPLAN, p. 32.

[92] See the contemporary Polish account quoted by Myxajlo HRUŠEVS'KYJ, *Istorija Ukraijny-Rusy*, 9, pt 1 (Kyjiv, 1928): 183.

[93] *Dopolnenija k Aktam istoričeskim*, 10: 311.

[94] *Ibid.*, 12: 329-330. The tradition continued ever since. The nuns of Sts Florus and Laurus still supported themselves by embroidery as late as the 1970's, cf. *Pravoslavnyj visnyk*, 1977, 6: 26-28.

[95] LAZAREVSKIJ, *Opisanie*, 2: 299.

[96] PETRUŠEVIČ, *Slovickij ženskij monastyr'*, p. 111-112.

of Lviv, the Theatine Jerome Moro, wrote in a report to Rome in 1748:

> The nuns go out whenever they wish, to get a miserable sustenance from
> the sale of cloth and thread and from work in the fields at harvest time...,
> very many still live from that, and there is no way of getting them to
> observe enclosure, given the lack of appropriate dwellings and a fund for
> the maintenance of the nuns[97].

Another very common work of the nuns for their support, though
again not very profitable, was baking prosfory (altar breads) and making candles. These two activities were usually found together in
monasteries; they were regulated by bishops. The Lviv nuns in 1669
received from bishop Joseph Šumljans'kyj exclusive rights to make
candles and to bake prosfory and to sell their products throughout
Lviv[98]. In 1635 Peter Mohyla authorized the Sts Peter and Paul
monastery of Minsk to bake prosfory[99], and from at least 1643 the nuns
of the Epiphany monastery of Mahilev had his authorization, confirmed
later by other hierarchs, to produce prosfory and candles[100]. We are
given to understand that in the Mahilev monastery the sale of prosfory
was poor and of the candles even more so.

In 1671 we hear of nuns selling candles in the church of the Holy
Trinity in Vilna, but this seems to have been only a temporary conces-
sion on the part of the monks, until a debt should be repaid to the
nuns[101]. Here as elsewhere, whoever in any one locality had the right to
sell candles was not tolerant of rivals. If the nuns could not be stopped
altogether from selling them, then at least a restraint was put on their
sales, such as that to sell only penny candles in Javoriv[102].

Monastery Schools

In a document of 1666 it is stated that the daughter of a Vilna merchant lived for a time at the sisters' convent, preparing to enter the
religious life[103]. She had a strong desire to become a nun, but was still

---

[97] *Acta S.C. de Propaganda Fide*, 4: 49.

[98] Mentioned in the confirmatory charter of Jan Sobieski in 1679, in C'OROX, p. 229.

[99] NIKOLAJ, p. 93.

[100] *IJuM*, 10: 495-498. Cf. ŽUDRO, *Bogojavlenskij bratskij monastyr'*, p. 35.

[101] *AS*, 12: 108.

[102] *Kataloh perhamentnyx dokumentiv Central'noho deržavnoho istoryčnoho arxivu
URSR u L'vovi 1233-1799* (Kyjiv, 1972), p. 483-484 (charter in favor of the brotherhood
at St George church in Javoriv).

[103] *AV*, 9: 203-204.

below the minimum age for entering (fifteen-sixteen). Both her parents had died; her guardian evidently had placed her in the monastery for instruction by the nuns.

Such allusions to monastery schools may be found in other documents of the period, but, as here, they never have further details. No doubt only the basic skills were taught, but the existence of such schools speaks in favor of literacy among the nuns. Paul of Aleppo mentions girls of different ages being brought up in the Kiev Ascension monastery. He says they were mostly orphans. He also reports that many of the girls brought up in that monastery later returned to become nuns there[104].

It is a pity that other sources on Kiev of the first half of the seventeenth century are silent about the school of the Ascension monastery. We can only guess that its establishement was somehow connected with the renaissance of Kiev as a cultural center. That a solitary foreign source is the only testimony to a school in Kiev that must have existed for decades, with girls form prominent families, should make us aware how imperfectly we know or can hope ever to know the range of cultural and religious life of the land.

That the pupils in Kiev were mostly orphans is plausible. If the mother died, the father might well send his daughter to be brought up either by relatives or by sisters. At Minsk, where there was a school at the Holy Trinity monastery practically from its beginnings (we hear of it already in 1639) we also see orphans[105], and the same must have been true of other monastery schools.

We hear of the teaching activity of Kievan nuns also from other sources, such as from a denunciation of hetman Brjuxovec'kyj ten years later (1663). Brjuxovec'kyj's tone was far from the admiring one of archdeacon Paul, but that was due to the hetman's ill-will towards the influential bishop of Mahilev (but resident in Kiev) Methodius Fylymonovyč, whose daughter was a pupil of the nun Angelina[105].

The royal confirmation for the transfer of the Mahilev St Nicholas monastery to a location outside the town in 1664 mentions that instruction to girls of the gentry and burgher classes was one of the purposes at its founding thirty years earlier[107]. At Xolm too there is mention of a school[108].

---

[104] Pavel ALEPPSKIJ, *ČOIDR*, 1897, 4: 58, 59.

[105] *AV*, 15: 23.

[106] Cf. ĖJNGORN, *ČOIDR*, 1893, 2: 253.

[107] *AS*, 2: 80.

[108] *AV*, 23: 308.

In the eighteenth century there are again bare references to teaching carried on by the sisters. A "monastery school" is noted at the Nižyn monastery in 1729[109]. A description of Podillja towards the end of the eighteenth century recorded that at the Vinnycja monastery there were several small classrooms for teaching children[110].

Towards the end of the eighteenth century, under official pressure to justify their existence by conducting schools, various monasteries introduced them. At the Vicebsk Holy Spirit monastery, for instance, a school was conducted around 1798[111].

In one fortunate instance a former pupil of a monastery school left brief but appreciative reminiscences about it. M. Maksymovyč, the noted ethnographer and historian and first rector of the Kiev University, received his first schooling at the Annunciation monastery in Zolotonoša, as did his mother and uncle before him and his cousins with him. The sisters taught the boys and girls of the neighborhood; the course of instruction was the traditional "hramatka, časlovec i psaltyr"[112]. Since the sisters were engaged in teaching from the time they moved there in 1760, perhaps they were continuing a practice begun already in their monastery in Korobivka.

A few words can here be said about what the nuns wore. Since reference to this are almost nonexistent, it can be assumed that they dressed more or less in the traditional eastern manner. From one document of the early seventeenth century we learn that the full monastic habit was considered to consist of the rjasa, mantle, and kamelaukion[113]. Even foreigners, mentioning the dress of nuns, pick out items that one would hardly think worth comment. Beauplan says of the nuns of the Kiev Ascension monastery that they wore black, and Paul of Aleppo that they wore long mantles.

Deviations from the norm cropped up occasionally. Elderly nuns in Xoroševe recalled that when they entered around 1800 there was no common habit in use at their monastery, but each sister dressed "as she could or would"[114]. The same could doubtless be said of other monasteries, especially of those without common life.

---

[109] VASILENKO, 1: 36.

[110] Cf. Myxajlo KARAČKIVS'KYJ, Materijaly do istoriji mist na Podilli naprykinci XVIII viku, *Istoryčno-heohrafičnyj zbirnyk*, 4 (1931): 175.

[111] In a list of the nuns from that year one is called mistress of the school ("mistrzynia pensyi"), WOŁYNIAK, p. 165.

[112] MAKSIMOVIČ, Vospominanija o Zolotonoše, p. 243.

[113] *IJuM*, 8: 415. The testimony is from Mahilev, 1625.

[114] *ISOXE*, 1: 133.

Enclosure

Some legal documents in 1 .huania present an interesting particular: town officials condescending to the observance by the nuns of not going out of the monastery unnecessarily. In 1709, for the legalities connected with a sale of property, town councillors and their assistants went to the Holy Trinity monastery in Vilna and there drew up the necessary document and collected the signatures of the sisters[115]. Again in 1755 it is expressly stated in a document that town officials were sent to this same monastery to draw it up because the nuns were bound by enclosure[116].

It is noteworthy that both instances (and others could be cited) regard the Vilna Holy Trinity monastery and that the examples come from both before and after the Synod of Zamość with its regulations on the keeping of enclosure by nuns. These instances depict the observance of that particular monastery and demonstrate as well that such observance was not a result of the Synod's regulations, but depended on other factors.

Even in Lithuania, court business often took nuns out of the monastery. Litigation was an integral part of the way of life of the citizens of the Commonwealth, and nuns were no exception. Court documents very often mention the presence of nuns at tribunals.

The Synod's categorical prohibition for sisters to go out of the enclosure has been cited earlier. Being unrealistic, it remained a dead letter, even though the bishops asserted their resolve to have it carried out. The members of the Synod of Zamość, in a series of questions put to the Propaganda, stated:

> Whether nuns may go out of the enclosure, with the faculties and dispensation of the bishops. The canons are ranged on the negative side, but practice in Poland is in its favor, which the Ruthenian bishops intend to abolish[117].

Tradition was a strong factor here. Strict enclosure in the western sense had been unknown, even under the best of circumstances, so that,

---

[115] *AV*, 9: 298; another instance on p. 301.

[116] "Coram nobilibus dominis Joanne Dubinski et Petro Kosobucki, consiliaribus Vilnens. pro recipienda recognitione ad claustrum religiosarum virginum recognoscentium obligalitatem claustralem a nobili officio consulari Vilnensi deputatis, totumque iudicium representantibus . . .", *ibid.*, p. 388.

[117] *EM*, 4: 89 (27 September 1720).

as we shall see a little below, even such a person as Josaphat Kuncevyč regarded it as self-understood that nuns would be going out of the monastery for various purposes.

Real poverty was often an obstacle to keeping the enclosure, even had there been a will to do so, just as poverty, in the concrete circumstances of those times, hindered the observance of common life. This is well brought out by Heraklij Lisans'kyj (later protoarchimandrite), who wrote in 1740 of the Mozoliv monastery, which had shortly before accepted the Union, but applied the same also to others:

> This alone is to be regretted, that [the nuns at Mozoliv] will be constrained to keep to the same mode of life, because of their great poverty, as they had before their conversion. The fact is that they have neither common life nor the enclosure prescribed by canon law; each is obliged to procure everything necessary for herself by the work of her own hands... Would that such a disorder might exist to this extent only in this one monastery, but (alas) in all the monasteries of nuns of our rite, subject to the ordinary jurisdiction of our archbishop (there are four in all), situated in this diocese [Polock], proper enclosure cannot be introduced on account of their small foundations and the extreme straits of the monasteries... Their great indigence makes it impossible to set up an enclosure for the professed nuns for the sake of discipline proper to their state[118].

Even when poverty was not extreme, economic affairs necessitated considerable trips, such as those of the Lviv nuns to Warsaw, already mentioned. Besides selling their products far afield, the nuns occasionally also had to defend their interests before distant tribunals. Two nuns from Smil'nycja, one of them the aunt of metropolitan Antony Vynnyc'kyj, are seen traveling to the one in Lublin in 1668[119].

Any number of reasons for making journeys, in fact, might crop up. A letter of metropolitan Athanasius Šeptyc'kyj of 1746 gives permission to the superior of the Minsk Holy Spirit monastery to go to Vilna, accompanied by another nun, to inspect there some of the monastery's property which needed repairs. In the same letter permission is given to another nun for a leave of three weeks to collect her inheritance[120]. The same Šeptyc'kyj, two decades earlier, as bishop of Lviv, had decreed for

---

[118] *LB*, 2: 69-70.

[119] Cf. *Arxiv JuZR*, pt. I, 10: 230. On the way the stopped at the metropolitan's residence in Lviv. To their misfortune, just then a party sent out by Vynnyc'kyj's rival Šumljans'kyj attacked the residence, and the nuns, together with all the other persons there, lost all their money, documents, and goods.

[120] *OAZM*, 2: 104 (no. 1429).

the Slovita nuns that they were not to go about markets and fairs to sell their wares, but send out laywomen associated with their monastery[121]. Perhaps time had shown him the futility of such categoric prescriptions.

The right of the Ruthenian Catholic bishops to grant permissions for nuns to go out of the enclosure was defended by metropolitan Hrebnyc'kyj in response to a question put to him by the nuncio to Poland Alberico Archinto. Behind the question lay an assumption which to the nuncio and his contemporaries appeared so natural as to exclude even the possibility of being challenged. The standards and norms of western women's monasteries, due to a different historical development and proceeding from a different tradition, applied equally well, so they took for granted, in the metropolitanate of Kiev. Behind the question also lay accusations of the Latin hierarchy against what it saw as too facile permissions accorded by the Ruthenian bishops. The Latin bishop of Luc'k Stephen Rupniewski, who in 1727 included this point in a goodly number of accusations against metropolitan Kyška[122], was not the only one to bemoan it.

Nuncio Archinto had asked:

> Can bishops give permission to nuns under their jurisdiction to go for a period of time out of the monastery when there are justifiable and reasonable causes?

Metropolitan Hrebnyc'kyj replied:

> The cases when nuns can go out of the enclosure with the permission of the bishops should be left to the authority and discretion of the bishop; there are quite a number of cases, especially for nuns who possess immovable property, as do the Basilians, when they must necessarily leave the enclosure[123].

The nuns, for their part, were accustomed to looking after their properties themselves, and it is doubtful if they applied to their bishop every time they had to make a trip[124].

Quite another matter was simple vagrancy, though it is difficult to

---

[121] In a document of 1721, published by A. PETRUŠEVYČ in *Vremennyk Instytuta Stavropihijskoho*, 7 (1870): 152.

[122] *EM*, 4: 142.

[123] *EM*, 4: 284.

[124] The chronicler of the Vilna Holy Trinity men's monastery notes under 24 August 1777: "Dnia 24. I. panna Bogumila Macewiczowna, starsza, naiąwszy furmana z dwoma socyuszami wyiechała do folwarku *Daukszyszek* nazwanego". *AS*, 10: 323.

draw strict distinctions. Calamities such as wars and fires encouraged the tendency of wandering from one monastery to another, endemic in the Christian East. It was a fairly common thing for nuns in such circumstances to go to stay with relatives—a temporary stay that was often prolonged beyond necessity.

In 1666 the bishop of Xolm Jakiv Suša reported that nuns who because of the war had gone to their relatives had still not returned to their monasteries (theirs again since 1661) and some had gone to Latin convents. He demanded that the nuncio use his authority to have them all return[125].

Some sixty years later matters were no different. The nuncio in 1728, Vincent Santini, accurately described them:

> The nuns of this rite have too much freedom given them by their ordinaries and obtain from them permission to go visiting their relatives, to ask them for the dowries due them, and for every other reason when they wish it, to go to sell their handwork in public markets, and to stay out of their monasteries whenever they feel like it[126].

This description applies equally to earlier as well as to later times and characterizes both Uniate and Orthodox nuns. Santini is not entirely just to the bishops, however; they did attempt to regulate such habits, but traditional ways proved stronger than the law. So the synod of the Peremyšl' eparchy in 1693 had already rules that the bishop's permission was necessary for going out of the monastery: "Without [the bishop's] permission the nuns are not to go out of their enclosures and wander about under any pretext whatsoever"[127]. Metropolitan Vynnyc'kyj in 1710 directed a visitator of monasteries to forbid all "unnecessary" trips to monastic properties and to the nuns' relatives, even under threat of excommunication[128]. That these and similar rulings proved ineffective is demonstrated by Santini's remark.

The seeking of alms often took nuns not only out of the monastery, but rather far afield. It was commonplace for the nuns of the impoverished monasteries to go begging in the neighborhood of their monasteries.

Such questing was not confined to the poorest of monasteries,

---

[125] *Ibid.*, 12: 89.

[126] *Congregationes particulares Ecclesiam Catholicam Ucrainae et Bielarusjae spectantes*, ed. Athanasius G. WELYKYJ, 1 (Romae, 1956): 252.

[127] *LE*, 4: 117.

[128] Acta Kisciana, 6, fol. 56r.

however. Josaphat Kuncevyč took it for granted that the nuns of the Polock monastery which he refounded and endowed would go out regularly to seek alms, especially in nature, and provided for their transportation[129].

In the late eighteenth century it is reported that the nuns of the Mahilev monastery of the Epiphany, which had no secure source of income, would go around the villages in the neighborhood of Mahilev begging for grain[130]. This seems to have been an annual procedure after the harvest, and bishop Volxovskyj adds that the nuns made a nuisance of themselves.

Many Orthodox monasteries regularly sent members to Moscow for alms, especially in the second part of the seventeenth century. Later, in the synodal period, in the Russian empire questing for alms was regulated by authorities. The restrictions passed by the Holy Synod affected Ukrainian monks and nuns if they intended to go to Russia to collect alms. New habits, however, were not acquired readily. When two nuns of the Nižyn monastery appeared in Moscow in 1742 and were asked if they had their hierarch's permission, they replied that they had not thought of asking it[131].

When the Xoroševe monastery burned down in 1744 permission was given to its nuns, at their request, to go begging; this was renewed in 1746, again by the bishop of Belgorod. Both times the bishop sent them a bound book with the seal of his consistory, in which each donor was to enter his donation[132]. The offerings received were neither large nor numerous; not only did the trip have to be repeated, but the cost of a new stone church was covered mainly by the donation of one of the entrants in the monastery[133]. A nun of the Barkalabava monastery had much the same experience at about the same time. She too had with her a bound book in which to enter donations; in four months of questing in Russia she collected only fifty rubles, though she was also given vestments and silver church vessels[134].

---

[129] In his grant to them in 1621 he wrote: ". . . ut Venerabiles Virgines Moniales, exeuntes pro acquirenda Elemosina, honestam possint habere vecturiam, adjungo ad hujusmodi servitium, ex altera villa dicta Bialousowa, Colonos tres, . . . qui tenebuntur, et ipsis venerabilibus Virginibus Monialibus exeuntibus pro acquirenda Elemosina, cum curru honesto inservire, et congregatam a Benefactoribus Elemosinam, ad illarum Monasterium advehere". Latin translation in APF, Miscellanee diverse, vol. 19, fol. 445r.

[130] ŽUDRO, *Bogojavlenskij bratskij monastyr'*, p. 35.

[131] Cf. *OASS*, 22: 294.

[132] *ISOXE*, 1: 115-117.

[133] *Ibid.*, p. 122.

[134] *OASS*, 21: 283.

Going about from monastery to monastery was almost an integral part of monastic life. In one case we have a direct statement from a nun, Domentijana Larska. She gives her reasons for leaving the Smolensk monastery and going to the one in Šumarovo. At Smolensk, with the monastery located in the center of the town, there was a constant stream of visitors. Dementijana's own relations lived nearby, moreover (though she herself was not from that region), and were forever either visiting her or inviting her to visit them. She had always desired a more secluded ("pustynne") life, and when, to top everything, the bishop of Smolensk expressed his intention of appointing her as superior, she quietly gathered her things and left. In her self-justification she added that she was glad to be away from such a well-known monastery and to be able to live tranquilly and on alms for Christ's sake in a "desert" monastery such as Šumarovo was. If the authorities insisted on her returning to Smolensk, they would have to keep her there "bound as in prison", as she would not remain otherwise.

Dementijana's wishes were for the most part fulfilled. She did not have to return to Smolensk, though she had to leave Šumarovo for Makošyn not far away, where, however, more or less the same conditions prevailed[135]. Here again we see the ineffectiveness of the hierarch's control. The bishop had been adamant in refusing his consent for her transfer, and theoretically his permission was necessary for admittance into another monastery.

Dementijana was impelled by a desire for a monastery with a less bustling way of life; in other instances the motive was not always so noble. This no doubt was often recognized and was a matter of concern in the monasteries themselves. The superior of the Sts Peter and Paul monastery in Minsk Eugenia Šembelev in her testament urged that if any of the nuns should want to leave for another monastery all the sisters and the ihumen should attempt to dissuade her. They should let her go only if she insisted violently or if she gave a justifiable reason to her spiritual father why she should not remain in that monastery any longer[136]. Her contemporary in Javoriv, Margaret (Macrina) Dyškevyč, in her testament when recommending obedience also singled out this point: without the superior's permission the sisters should not so much as set foot outside their monastery, much less go off to another one[137].

---

[135] *Ibid.*, p. 464-465.
[136] *VZR*, 2 (1863), November, 15.
[137] C'OROX, p. 244: "Siostrzyczki . . . bez woliey [Starszey] aby nie tylko z Manastyra tego do drugiego na insze Miasta i Mieysca, ale y na stopę wychodzić y występować niewazyły się".

The negative side of the wandering about from monastery to monastery can be seen in the case of Mykulynci in Podillja. In 1773 the visitator there noted down in which monastery each of its nine nuns had made profession and in what monasteries she had lived. The results do not testify to a love for stability. Each nun had been in at least two, one had been in six different monasteries. Concerning several nuns the visitator remarked that they had left a particular monastery because they did not want to accept the superior or certain of the superior's regulations. As could be expected, the visitator found in the Mykulynci monastery a great deal in need of correction[138].

We obtain a general picture of the life of the nuns: prayer, handwork, sometimes other occupations. An example of a monastery schedule, a description of a day in at least a few monasteries would fill in the details. As so often, though, we again have to complain of a lack of sources.

---

[138] SECINSKIJ, p. 346-348. Other examples abound; in the documents that report them all their negative features loom large, as in the following two from Acta Kisciana, vol. 6. A nun at Vicebsk in 1710 had been in six other monasteries (fol. 29r). The Minsk and Vilna Catholic monasteries had a great deal of bother around 1710 over the case of Antonina Ostrejko who passed from one to another (passim).

Chapter VIII

SUPPRESSIONS

A large number of monasteries were closed or died out in the eighteenth century, and some others ceased to exist in the first decades of
the nineteenth. There were several movements to close down
monasteries, with quite different motives.

The Merging of Small Monasteries

The problem of what to do with small and impoverished
monasteries was brought up several times during the eighteenth century.
Already the Synod of Zamość discussed it in 1720. The Synod decreed
that monasteries which did not have a sufficient endowment should be
abolished and their members, together with the goods of the monasteries
concerned, be transferred to other larger ones[1].

The women's monasteries concerned were primarily those in
Halyčyna and Podillja, which could not carry on a proper monastic life
with their small numbers and still smaller funds. Whether in fact any
monasteries were closed as a result of this ruling remains unknown; it
seems that no action followed the Synod's decision.

In 1744, however, pope Benedict XIV in his constitution *Inter
Plures* called for the closing of very small monasteries, and similar
resolutions on the part of the Basilian monks followed[2]. In the 1740's
and 1750's then there occur some instances of monasteries being closed:

---

[1] *SPR*, p. 111.
[2] For this, cf. VAVRYK, p. 24-25.

Žovkva, Kulykiv, Sasiv in Halyčyna[3], Mykulynci in Podillja[4]. (The closing of Mykulynci, though, was not permanent). Probably others were
closed; since a few nuns from the Dobrotvir (Jazvyn) monastery came to
Slovita in 1758/1759[5], it too must have been closed then. Perhaps later
closings, such as that of the Transfiguration monastery in Rohatyn in
1768, can be traced to the same rulings.

The reasons for the closings can be understood if one considers the
case of Mykulynci. Its penury was extreme, so the nuns had to go out
frequently to beg alms, more or less abandoning even the semblance of
religious life. This in turn scandalized the population, making it little
disposed to aid the nuns. Some of the small monasteries about which we
know little more than their names must have eked out a similarly
miserable existence before becoming noiselessly extinct.

State Suppressions

The period of large scale suppressions began in the 1780's, prompted by quite different motives. Now it was not a question of aiding
monasteries by combining their numbers, but of computing their
utilitarian value to the state. The properties of monasteries were to be
confiscated by the state with an obligation to maintain a limited number
of monks and nuns in a limited number of monasteries.

Halyčyna came under the Hapsburg monarchy after the first partition of Poland in 1772. Its monasteries were affected in the 1780's by
the project of Joseph II to close all monasteries not socially useful.

In Kiev and the Left Bank the reform of Catherine II that had as
its object the abolition of all particularities in that territory brought
about necessarily also the suppression of monasteries considered useless.
This began in 1786, as it had already been carried out in Russia in 1764.

As regards Belorussian and Ukrainian lands that become part of the
Russian empire after the partitions of Poland, the period of suppressions began in 1795. At first it involved Orthodox monasteries as well as
Uniate ones that had once been Orthodox. It continued to the time of
the apostasy of the bishop of Lithuania Joseph Sjemaško in 1839, when

---

[3] KOSSAK, p. 206, says there was talk of it already in 1743, but on p. 209, speaking of
Sasiv, he says that the transfer of the nuns to Slovita took place in 1759. In 1763 nuns
from Sasiv were present in Slovita, cf. C'OROX, p. 234.

[4] Officially closed in 1747, cf. SECINSKIJ, p. 340.

[5] Cf. the list in C'OROX, p. 233-234.

the final Uniate monasteries were closed. These several waves of the closing of monasteries will be examined in turn.

Monasteries in Halyčyna were affected by the decision to close all monasteries that did not have schools attached to them. The monasteries were so small and poor that it was difficult even to collect reliable and stable statistics about their number; evidently eparchial officials themselves were not sure what to consider a monastery, so the number varies between six and thirteen.

Government officials proposed in 1782 to close all the monasteries except the one in Lviv, transfer all the nuns as well as the monastery funds there, and have a school for Greek rite girls opened. The Lviv monastery on closer examination turned out to be too small for the projected move, and other practical obstacles arose to the execution of the project. The chief difficulty was to find means of support for all the nuns (around forty) in the unified monastery. After various calculations it was decided in 1784 to permit the monasteries to remain as they were, but they were forbidden to accept any more novices and thus were destined to die out. In fact, by the end of that century, only two remained, in Slovita and Javoriv.

At Smil'nycja household items, the rundown monastery building, and the church were all sold at auction. At Bus'k the decaying church was dismantled. The church icon and church vessels were transferred to the local parish church and two garden plots were given to the pastor[6]. The fate of other closed monasteries was similar.

For Slovita and Javoriv efforts were made in the early nineteenth century to legalize their continued existence and to permit them to take in new members. It was decades before they revived, however[7].

In Kiev and the Left Bank suppression of monasteries was embarked upon in 1786. On 10 April of that year Catherine II issued an ukaz setting out in detail the new order of things. The purpose was to bring Ukrainian church institutions into conformity with those of Russia, that is, to extend the ukaz of 1764 to Ukrainian territory[8]. Quite a number of the provisions of the ukaz were rather far-fetched and never carried out. But as concerns women's monasteries, all those marked for closing were in fact shut down, and even several of those permitted to continue came to their end within a few years.

---

[6] PETRUŠEVIČ, *Svodnaja letopis' 1600-1700*, p. 12.

[7] The history of the suppressions of women's monasteries in Halyčyna is set out in detail on the basis of archival materials by CHOTKOWSKI, p. 135-149.

[8] The ukaz, with a brief discussione of it, is printed by F.A. TERNOVSKIJ, Izlišnie malorossijskie monaxi konca XVIII st. *KS*, 2 (1882, 2): 329-337. It may be compared with

Of the nineteen monasteries concerned, six became *štatnye*, that is,
the state, in compensation for the confiscation of the monastery's property obligated itself to support there a limited number of nuns. These six
were to be: Kiev—Sts Florus and Laurus (1st class); Kiev—St John (2nd
class); Korobivka, Kozelec', Nižyn, and one more to be chosen in the
territory of the stillborn eparchy of Novhorod Sivers'kyj (3rd class)[9].

The unnamed monastery that was left open was Kamens'kyj Xutor.
There the men's monastery had closed some time previously. In 1786
nuns from Pečenyky were moved there, probably because the buildings
at Kamens'kyj Xutor were in a better state of repair.

The differences between the classes were to be the same as those af-
fecting Russian monasteries according to the ukaz of 1764. They regarded chiefly the number of members permitted and the funds alloted.
Monasteries of the first class were allowed 100 members and received a
greater allotment. Monasteries of the second and third classes were to
have only 17 members in each, that is, the funds allocated by the state
were limited to providing only for that number. Additional members
had to be provided for by other means.

The ukaz of 1786 did not mention any monasteries with small properties that could be left to continue as self-supporting (*zaštatnye*).
This possibility had been left open in the ukaz of 1764 and apparently it
was also applied to Ukrainian monasteries. Amvrosij says that five
women's monasteries in Ukraine were left as *zaštatnye* and lists them as:
Čyhyryn, Kozelec', Ladyn, Lebedyn, and Puškarivka . He is right about
the number. But the one monastery in Kozelec' became state-supported
(though only for twenty years). The fifth self-supporting monastery was
Pysarevščyna. It did not become a second class monastery in 1786, as
Zverinskij says[10], but in or after 1789, when it was permitted for a small
number of monasteries in Ukraine to change their status from *štatnye* to
zaštatnye[11].

The rest of the monasteries were to be abolished and were in fact
suppressed. A project to replace the St Paraskeva monastery of Černihiv
by a "Latin school" had already been made in 1739 by the bishop of
Černihiv Nikodym Srebnyc'kyj[12]. The monastery was closed in

the ukaz of 1764 in *PSPR*, Catherine II: 1: 166-200.
   [9] TERNOVSKIJ, p. 330-331.
   [10] AMVROSIJ, 2: cxxv-cxxvii.
   [11] ZVERINSKIJ, 1: 269. Cf. the resolution of 3 August 1789 in *PSPR*, Catherine II, 3: 292-297.
   [12] Cf. *PSPR*, [1st series], 10: 297-298. It appears that the bishop was not well-disposed towards this monastery, located only a few steps away from his residence.

1786—but the school which the ukaz decreed to be installed in its buildings never did materialize.

Three monasteries of the Kiev eparchy named in the ukaz as being permitted to continue—Kiev—St John the Evangelist, Kozelec', and Korobivka—did not exist very much longer. The latter two were closed in the early years of the nineteenth century, while the St John the Evangelist monastery of Kiev was transferred in 1789 to the empty monastery of Krasnohora on the grounds that its location in Kiev was "inconvenient"[13]. There, however, it began a new life and was still open in the 1970's.

The Jordan monastery of Kiev remained open for a short time since superfluous("zaštatnye") nuns form closed monasteries for whom there was no place in those allowed to continue were sent there to live out their days[14]. These nuns were given an annual allowance from confiscated properties of ten rubles each. Hierarchs had to report twice yearly on how many of such nuns (and monks, as the same directives concerned both) had died since the preceding report, so that their allowances would not continue to be sent out[15].

In 1786 church life and civil life in Slobidščyna, as in hetmanate Ukraine, was normalized from the point of view of the Russian state; it too became subject to the same laws that were in force in the Russian gubernijas. Of the three women's monasteries in that territory, two were closed (Ostrogožsk and Sumy), and only the one in Xoroševe remained.

In the course of the suppressions projects were formed concerning the use to be made of the evacuated monastery buildings, properties were examined and described, funds were allocated to feed the surviving nuns, but the wishes and feelings of the nuns themselves were left totally out of consideration. In more than one instance it must have been painful to leave behind a monastery, however small and poor it might have been, and not everyone was capable of it. When the monastery of Zolotonoša-Korobivka was closed in 1817, its nuns were to go to Ladyn. But close to thirty years later there were still several of them living in the vicinity of the suppressed monastery. One of them had managed to establish herself as caretaker of the monastery church, which now served as a parish, while another had put up a lean-to against a nearby Cossack house and there continued to teach children of the vicinity[16].

---

[13] *PSPR*, Catherine II, 3: 289-291, 308; DUMITRAŠKO, p. 21; P.L-v, p. 243.
[14] *PSPR*, Catherine II, 3: 289-291.
[15] TERNOVSKIJ, p. 334; P,L-v, p. 243.
[16] MAKSIMOVIČ, Vospominanija o Zolotonoše, p. 423-425.

Suppressions in Territories under Russia after the Polish Partitions

A number of Uniate monasteries in territories that went to Russia in the partitions of Poland survived until the times of Sjemaško, who took an active part in closing them, both before and after his open apostasy. Others were closed almost immediately, or, as an alternative, were turned temporarily into Orthodox ones.

This fate befell the monasteries that had at any time in the past been Orthodox, such as Mozoliv, which had accepted the Union only in 1727 and was therefore revindicated for the Orthodox. The Orthodox archbishop of Mahilev George Konys'kyj already in 1789 had introduced Orthodox nuns into the monastery. But no one among them was capable of being a superior, and he turned to the Holy Synod for permission to take one from elsewhere. His choice fell on a certain Domentijana Von-ljarska, who had once been an ihumenja and who was then living in the Ascension monastery in Smolensk. It is not said where Domentijana had been superior, but there can be no doubt that she was from Belorussia. The Synod, in consideration of the state policies that were closing monasteries and not opening them, asked for more information before giving its authorization[17]. The official decision to make it into an Orthodox monastery followed in 1795[18].

Korec' too had a monastery founded by the Orthodox Korec'kyj family, and its Uniate nuns were forced to leave in 1795. A contemporary writes thus of their expulsion:

> At this time the monastery of our Basilian nuns in Korec', which was very well built, better than others, in force of that ukaz was taken for nuns of the state religion. Three days they kept our nuns as if under siege, because they had shut themselves up in their monastery; they gave them neither bread nor water. Even the Lutherans took pity on them and would throw bread to them through the windows. Finally, hunger and oppression constrained them to come out, under jeers and abuse, and to go to the residence of the Latin priest there, where they are still living, praising God and living only from alms, because their endowment was entirely taken away, their own funds perished, and they were forced out of the monastery with nothing but the clothes on their backs; if compassionate Lutherans had not given them their carriages, they would have had to go on foot[19].

---

[17] *PSPR*, Catherine II, 3: 278-279.
[18] *AV*, 16: 8-9.
[19] The account of the expulsion of the Uniate nuns written in Polish by the Basilian

Eventually, these sisters came to Derman', where during their short stay they engaged in teaching, then found shelter in other Uniate monasteries.

But a pretext of an Orthodox foundation was not always necessary. The nuns of the Holy Spirit monastery of Minsk were sent to join those at the Holy Trinity monastery in the same town: one Uniate women's monastery there was enough. In 1834 the sisters were sent to Miadziol, to what had once been a Carmelite monastery, but by 1844 the monastery came to a definite end.

As in this case, the suppression often proceeded by degrees. At Polonne the monastery church was taken by the authorities in 1795, though the monastery itself continued to exist until 1839 as Uniate and then until 1858 as Orthodox[20]. A similar thing happened at Dubno, where the monastery's property was confiscated in 1812. This placed the nuns in a very difficult position: they had nothing with which to procure necessities for themselves and to pay their hired help and so ran up debts. Earlier they had had a priest living by their monastery, but by 1818 a priest from a distance came around only once a month to celebrate the Divine Liturgy[21].

The Uniate nuns were generally firm in refusing to accept the state religion. In Podillja, where already in 1773 steps were taken towards "reunion with Orthodoxy"[22], Uniate nuns, principally from Vinnycja, who did not want to accept the new official religion took refuge in the monastery of Mykulynci and the woods around it. Their presence there was not tolerated for long, and an end to this state of things was put in 1796[23].

At times Orthodox nuns were settled in formerly Uniate monasteries because it would have seemed too abrupt to go about closing monasteries altogether, but they were not allowed to remain there long. Thus at Mykulynci the official Orthodox community was told in 1796, only a short time after it had been established, to move to Vinnycja. The nuns were not prompt in obeying this order: it had to be repeated in 1798 and this time was executed[24].

---

monk Luke Sulžyns'kyj was published by N. PETROV (in a Russian translation) in Kratkija izvestija o položenii bazilianskogo ordena i raznyx peremenax v ego upravlenii, ot 1772 g. do 1811 g., *TKDA*, 9 (1868, 3): 165-166.

[20] Cf. WOŁYNIAK, p. 157-158; ZVERINSKIJ, 1: 278 (no. 550).

[21] There the sisters turned their refectory into a chapel when their church with all its furnishings was taken, cf. SKRUTEN', p. 354-355, 359.

[22] Cf. *OAZM*, 2: 288.

[23] Secinskij, p. 342.

[24] *Ibid.*

Occasionally the tenacity of the nuns won out. In the same year 1796 the Braclav consistory ordered that the superior and some of the nuns of the Nemyriv monastery be moved to Vinnycja, together with some of their possessions and church furnishings. Evidently a total closing was intended (perhaps the Vinnycja monastery could not hold all the nuns of the suppressed monasteries of Podillja immediately). But the community still left at Nemyriv petitioned for official recognition and the return of its possesions. The founder of the monastery gave it some land, and in 1798 the Holy Synod classified it as a monastery of the third category, instead of a projected one in Kamjanec' Podil's'kyj[25].

Other Orthodox monasteries were also closed at this time. In 1795 the nuns of the Vilna Holy Spirit monastery were transferred to the Sluck monastery[26]. It must be admitted that there was a good case for closing this monastery: there were only two nuns, and the monastery buildings were in a sad state of disrepair[27].

In Mahilev the Epihany women's monastery fell a victim to the animosity between the moribund brotherhood that had founded it and still claimed patronage over it and the bishop of Mahilev Athanasius Volxovskyj. The nuns could choose where they wanted to go—their choices were the monasteries of Kutejno, Barkalabava, and Mozoliv—and the small funds of the monastery were divided by the bishop among the nuns. Because of protests by the brotherhood the Holy Synod ordered an investigation by the successor of Athanasius, Anastasius Bratanovs'kyj, and his consistory, which upheld the closing. The monastery building, although dilapidated, was turned over to the cathedral singers[28].

Eleven Uniate monasteries survived a few more decades in the Russian empire: Brahin, Dubno, Hrodna, Minsk—Holy Trinity, Navahrudek, Orša, Pinsk, Polonne, Vicebsk, Vilna—Holy Trinity, Volodymyr Volyns'kyj. In 1825 the nuns numbered 87; by 1834 the number was down to 74[29]. One by one these monasteries were closed by

---

[25] Ibid., p. 333-334. While it may seem strange that in a period of general closings of monasteries a new one should be considered, the explanation is simple. In Kamjanec' Podil's'kyj there was a large new building destined for the Uniate cathedral chapter (krylos) and seminary. After some discussion about the use to which to put it now, it was decided to transfer there nuns from various monasteries.

[26] Cf. ŠČERBICKIJ, Vilenskij Svjato-Troickij monastyr', p. 129.

[27] In July 1793 a church warden reported to the bishop of Perejaslav Victor Sadkovs'kyj that there was danger of the nuns' church caving in, AS, 11: 195.

[28] Ibid., 2: lxxv (Zapiski igumena Oresta); ŽUDRO, Bogojavlensij bratskij monastyr', p. 31.

[29] [Augustin THEINER], Die neuesten Zustände der Katholischen Kirche beider Ritus in

Sjemaško. Volodymyr-Volyns'kyj was closed between 1833-1836. In the Dubno monastery in 1834 there were 10 nuns, 4 old women under their care, 15 orphans, and 10 older girls; it was closed around 1833 as was also the monastery in Brahin. In 1839 Sjemaško's apostasy became open, and the Uniate Church of Belorussia and Volyn' was declared officially reunited with Orthodox. This meant the end of all Uniate monasteries. Of the 8 still left most were closed in 1839-1840; by 1845 no Uniate monasteries remained in the Russian empire.

Efforts were made to induce the nuns of these monasteries to receive the sacraments from an Orthodox priest; this was considered as the sign of their passage to Orthodoxy. They were not required to sign a formal declaration as were secular priests and Basilians. Most of the nuns remained faithful to the Catholic Church. The surviving nuns were permitted to go to relatives to live out their days[30].

Polen und Russland (Augsburg, 1841), p. 336 (official statistics).

[30] WOŁYNIAK, in his "Z przeszłości Zakonu Bazyliańskiego", under each monastery says something about its closing. A general account of these closings is given by G. Ja. KIPRIANOVIČ, *Žizn' Iosifa Semaški mitropolita litovskogo i vilenskogo i vossoedinenie zapadnorusskix uniatov s pravoslavnoju cerkoviju v 1839 g.* (2nd ed., Vil'na, 1897), p. 277-280. No documentation on the fate of Uniate women's monasteries has been published. Although Sjemaško appends numerous documents to his memoirs, only one item regards Uniate nuns, *Zapiski Iosifa mitropolita litovskogo*, 2 (Sanktpeterburg, 1883): 335-342. This is a self-defense of 6 December 1845, called forth by an article that had appeared in the Parisian paper *Le Siècle*. The information Sjemaško here gives is not entirely reliable; he contradicts himself on several points.

CHAPTER IX

CONCLUSION

About the origins of monasteries in Ruthenian lands and about their early developement we have very few notices. We cannot, for that reason, reconstruct the early stages, but have to be satisfied with recording a few bare, isolated facts. Loss of documentation can be blamed. But everything that we do know points to the conclusion that monasticism did not flourish there. Had we even more sources from the early period, our general picture of monasticism would not change. At most, we might have had more details on the larger and more famous monasteries. This state of monasticism in Ruthenian lands lasted almost to the end of the sixteenth century.

About the time of the Union of Brest a change begins to take place. At the very end of the sixteenth and through the first half of the seventeenth centuries women's monasticism shares in the upsurge of church life in the Kievan metropolitanate. But from about the middle of the seventeenth century it fails to keep pace with the general development of the Church.

Dividing women's monasteries in Ukraine and Belorussia into Catholic and Orthodox does not show up differences among them. The differences that did exist were regional and were due to social and economic factors.

Even at its most flourishing the number of monasteries and of monks and nuns never becomes very large in proportion to territory and population. This is true not only of Ukraine and Belorussia, but of Russia as well. It is difficult to make direct comparisons, as statistics except for the most recent period have not been computed or even approximated (an extremely difficult task in any case).

If one computes the statistics of nuns at the end of the eighteenth century by counting the figures known and then making allowances for monasteries for which no figures are available, the total reached is probably not much over 600 for the entire territory of Ukraine and

Belorussia. In 1772-1773 the Basilian monks numbered about 1370[1]. It is difficult to compute how many Ruthenian Orthodox monks there were at the same time. When a closed number of monks and nuns was established for Ukrainian monasteries in 1786, no figures were given for the actual numbers at that time. If one relies on Ternovskij who says that the three eparchies of Kiev, Černihiv, and Novhorod Sivers'kyj (the last projected but never actuated) had more than 466 monks over the established number, and computes that the state lists allowed for 356 monks, then makes allowances for monasteries in Slobidščyna (subject to state limitations also in 1786), Belorussia, and Podillja, one reaches the figure of about 1000 Orthodox monks[2].

For purposes of comparison we can quote figures of Russian monastic membership just before the confiscation of church properties in 1764 and as determined in that year. In 1762 there were about 9500 professed members in Russian monasteries; the numbers of monks and nuns are not given separately[3]. The ukaz of 1764 set the number at 4180[4], but one has to add about 2000 more in the monasteries that were allowed to continue without state support. The population is difficult to determine, but it may be taken as about 18 million Orthodox.

In Poland, at the same period (in 1772) there were 14.200 religious men and 3211 religious women, for a population of about 7 million Latin Catholics[5].

These figures tell us that in this period everywhere women religious were far less numerous than men religious. If then one takes the figures in relation to the population, the number of monks and nuns in eastern Slavic lands is much smaller than that in Poland (or in other western countries).

The low figures can be ascribed to various causes. Chief among them and one which then involved other causes, was the economic situation. This took on different aspects in different regions, but it always had a limiting, negative effect on monasteries.

---

[1] VAVRYK, p. 49.

[2] TERNOVSKIJ, p. 334. The ukaz of 1786, the text of which Ternovskij gives, did not give figures for Ukrainian monasteries, but merely divided them into three categories plus the Kiev Lavra and said that they were to follow the prescriptions given to Russian monasteries in 1764.

[3] According to official statistics, in Aleksej ZAV'JALOV, *Vopros o cerkovnyx imenijax pri imperatrice Ekaterine II* (S.-Peterburg, 1900), p. 346-347.

[4] *PSPR*, Catherine II, 1: 174.

[5] Jan KOCENIAK, Zakony, *Historia Kościoła w Polsce*, 1, pt. 2 (Poznań-Warszawa, 1974): 442.

In Lithuania a monastic foundation was often made for a specific number of persons. This held for Basilians, it held for Orthodox monks. It also held for the nuns. An endowment sufficed to support a certain number of persons—and 15 was already considered a large number. The buildings were then also constructed with that number in mind. Since means did not allow more members, obviously no efforts were made to attract them. If they came, they were turned away.

In Halyčyna, on the other hand, most monasteries suffered from having no endowment at all or a paltry one at best. Numerous monasteries arose in the course of the seventeenth and eighteenth centuries, but they vanished almost as quickly as they sprang up. There was no class sufficiently wealthy among the Ruthenian population to found monasteries and endow them.

The relative superiority in numbers in the monasteries of Kiev and the Left Bank can be traced directly to the better economic and social standing of the population. True, in the 1720's various restrictions put an end to new endowments in favor of church institutions. But by that time the monasteries of Kiev, the hetmanate, and Slobidščyna had acquired sufficient properties for economic security and buildings large enough to accomodate good-sized communitites.

As economics were so important in the life of monasteries, the danger existed of their becoming an overriding concern, to the detriment of other qualities of community life. If the economic circumstances were miserable, as in Halyčyna, the most pressing problem of the nuns was to provide themselves with basic necessities. If a monastery had properties, the mania of litigating with neighbors which no property-holder in Poland-Lithuania could resist, soon took its toll of the monastery's wealth. In the Left Bank the ownership of land made of monasteries more economic than religious institutions, as Lazarevs'kyj justly observed[6]. As such they had neither great influence on the religious life of the people nor offered ideals that would attract numbers of entrants.

Another factor that played a role in determining the number of persons entering monastic life was the level of culture, and in particular the low level of religious culture. If Halyčyna had smaller numbers than other regions it was because, among other things, it was at this time more backward culturally (which in turn was again due to economic and social factors). Even more backward was the Carpathian region, where there was no women's monastery until modern times (in the period we are considering the monks numbered about 100)[7].

---

[6] Lazarevskij, *Opisanie*, 2: 299.
[7] Vavryk, p. 49.

Although monasticism as a whole was not flourishing in Ruthenian lands, the condition of women's monasteries was much worse off than that of men's. In western Ukraine, while there were about 620 monks, there were only about 40 nuns in 1772-1774.

Much smaller proportions of nuns are seen, however, everywhere: Orthodox monasteries in Ukraine and Belorussia, Russian monasticism, religious life in Poland. It is clear, then, that the proportion is due to a more general cause than particular circumstances in Ruthenian lands. Obviously, the position of women in society and in church life played a great role here.

Unfortunately, the history of women's monasteries in Russia before the nineteenth century is entirely unexplored[8]. We have to turn to comparisons with the conditions in Poland, for which there is an ever increasing number of studies on women religious. In general, the development there is strikingly similar to that of women's monasteries in the metropolitanate of Kiev. While in the first half of the seventeenth century there is an extremely rapid rise in the number of Latin sisters in Poland-Lithuania, from 1650 to 1772 there is hardly any growth at all, and if fuller statistics were available for 1650, they might show that there was on the contrary a decline in numbers[9].

Hasty conclusions should be avoided. To give an idea of the complex factors involved, it should be recalled that the period from 1648 through the first decade of the following century was one of constant wars (Xmel'nyc'kyj's uprising, the Russian-Polish war, Cossack wars, the Northern war—and Tatar incursions in addition). The population in the territories involved declined drastically. There could be no increase in monastic population under the circumstances.

In the eighteenth century religious life in Poland offered a greater scope for the activity of women than life outside the convents. However, the efforts of church authorities with regard to women's monasteries were almost entirely devoted to enforcing, not very successfully, total enclosure. The only communities of women religious in Poland that registered a growth in the eighteenth century were those that evaded the obligation of enclosure by renouncing the canonical status of nuns (Sisters of Charity and others) and could thus devote themselves to charitable and educative work.

---

[8] The major survey of Russian monasticism, Igor Smolitsch, *Russisches Mönchtum* (Das östliche Christentum, NF, 10-11; Würzburg, 1953), completely ignores women's monasteries prior to the nineteenth century.

[9] Cf. Elżbieta Janicka-Olczakowa, Zakony żeńskie w Polsce, *Kościół w Polsce*, 2 (Kraków, 1969): 770-771.

Women's monasteries of the eastern rite in Poland-Lithuania suffered for the same reasons. While the figures for the Basilian monks at the time of the partitions of Poland are not striking, they do nevetheless represent a steady advance in numbers. The Basilians continued to widen their field of activity and to provide for the religious needs of the people. At the end of the eighteenth century this pastoral activity is very marked and very beneficial. In a sense, the Basilians provided that which in the Latin Church was provided by the variety of orders and congregations. This met the needs of the Church; it also met the varied aspirations of those entering.

A similar development among the nuns was entirely absent. The impulse to it had to come from outside the monasteries, but such guidance was lacking. The state of church life and of social life as a whole could not provide it.

It is the common procedure, whether studying one aspect or one subperiod of the Ukrainian-Belorussian Church after the Union of Brest, to give one's attention either to the Catholic or to the Orthodox side to the exclusion of the other. Such an approach makes it convenient to idealize one side or to emphasize the shortcomings of the other, as one's sympathies lie. But the exclusivity of this method becomes an obstacle to a comprehension of the common heritage of both Churches and blinds one to the fact that many characteristics—both strong and weak points—of church life were surprisingly the same on either side.

Women's monasteries illustrate this point. One can note two basic types, but they are distributed not between Catholics and Orthodox, but territorially, or, to put it another way, they were due to the social and cultural milieu in which they arose.

To understand the first type it is necessary to point out some parallels. Monastic reform among the Uniates is largely the work of Joseph Veljamyn Rutskyj, who recognized its importance even before he himself enetered a monastery and who pursued it as metropolitan and protoarchimandrite. The most prominent features of his reform were, with regard to the internal life of monasteries, a reintroduction of common life and externally, the unification of monasteries into an order for the sake of common support and strength. The efforts of Orthodox monastic reformers were distinguished by the same features. Here there was not one united drive but several, contemporary with that of Rutskyj. The monasteries founded by the Stetkevyč family in eastern Belorussia, organized and directed by Joil Trucevyč, and the Vilna Holy Spirit grouping of monasteries both display the same features of Rutskyj's reform. The effects of these reforms, both among the Catholics and the Orthodox, were also felt by women's monasteries. All of these

were in Belorussia, where one sees a number of well-organized, struc-
tured monasteries.

For the rest of the monasteries, whether Catholic or Orthodox,
whether in the seventeenth or the eighteenth century, and in whatever
region, one sees monasticism in an incipient stage, in a certain sense.
These monasteries of the second, much more common type, display an
amorphous community, nuns living alone or by twos in small cottages,
new members settling down with older nuns, handwork, sale of the
handwork in markets nearby, hiring oneself out for work in the fields.
The task of the superior in such monasteries was confined to looking
after the economic interests of the monastery as a whole and to taking
care of official dealings with civil and ecclesiastical authorities.

The difference in the two types of monasteries is again partially due
to economic differences. But some of the monasteries of the second type
that existed in hetmanate Ukraine were just as prosperous as the town
monasteries of Belorussia. The difference is due above all to a lack of
real guidance in monastic life. Monastic literature was meager in the
monasteries. And regulations such as those of the Synod of Zamość, so
far removed from the reality of life in, for instance, the little
monasteries of the Lviv eparchy, had little chance of being applied.
Thus monastic life continued without change with the characteristics it
had developed perhaps already in pre-Mongolian times.

As religiosity in general in these lands paid most attention to external rites, there was a tendency to see the essence of monasticism in its
external forms. Monastic literature, which could contribute to a deeper
understanding of monastic life, was not abundantly available, especially
in women's monasteries. In the West the religious were led to reflect on
the purpose of their life; in the East such reflection, so necessary for
any deepening of the spiritual side to monasticism, was lacking. The
monastic enclosure, the habit, and church services sufficed to make up
the general conception of monastic life, both for those outside and those
inside the monasteries.

Amidst these general conditions there were undeniably examples,
and perhaps numerous ones, of individuals who entered monasteries and
lived out their lives there in a spirit of sacrifice and prayer. Available
records give us little more than a glimpse of the spiritual side of
monastic life. But this aspect must not be forgotten in any correct ap-
praisal of these women's monasteries.

A SUMMARY TABLE OF MONASTERIES

PLACE	REGION	NAME	PERIOD
1. Barkalabava	Mahilev terr.	Ascension	c. 1641-XX cent.
2. Baturyn	Černihivščyna	Holy Cross	c. 1650-1683
3. Biała Podlaska	Pidljaššja		late XVIII cent.
4. Bibrka	Halyčyna		late XVII cent.-bef. 1746
5. Bil'če	Halyčyna	Birth of BVM	c. 1608
6. Bilylivka	Volyn'		bef. 1626-after 1710
7. Borejky	Mscislav terr.	Dormition	c. 1728-1751
8. Brahin	Minsk terr.	Annunciation	c. 1609-1844
9. Braslav	Vilna terr.		XV cent.
10. Bučyna	Halyčyna	Dormition	XVII cent.
11. Bus'k	Halyčyna		c. 1602-c. 1780
12. Bycen'	Brest terr.		c. 1607-c. 1613
13. Bystrycja	Poltavščyna	Dormition	1709-c. 1786
14. Čerčyci	Volyn'	Savior	bef. 1597-c. 1795
15. Cerkovišče	Mahilev terr.		XVIII cent.
16. Černihiv	Černihivščyna	St Paraskeva	after 1600-1786
17. Četvertnja	Volyn'		1618-after 1793
18. Čyhyryn	Kyjivščyna	Holy Trinity	after 1708-XX cent.
19. Dobrotvir	Halyčyna		XVII cent.-1759
20. Drohyčyn	Brest terr.	Holy Trinity	1659-after 1780
21. Dubno	Volyn'	Holy Trinity	1592-c. 1833
22. Forošča	Halyčyna		XVII cent.
23. Fyrlijiv	Halyčyna		XVII cent.
24. Hamalijivka	Černihivščyna	St Charlampius	1702-1733
25. Hluxiv	Černihivščyna	Transfiguration	1670-1784
26. Holoskiv	Pokuttja		c. 1774
27. Horodyšče	Halyčyna		bef. 1628-early XVIII cent.
28. Hrodna		Birth of BVM	c. 1635-XX cent.
29. Jaseniv	Halyčyna		XVIII cent.
30. Jasnohorod	Volyn'	Holy Trinity	XVI cent.-after 1804
31. Javoriv	Halyčyna	Pokrov	1621-1940's
32. Kamens'kyj Xutor	Černihivščyna	Dormition	1786-XX cent.
33. Kaminka Strumylova	Halyčna	Annunciation	bef. 1666-c. 1782
34. Kascjukoviči	Mahilev terr.		1665-after 1720

35. Kiev		St Irene	XI cent.
36. Kiev		St Nicholas	XI cent.
37. Kiev		St Andrew	XI cent.
38. Kiev		St Lazarus	XII cent.
39. Kiev		Sts Florus & Laurus	1566-
40. Kiev		Ascension	bef. 1586-1707
41. Kiev		Jordan	c. 1615-1808
42. Kiev		St Michael/St John	c. 1621-1790
43. Klynec'	Volyn'	Holy Cross	bef. 1664-after 1740
44. Knjaže	Halyčyna	St Paraskeva	to 1781
45. Korec'	Volyn'	Resurrection	c. 1571-
46. Korobivka	Poltavščyna	Annunciation	after 1719-1817
47. Korop	Černihivščyna		XVII cent.
48. Kozelec'	Kyjivščyna	Epiphany/St John	early XVIII cent.-1808
49. Krasnohora	Poltavščyna	St John Evangelist	1790-
50. Krylos	Halyčyna	St Elias	bef. 1654-after 1763
51. Kulykiv	Halyčyna	St Demetrius	bef. 1680-1743
52. Kutejno	Vicebsk terr.	Dormition	1631-XX cent.
53. Ladyn	Černihivščyna	Pokrov	1619-XX cent.
54. Lebedyn	Kyjivščyna	St Nicholas	1779-XX cent.
55. Lisovyči	Kyjivščyna	St George	XVII cent.
56. Lviv	Halyčyna	St Catherine	1591-c. 1800
57. Mahilev		Savior	1447-after 1625
58. Mahilev		Epiphany	bef. 1643-1795
59. Mahilev		St Nicholas	1634-late XVIII cent.
60. Makošyn	Černihivščyna	St Nicholas	1640-1786
61. Maraščanka	Halyčyna		XVII cent.
62. Mazyr	Polissja	St Paraskeva	XVIII cent.
63. Mena	Černihivščyna		XVII cent.
64. Minsk		Sts Peter & Paul	1612-1796
65. Minsk		Holy Trinity	1630-1834
66. Minsk		Holy Spirit	1650-1795
67. Mozoliv	Mahilev terr.	Dormition	1675-XX cent.
68. Mutyn	Černihivščyna	Savior	1733-1786
69. Mykolajiv	Halyčyna	St Nicholas	XVII cent.
70. Mykulynci	Podillja	Holy Cross	1716-1796
71. Navahrudek	Hrodna terr.	Sts Boris & Hlib	1629-1835
72. Nemyriv	Podillja	St Nicholas	1783-XX cent.
73. Nižyn	Černihivščyna	Presentation	early XVIII cent.-XX cent.
74. Nova Hreblja	Halyčyna		XVII cent.
75. Novi Mlyny	Černihivščyna	Dormition	1658-early XIX cent.
76. Oles'ko	Halyčyna		XVII cent.
77. Ombyš	Černihivščyna	Presentation	1st half XVII cent.
78. Orša	Vicebsk terr.	Pokrov	1642-1839
79. Ostrogožsk	Slobidščyna	Dormition	c. 1663-1786
80. Ovruč	Volyn'	Birth of BVM	XV-XVI cent.
81. Ovruč		Sts Joachim & Anna	XV cent.
82. Pečenyky	Černihivščyna	Dormition	1693-1786
83. Peresopnycja	Volyn'		XVI cent.
84. Pidhajci	Halyčyna		XVII cent.
85. Pidluby	Halyčyna		XVII cent.
86. Pikulice	Halyčyna		XVII cent.

87. Pinsk	Polissja	St Barbara	bef. 1521-after 1839
88. Polock		Savior/St Sophia	bef. 1128-XX cent.
89. Polock		St Michael	late XV cent.
90. Polonne	Volyn'	Dormition	c. 1612-1858
91. Popivka	Volyn'	St Nicholas	1646-1836
92. Puškarivka	Poltavščyna	Pokrov	1676-late XVIII cent.
93. Pustel'nyky	Halyčyna		XVII cent.-after 1732
94. Pysarevščyna	Poltavščyna	Transfiguration	bef. 1679-XX cent.
95. Ripjanka	Halyčyna	Dormition	XVII cent.-1756
96. Rohatyn	Halyčyna	Ascension	to 1784
97. Rohatyn		Transfiguration	to 1768
98. Rozhirče	Halyčyna		after 1693-1789
99. Rusec'	Halyčyna		XVIII cent.
100. Sasiv	Halyčyna		to 1759
101. Šelexove	Podillja		XVIII cent.
102. Šklov	Mahilev terr.	Dormition	bef. 1665-XVIII cent.
103. Slovita	Halyčyna	Holy Cross	bef. 1581-1940's
104. Sluck		St Elias	1611-1855
105. Smil'nycja	Halyčyna		XVII cent.-1789
106. Sosnycja	Černihivščyna	St John Evangelist	1751-1786
107. Stanyslaviv	Halyčyna	Dormition	XVIII cent.-c. 1782
108. Staryj Sambir	Halyčyna		XVIII cent.-bef. 1761
109. Sudova Vyšnja	Halyčyna		XVII cent.
110. Šumarovo	Černihivščyna	Pokrov	c. 1690-1786
111. Šums'ke	Volyn'		XVII cent.
112. Sumy	Slobidščyna	St John Baptist	bef. 1658-after 1786
113. Terebovlja	Halyčyna		XVII cent.
114. Univ	Halyčyna	Savior	bef. 1644-after 1761
115. Utiškiv	Halyčyna		XVII cent.
116. Vicebsk		Birth of BVM	XVI cent.
117. Vicebsk		Holy Spirit	bef. 1710-after 1844
118. Vilna		Holy Trinity	bef. 1589-1841
119. Vilna		Holy Spirit	c. 1605-1795
120. Vinnycja	Podillja	Annunciation	1635-1845
121. Vlodava	Pidljaššja		XVIII cent.
122. Volja Arlamivs'ka	Halyčyna		XVII cent.
123. Volodymyr Volyns'kyj	Volyn'	St Elias	1772-1833
124. Volsvyn	Halyčyna		XVII cent.
125. Vyšhorod	Kyjivščyna	St Nicholas	XII cent.
126. Xolm	Pidljaššja	Dormition	c. 1650-after 1779
127. Xoroševe	Slobidščyna	Ascension	c. 1656-XX cent.
128. Zahvizdja	Halyčyna	Holy Trinity	bef. 1669-1789
129. Žovkva	Halyčyna	Holy Cross	bef. 1627-c. 1743
130. Žydyčyn	Volyn'	Holy Spirit	c. 1621

Appendix II

STATISTICS OF INDIVIDUAL MONASTERIES

Monastery	Date	No. of Nuns	Source
Borejky	1750	14	*OASS*, 31: 175
Bus'k	1776	2	Petruševič, *Svodnaja letopis' 1600-1700*, p. 11
Bycen'	1610	11	*AS*, 9: 459
Bystrycja	1745	26	*OASS*, 20: 593
Černihiv	1739	15	*PSPR*, [1st series], 10: 297
	1740	15	*OASS*, 19: 507
	1745	36	*OASS*, 20: 612
Čyhyryn	1766	44	*Arxiv JuZR*, pt I, 3: 242
Hluxiv	1745	8	*OASS*, 20: 593
Holoskiv	1774	6	Chotkowski, p. 136
Hrodna	1650	10	*OAZM*, 1: 291
	1744	7	*OAZM*, 2: 92
Javoriv	1774	5	Chotkowski, p. 136
	1782	5	Chotkowski, p. 144
Kiev			
St Florus	1745	117	*OASS*, 20: 592
	1777	123	Xarlampovič, p. 631
Ascension	1586	33	Xarlampovič, p. 13
Jordan	1745	100	*OASS*, 20: 592
St John Ev.	1712	26	P.L-v, p. 241
	1745	68	*OASS*, 20: 592-592
	1789	70	*PSPR*, Catherine II, 3: 290
Korobivka	1745	25	*OASS*, 20: 606
Kozelec'	1745	3	*OASS*, 20: 593
Kutejno	1743	74	*OASS*, 23-36
Ladyn	1745	25	*OASS*, 20: 593
	1786	49	Šafonskij, p. 499
Lisovyci	1654	30	*Akty JuZR*, 10: 792
Lviv	1774	6	Chotkowski, p. 136
	1782	11	Chotkowski, p. 138
	1790	5	Chotkowski, p. 144-145
Mahilev			
Epiphany	1795	10	Žudro, *Bogojavlenskij bratskij monastyr'*, p. 31
Makošyn	1654	16	*Akty JuZR*, 10: 823
	1740	36	*OASS*, 19: 509
	1745	35	*OASS*, 20: 612

Minsk			
Holy Trinity	1749	7	*LB*, 2: 189
Holy Spirit	1749	25	*LB*, 2: 189
Mutyno	1745	10	*OASS*, 20: 593
Mykulynci	1716	12	Secinskij, p. 343-344
	1773	9	Secinskij, p. 346-348
Nižyn	1745	7	*OASS*, 20: 593
	1786	18	Šafonskij, p. 462
Novi Mlyny	1745	15	*OASS*, 20: 593
	1777	27	Lazarevskij, *Opisanie*, 2: 298
Orša	1797	9	Wołyniak, p. 78
Pečenyky	1740	42	*OASS*, 19: 509
	1745	40	*OASS*, 20: 612
Polock	1614	12	Susza, *Cursus vitae b. Jasaphat*, p. 55
	1623	35	Susza, *Cursus vitae b. Josaphat*, p. 55
	1775	20	*AV*, 16: 425
Puškarivka	1745	13	*OASS*, 20: 612
Pysarevščyna	1745	11	*OASS*, 20: 612
Rohatyn	1774	11	Chotkowski, p. 136
Rusec'	1774	9	Chotkowski, p. 136
Slovita	1763	10	C'orox, p. 233-234
	1764	11	Petruševič, *Slovickij ženskij monastyr'*, p. 118
	1774	7	Chotkowski, p. 136
Smil'nycja	1764	8	C'orox, p. 67
	1789	7	Chotkowski, p. 143
Sosnycja	1750	14	*OASS*, 31: 175
Šumarovo	1740	17	*OASS*, 19: 510
	1745	22	*OASS*, 20: 612
Sumy	1745	37	*OASS*, 20: 608-609
Vicebsk	1798	9	Wołyniak, p. 165
Vilna			
Holy Trinity	1749	15	*LB*, 2: 187
Holy Spirit	1750	7	*OASS*, 31: 424
	1778	3	*AV*, 9: 547
Vinnycja	1786	2	Wołyniak, p. 164
	1792	2	Secinskij, p. 266
Volodymyr Vol.	1775	12	*EM*, 6: 458
Xoroševo	1745	40	*OASS*, 20: 608
Zahvizdja	1774	6	Chotkowski, p. 136

Appendix III

ALTERNATE NAMES FOR MONASTERIES

The first column contains place names by which the monasteries are otherwise known, the second, as they are listed in this book.

BEREZNJA	SOSNYCJA
BIELIŁÓW	BILYLIVKA
BILA	BIAŁA PODLASKA
BOBRKA	BIBRKA
BOBRYK(OVSKIJ)	NOVI MLYNY
BORKOLABOVO	BARKALABAVA
BOROV	BOREJKY
BRAHYNO-SIDLCI	BRAHIN
BUDYŠČA VELYKI	PYSAREVŠČYNA
BUKTRINSKIJ	BYSTRYCJA
BYSTRINSKYJ	BYSTRYCJA
BYTEN'	BYCEN'
ČERNEČYJ JAR	PYSAREVŠČYNA
HNOJINA	POPIVKA
JAZVYN	DOBROTVIR
KERBUTOVSKIJ	NOVI MLYNY
KOSTJUKOVYČI	KASCJUKOVIČY
LUC'K	ČERČYCI
LUKY	SUMY
MAROŠANKA	MARAŠČANKA
MOGIL'NO	POPIVKA
MOHYL'NA	POPIVKA
MYRONOVSKIJ	SOSNYCJA
NOVOGRUDOK	NAVAHRUDEK
PEČENIHY	PEČENYKY
PIDBIRCI	DUBNO

PIDHIRS'KYJ	LADYN
POČERPYC'KYJ	PEČENYKY
PODBÓRCE	DUBNO
PODHORS'KYJ	LADYN
POLTAVA	PUŠKARIVKA
POPIV MLYN	POPIVKA
PRYLUKY	LADYN
RIŽOK	MYKULYNCI
SELEC'	BRAHIN
SILEC'	BRAHIN
SOSNYCJA	MAKOŠYN
STARA ČETVERNJA	ČETVERTNJA
STARODUB	PEČENYKY
UTIXIV	UTIŠKIV
VARKALABOVO	BARKALABAVA
VELYKI BUDYŠČA	PYSAREVŠČYNA
VOLODAVA	VLODAVA
VORKOLABOVO	BARKALABAVA
XARKIV	XOROŠEVO
XARLAMPIEVS'KA PUSTYNJA	HAMALIJIVKA
ZAZULOVSKIJ	KOROBIVKA
ZOLOTONOŠA	KOROBIVKA or KRASNOHORA

Appendix IV

LIST OF TERMS DEFINED IN TEXT

duxovnyj otec	p. 176	prosfory	p.	184
duxovnyk	176	prydil		85
ihumen	177	pud		74
ihumenja	151	rjasa		123
koloda	72	rjasoforna		124
kopa	72	skyt		57
korec'	74	soborna starycja		155
krylos	172	starša		147
krylošanka	172	staršyna		61
ktytor	68	starycja		123
ktytors'kyj ustav	68,108	štatnyj		198
namisnycia	151,156	sxymnycja		123
pomjanyk	16	universal		18
poslušnycja	123	voloka		74
postryženie	123			

BIBLIOGRAPHY

A.D. z Valjavy. Sostojanie Eparxii ruskoi Peremyskoi pered stoma lity, *Halyčanyn*, 2 (1863): 79-87.
Although the title suggests a brief article, this is, in fact, a publication of a report written by the bishop of Peremyšl' Onufrij Šumljans'kyj on 23 August 1761 concerning the state of his eparchy.

Akty istoričeskie. Sobrannye i izdannye Arxeografičeskoju Kommissieju. 5 vols. Sanktpeterburg, 1841-1845.
Volumes 4 and 5 are especially useful for the study of monasteries, with documents from 1645 to 1700.

Akty izdavaemye Kommisieju vysočajše učreždennoju dlja razboru drevnix aktov v Vil'ne. 39 vols. Vil'na, 1865-1908.
Almost all the volumes in this series contain documents which shed light on the economic as well as other aspects of monastic life, chiefly in western Belorussian territories. The entire series is well edited; each volume has its own introduction, often of great service, and indices of personal names, place names, and subjects.

Akty otnosjaščiesja k istorii južnoj i zapadnoj Rossii. Sobrannye i izdannye Arxeografičeskoju Kommissieju. 15 vols. Sanktpeterburg, 1863-1892.
This collection offers much information on monasteries in Kiev and the Left Bank, principally in the seventeenth century.

Akty otnosjaščiesja k istorii zapadnoj Rossii. Sobrannye i izdannye Arxeografičeskoju Kommissieju. 5 vols. Sanktpeterburg, 1840-1853.
All these volumes contain documents regarding women's monasteries in the sixteenth and seventeenth centuries.

Alekseev, L.V. *Polockaja zemlja.* Očerki istorii severnoj Belorussii v IX-XIII vv. Moskva, 1966.
A good amount of information on Euphrosine of Polock and her monastery is contained in this excellent book by an archaeologist. An index would have added greatly to its usefulness.

Amvrosij [Ornackij]. *Istorija rossijskoj ierarxii.* 6 vols. in 7. Moskva, 1807-1815. Vol. 1-2 reprinted, Copenhagen, 1979.
Volume 1 contains a list of hierarchs and related chapters; the remaining volumes deal alphabetically with all the monasteries in the territory of the Russian empire. Early as the compilation is, it has never been entirely superseded, since later compilers simply copied its entries.

Archiwum domu Sapiehów. Vol. 1. Lwów, 1892.
Volume 1 is the only one to have been published. It contains letters of the family

from 1575 to 1600, when most members were still of the eastern rite. These shed much light on church affairs, including monastic life, in that period.

Arxeografičeskij sbornik dokumentov otnosjaščixsja k istorii severozapadnoj Rusi. 14 vols. and index. Vil'na, 1867-1904.
Most of these volumes are useful for the study of women's monasteries in the seventeenth-eighteenth centuries in Belorussia.

Arxiv jugo-zapadnoj Rossii. Part I. 12 vols. Kiev, 1859-1904.
Part I of this collection of documents published by the Vremennaja Kommissija deals specifically with church matters. The volumes especially helpful for the study of monasteries are: 4, 5, 6, 10, 11.

BARSOV, E.V. Opisanie aktov arxiva Markeviča, otnosjaščixsja k istorii južno-russkix monastyrej, *ČOIDR*, 1884, 2: 1-35.
This is a list of briefly described documents concerning the properties of monasteries in Kiev and the Left Bank.

BEAUPLAN, Guillaume. *Description de l'Ukraine.* Paris, 1861.
Guillaume Le Vasseur, sieur de Beauplan (c. 1600-1670) was a French military engineer in the employ of Poland, for which he constructed, among other things, the fortress Kodak on the Dnieper river. His description of Ukraine, its inhabitants, and their customs first came out in Rouen in 1650.

BIDNOV, V. Marija Mahdalyna, maty het'mana Mazepy, *Mazepa.* Zbirnyk. 1 (Warszawa, 1938): 35-42.
The author has collected information on hetman Mazepa's mother, ihumenja of the monasteries of Kiev-Ascension and Hluxiv. His article, however, does not take account of all possible sources.

BIEŃKOWSKI, Ludomir. Organizacja Kościoła Wschodniego w Polsce, *Kościół w Polsce*, 2 (Kraków, 1969): 779-1049.
This is a general survey of the Eastern Church in the Polish-Lithuanian Commonwealth in the sixteenth-eighteenth centuries. The section that regards women's monasteries (p. 1025-1031) relies too much on antiquated works and is frequently inaccurate.

BODJANSKIJ, O., ed. Rospis' Kievu, *ČOIDR*, 1858, 2: 59-68.
The topographic description of Kiev from 1682 which is published here provides data on its monasteries.

BUCMANJUK, Ivan. *Univ i jeho monastyri.* Žovkva, 1904.
The publication in recent decades of documents referring to the Ukrainian Church, with a great deal on the Univ archimandria, makes this book outdated historically. It is valuable, however, in recording local traditions about the Univ monasteries, especially for the times from which no documentary evidence exists.

CHOTKOWSKI, Władysław. *Historya polityczna dawnych klasztorów panieńskich w Galicyi.* Kraków, 1905.
The author, on the basis of official documents, recounts the history of the suppression of women's monasteries, both Latin and Uniate, under Austrian rule, as well as the fate of those that survived. His work covers the years 1773-1848.

C'OROX, Salomija. *Pohljad na istoriju ta vyxovnu dijal'nist' monaxyn' Vasylijanok.* L'viv, 1934. Reprinted, Romae, 1964.
This work gives a detailed history of monasteries of Basilian nuns in the nineteenth and twentieth centuries to the 1930's by one who had personal knowledge of them and access to their archives. The introductory remarks on the earlier history of

monasteries are based, however, only on a limited number of secondary sources. The documents published in the appendix are valuable sources on monasteries in Halyčyna.

DENISOV, L.I. *Pravoslavnye monastyri rossijskoj imperii*. Moskva, 1908.
Before setting out to compile this illustrated catalog, the author sent a detailed questionnaire to all the monasteries in the Russian empire. About a fourth of the monasteries responded. Thus, the work did not turn out to be the definitive catalog as intended. Many of the entries here are a word-for-word copying of notices found elsewhere, principally in Zverinskij, whom, however, Denisov occasionally corrects. The bibliography is extremely limited.

Devjatisotletie pravoslavija na Volyne. 2 vols. Žitomir, 1892.
This commemorative edition contains a listing of monasteries, whether extinct or functioning, in Volyn' with brief historical notices about them. Regrettably, the introductory admission of the compilers that in preparing these volumes they "did not go into any scholarly researches" is fully borne out by the uncritical and inaccurate information contained in them.

DOMONTOVIČ, M. *Černigovskaja gubernija*. Sanktpeterburg, 1865.
This volume enters into the series *Materialy dlja geografii i statistiki Rossii, sobrannye oficerami general'nogo štaba*. Depending on the author, historical and descriptive information in the volumes is more or less complete. The present volume contains brief, but factual and accurate notices on monasteries and gives interesting statistics for the mid-nineteenth century.

Dopolnenija k Aktam istoričeskim. Vol. 10, 12. Sanktpeterburg, 1867, 1872.
The series of 12 volumes deals mostly with Russian matters. Some documents on Ukrainian monasteries, chiefly Kievan, are found in the two volumes noted.

DUMITRAŠKO, Nikolaj. *Istoriko-statističeskij očerk Zolotonošskogo Krasnogorskogo Bogoslovskogo vtoroklasnogo ženskogo monastyrja (Poltavskoj eparxii)*. Poltava, 1859.
The author was a descendent of one of the monastery's early benefactors, the polkovnyk of Perejaslav Demetrius Dumytraško-Rajče. His brief study collects all the information available about the monastery.

ÉJNGORN, Vitalij. O snošenijax malorossijskogo duxovenstva s moskovskim pravitel'stvom v carstvovanie Alekseja Mixajloviča, *ČOIDR*, 1893, 2: i-xiv, 1-370; 1894, 3: 371-570; 1898, 4: 571-794; 1899, 1: 795-922; 2: 923-1072.
This detailed study is a basic source on the relations of Ukrainian monasteries with Muscovy in the given period.

Epistolae metropolitarum Kioviensium Catholicorum. Ed. Athanasius G. WELYKYJ. 9 vols. Romae, 1952-1980.
References to women's monasteries in the letters are infrequent, but provide official data.

GOLUBINSKIJ, E.E. *Istorija russkoj Cerkvi*. Vol. 1, pt. 2. Moskva, 1904.
This volume contains the fullest and most detailed survey of monasticism in pre-Mongolian Rus'.

HOLUBEC', M. Materijaly do katal'ogu vasylijans'kyx monastyriv u Halyčyni, *AOSBM*, 3, no. 1-2 (1928): 165-170.
Very brief notices on 47 monasteries.

HRUŠEVS'KYJ, Ol. Het'mans'ki zemel'ni universaly 1660-1670 rokiv; *Istoryčno-heohrafičnyj zbirnyk*, 1 (1927): 53-92.
The author examines the reasons for the land grants accorded by hetmans, many of

them to monasteries, as well as the light they throw on the relationship between the authority of hetmans and of tsars.

——. Universaly ta hramoty v zemel'nyx spravax z 1650-1660 rokiv, *Zapysky Ukrajins'koho Naukovoho Tovarystva v Kyjevi*, 20 (1926): 110-136.
A concise account of the circumstances that led monasteries to seek material aid from the tsar and the consequences of this.

——. Z ekonomičnoho žyttja ukrajins'kyx manastyriv XVII-XVIII vv. Perši het'mans'ki universaly, *Ukrajina*, 1914, 4: 42-48.
Some general observations based on published sources. Here, as in his other articles, the author does not give enough references to the sources.

Istoriko-arxeologičeskie muzei severo-zapadnogo kraja, *Zapiski severo-zapadnogo otdela imperatorskogo russkogo geografičeskogo obščestva*, 1 (1910): 222-236.
In this notice on several Belorussian museums and their collections some objects that had come from monasteries are described.

Istoriko-juridičeskie materialy, izvlečennye iz aktovyx knig gubernij Vitebskoj i Mogilevskoj, xranjaščixsja v central'nom arxive v Vitebske. 32 vols. Vitebsk, 1871-1906.
This collection offers valuable and abundant sources for many aspects of the history of the Vicebsk and Mahilev regions, but it has been little utilized on account both of its rarity and its uninviting composition. The earlier volumes lack indices and even a simple numbering of the documents published. Titles of documents, where there are tables of contents, are of the most generic kind. Misprints are common; occasionally the same sources (from the same archival volume) are published twice (cf. vol. 23, no. 126, and vol. 29, no. 60).

Istoriko-statističeskoe opisanie Černigovskoj eparxii. Vol. 5-6. Černigov, 1874.
The listed volumes were the only ones available for consultation. The author of this work was Filaret Gumilevskij, archbishop of Černihiv (1859-1866). This work is widely quoted as an authority, but is not entirely reliable (cf. Al. Lazarevskij, *Opisanie staroj Malorossii*, 1: xv-xvi; 2: iii, for examples).

Istoriko-statističeskoe opisanie Xar'kovskoj eparxii. Vol. 1. Xar'kov, 1859.
Filaret Gumilevskij, who was bishop of Xarkiv in 1848-1859, is also the author of this work, much more reliable than the one on the Černihiv eparchy. It consists of 5 volumes, but only the first has material about monasteries, which are described individually. There are many citations from primary sources and abundant statistics.

K portretu Savvy Grigor'eviča Tuptalo, *KS*, 3 (1882, 3): 194-198.
A portrait of the father of Demetrius Tuptalo occasions comments on him and his family, including his three daughters who were nuns.

Karačkivs'kyj, Myxajlo. Materijaly do istoriji mist na Podilli naprykinci XVIII viku, *Istoryčno-heohrafičnyj zbirnyk*, 4 (1931): 161-187.
The excerpts published here from administrative-economic (*kameral'nye*) and topographic descriptions include brief notices on monastery buildings.

Karger, M.I. *Drevnij Kiev. Očerki po istorii material'noj kul'tury drevnerusskogo goroda.* 2 vols. Moskva, 1958-1961.
This detailed exposition of the findings of archaeology concerning pre-Mongolian Kiev includes a full discussion about the location of its monasteries.

Karpovyč, V. Skal'nyj monastyr u Rozhirči, *AOSBM*, 3, n. 3-4 (1930): 562-573.
A description of the monastery with illustrations.

Kievo-Podol'skie monastyri i cerkvi sto let tomu nazad, *Kievskija eparxial'nyja vedomosti*, 51 (1912), no. 9-12: 194-197, 214-217, 242-246.

The relation of the effects of the great fire of 9 July 1811 describes the church buildings damaged or destroyed.

Kievo-Zlatoverxo-Mixajlovskij monastyr'. Istoričeskij očerk ot osnovanija ego do nastojaščogo vremeni. Kiev, 1889.
A reliable survey, put out by the St Michael monastery.

KOSSAK, N. Mykolaev. Korotkyj pohljad na monastyry i na monašestvo ruske, *Šematyzm provynciy Sv. Spasytelja Čyna sv. Vasylija Velykoho v Halyciy*. L'viv, 1867.
After a historical survey the author lists women's monasteries alphabetically with brief notices on each. The list is confined to territories then in the Hapsburg monarchy.

KRYPJAKEVYČ, Ivan. Serednevični monastyri v Halyčyni, *AOSBM*, 2, no. 1-2 (1926): 70-105.
A provisional catalog of monasteries supposed to have existed in the twelfth to the fifteenth centuries.

LAZAREVSKIJ, A. Akty po istorii monastyrskogo zemlevladenija v Malorossii (1636-1730 gg.), *ČN*, 5 (1891): 49-92.
Here is collected a series of documents concerning land ownership of several monasteries in hetmanate Ukraine.

——. Dokumental'nyja svedenija o Savve Tuptale i ego rode, *KS*, 3 (1882, 3): 382-384.
The document concerned is the last will and testament of Paraskeva Tuptalo, ihumenja of the Jordan monastery in Kiev.

——. *Obozrenie Rumjancovskoj opisi Malorossii*. Polk Černigovskij. Černigov, 1861 (Reprinted from *Černigovskija gubernskija vedomosti*, 1861).
In the 1760's a thorough economic census of hetmanate Ukraine was undertaken. The present work describes its findings for the Černihiv polk. It was later included in the series published under the same title by A. Lazarevskij and N. Konstantinovič in 1866-1875, a work difficult to find.

——, *Opisanie staroj Malorossii*. Materialy dlja istorii zaselenija, zemlevladenija i upravlenija. 3 vols. Kiev, 1888-1902.
The three volumes deal respectively with the Starodub, Nižyn, and Pryluky polky. The work is an excellent study of land ownership in the hetmanate period. The author provides lengthy introductions on the territory, administrative history, and the officials of these territories.

Letopis' o pervozačatii i sozdanii Gustinskogo monastyrja, ed. O. BODJANSKIJ, *ČOIDR*, 1848, 8: i-iv, 1-76, and separately.
The chronicle of the Hustyn' monastery recounts also the beginnings of its associated monasteries Lubny and Ladyn. This edition contains also other documents that refer to these monasteries.

Litterae Basilianorum in terris Ucrainae et Bielarusjae. Ed. Athanasius G. WELYKYJ. 2 vols. Romae, 1979-1980.

Litterae episcoporum historiam Ucrainae illustrantes. Ed. Athanasius G. WELYKYJ. 5 vols. Romae, 1972-1981.
The series is being continued. References to women's monasteries are sparse, but valuable.

LIXAČEV, D.S., ed. *Povest' vremennyx let*. 2 vols. Moskva, 1950.
The best critical edition of the Laurentian recension of the primary chronicle, the main source on monasteries in pre-Mongolian Rus'.

MAKSIMOVIČ, M. Obozrenie starogo Kieva, *Kievljanin*, 1 (1840): 5-59.
Although this article gives only brief, general descriptions of Kievan monasteries, it is

worth noting, since these are then copied word for word by all later compilers.

——. Vospominanie o Zolotonoše, *Žurnal Ministerstva Vnutrennyx Del*, 23 (1848): 410-428.
These reminiscences provide detailed information about the locality and the monastery.

Materialy dlja statistiki rossijskoj imperii. Izdavaemy s vysočajšogo soizvolenija, pri statističeskom otdelenii soveta ministerstva vnutrennyx del. S.-Peterburg, 1841.
The first part contains a long article by A. GLAGOLEV, Kratkoe obozrenie drevnix russkix zdanij i drugix otečestvennyx pamjatnikov. (Cerkvi i monastyri), p. 3-204.

MJAKOTIN, V.A. *Očerki social'noj istorii Ukrajiny v XVII-XVIII vv.* Praga, 1924-1926.
The work was planned in three volumes, but only the first, in three parts, was published. It is based on archival materials and is devoted to the history of land ownership in Left Bank Ukraine. It thus treats of monasteries as proprietors.

NIKOLAJ [TRUSKOVSKIJ]. *Istoriko-statističeskoe opisanie Minskoj eparxii.* Sanktpeterburg, 1864.
This historical-descriptive work has a wealth of information on monasteries, though some details stand in need of correction (as the list of superiors of the Pinsk monastery on p. 143-144).

Opisanie dokumentov arxiva zapadnorusskix uniatskix mitropolitov. 2 vols. S.-Peterburg, 1897.
The concise summaries of this catalog provide much information on many aspects of church life, including monasticism.

Opisanie dokumentov i del xranjaščixsja v arxive Svjatejšogo Pravitel'stvujuščogo Sinoda. Sanktpeterburg, 1868-1914.
Volume 50 was the last one to come out, but some preceding ones were never published. Since it contains detailed analyses of the archives of the Synod, following each case from beginning to end, this series is basic for any study of the Church in the Russian empire in the synodal period.

P.L-v. Istoričeskija zametki o Kieve, *KS*, 12 (1884, 4): 238-241.
Historical comments about some sites in Kiev, including several churches and monasteries.

Pamjatniki. Izdannye Vremennoju Kommissieju dlja razbora drevnix aktov. 4 vols. Kiev, 1848-1859.

Pavel ALEPPSKIJ. Putešestvie antioxijskogo patriarxa Makarija v Rossiju v polovine XVII veka, tr. G. MURKOS, *ČOIDR*, 1896, 4: i-x, 1-156; 1897, 4: i-vi, 1-202; 1898, 3: i-iv, 1-208; 4: i-x, 1-195; 1900, 2: 1-v, 1-245.
A start was made to publish the original Arabic text with a French translation by Basile Radu in *Patrologia Orientalis*, vol. 22, 24, 26 (Paris, 1930-1945), but this edition did not get very far.
Archdeacon Paul of Aleppo accompanied patriarch Macarius in his travels. In 1654-1656 they were in Ukraine, Russia, and again Ukraine. Paul of Aleppo was an acute observer and his descriptions are among the most valuable sources for the study of church practices in the territories and period concerned.

PETRUŠEVIČ, A.S. Slovickij ženskij monastyr' Činu Sv. Vasilija V. i ego devičoe vospitališče, *Zorja Halycka*, 1851, no. 13-15.
The author gives a history of the monastery and describes it as it appeared in his time.

——. *Svodnaja galicko-russkaja letopis'.* L'vov, 1874-1897.
Three volumes of the *Letopis'* and three volumes of its *Dopolnenija* cover the period

from 1600 to 1800. The lack of indices hampers the use of this collection of excerpts from the most varied primary sources, which deal with all facets of church life.

Polnoe sobranie postanovlenij i rasporjaženij po vedomstvu pravoslavnogo ispovedanija rossijskoj imperii.
[1st series] 1721-1741. 10 vols. Sanktpeterburg, 1879-1911.
[2nd series] Elizabeth. 4 vols. Sanktpeterburg, 1899-1912.
[3rd series] Catherine II. 3 vols. Sanktpeterburg, 1910-1915.
This series was conceived as a complement to *OASS*. Here only decisions are given without full case histories.

Prixody i cerkvi Podol'skoj eparxii, *Trudy Podol'skogo eparxial'nogo istoriko-statističes-kogo komiteta*, 9 (1901).
Whatever monasteries, or at least remains of monastery churches in the case of extinct monasteries existed in Podillja in 1901 are carefully noted in this references work that comprises the whole of one good-sized volume of the *Trudy* with indices (23 + 1064 + 175 p.).

Putešestvie stol'nika P.A. Tolstogo 1697-1699, *Russkij arxiv*, 26 (1888), bk. 1: 161-204, . . . bk. 2: 369-400.
Sent abroad by Peter I to learn navigation, Tolstoj both on his way to and from Italy traveled through Poland-Lithuania where he visited Orthodox and Uniate monasteries and recorded his impressions.

ŠAFONSKIJ, Afanasij. *Černigovskogo Namestničestva topografičeskoe opisanie s kratkim geografičeskim i istoričeskim opisaniem Malyja Rossii.* Ed. M. SUDIENKO. Kiev, 1851.
The author, a native of Černihivščyna, compiled his work in 1786, four years after nine polky had been reorganized into three namestničestva and the tenth, Poltava, entered as part of the Novorossijskaja gubernija. He provides valuable contemporary information on the Černihiv namestničestvo. For its monasteries he lists, as far as he could ascertain, when and by whom they were founded, how constructed, what they possessed "worthy of note", how far they were from towns, how many members they had, what they owned before the confiscation of monastery properties in 1786. Valuable maps of the territory before and after the administrative reorganization are provided.

Sapiehowie. Materjały historyczno-genealogiczne i majątkowe wydane nakładem rodziny. 3 vols. Petersburg, 1890-1894.
This work consists of biographical notices about individual members of the Sapieha family. Each volume includes also supporting documents.

ŠČERBICKIJ, O.V. *Vilenskij Svjato-Troickij monastyr'.* Vil'na, 1885. (Reprinted from the *Litovskija eparxial'nija vedomosti*).
A concise history of the monastery, as accurate as the author could make it, but materials published after it came out render it in need of correction in some details and add further data.

SECINSKIJ, E. Materialy dlja istorii pravoslavnyx monastyrej Podol'skoj eparxii, *Trudy Podol'skogo eparxial'nogo istoriko-statističeskogo komiteta*, 5 (1890-1891): 207-444.
This is a brief exposition of the history of individual monasteries based on archival materials, the most important of which are printed in full.

SKRUTEN', J. Vizyta dubens'koho monastyrja SS. Vasylijanok 1818 r., *AOSBM*, 2, no. 3-4 (1927): 354-361.
Gives a detailed account of the state of the Dubno monastery in 1818.

SNITKO, Andrej. Opisanie dokumentov, sostavljajuščix I-yj tom Sluckogo Trojčanskogo arxiva, *Minskaja starina*, 4 (1913).

This catalog comprises the entire volume (iv + 200 + 39 p.). Among the documents described are those of the St Elias women's monastery in Sluck.

STEBELSKI, Ignacy. *Dwa wielkie światła na horyzoncie połockim, czyli żywoty świętych Ewfrozyny i Parascevii z chronologią i przydatkiem niektórych służących do tego pożytecznych krajowych wiadomości.* 3 vols. Lwów, 1866-1867.
The title describes the varied contents of this work which first came out in 1781. Stebelski has served as a source for numerous later authors, though his information on monasteries is scanty and imprecise.

Synodus provincialis Ruthenorum. Habita in Civitate Zamosciae Anno MDCCXX. Romae, 1724.
The decisions of the Synod of Zamość were reprinted in Rome in 1838 and 1883. This legislation remained in force in the Ruthenian Catholic Church for over 200 years. The section that regards women's monasteries, however, has more value as a testimony of the desires of the hierarchy than as a model of the course the monasteries took.

TERNOVSKIJ, F.A. Izlišnie malorossijskie monaxi konca XVIII st., kakix oni byli kačestv i kak doživali svoj vek, *KS*, 2 (1882, 2): 329-337.
This brief study, based on archival materials of the Holy Synod, discusses the ukaz of 1786 which confiscated church properties in Ukraine and the extent to which it was carried out.

Ukrajins'kyj arxiv. Vol. 1. Kyjiv, 1929.
Documents of the hetmanate are printed here; some of them regard monasteries. Volumes 2 and 4 have little regarding the Church; volume 3 seemingly never came out.

VASILENKO, N.P., ed. *Materialy dlja istorii ekonomičeskogo, juridičeskogo i obščestvennogo byta staroj Malorossii.* 3 vols. Černigov, 1901-1909.
A lengthy study precedes the publication of materials dealing with the Nižyn and Černihiv polky from what is known as the "General'noe sledstvie o maetnostjax" of 1729-1731. The purpose of this was to distinguish hereditary holdings from those due to rank and service in the hetmanate. A great deal of information on monastery-owned lands is provided.

VYNOHRADS'KYJ, Ju. Marija Dorošyxa. (Z Sosnyc'koji staryny), *Istoryčno-heohrafičnyj zbirnyk*, 1 (1927): 32-39.
This article collects information about hetman Peter Dorošenko's mother, a nun, and the monastery with which she was associated, Makošyn.

WOŁYNIAK [Jan Marek GOZDAWA GIŻYCKI]. Z przeszłości Zakonu Bazyliańskiego na Litwie i Rusi, *Przewodnik naukowy i literacki*, 32 (1904): 65-82, 157-172, 249-268, 353-360, 449-463.
The author limits himself to monasteries that in his time were within the Russian empire and that, moreover, at least for a time had been Uniate. His accounts are good, but based as they are on secondary literature, only as reliable as his sources.

XARLAMPOVIČ, K.V. *Malorossijskoe vlijanie na velikorusskuju cerkovnuju žizn'.* Kazan', 1914.
Only the first volume, which deals with the seventeenth century, of a projected 3-volume study appeared. Its value lies in its wide use of primary sources, many of them unpublished.

ŽUDRO, F.A. *Bogojavlenskij bratskij monastyr' v g. Mogileve.* Mogilev, 1899. (Reprinted from the *Mogilevskija gubernskija vedomosti*, 1898-1899).
A detailed history of the monastery.

Žverinskij, V.V. *Material dlja istoriko-topografičeskogo issledovanija o pravoslavnyx monastyrjax v rossijskoj imperii.* S bibliografičeskim ukazatelem. 3 vols. S.-Peterburg, 1890-1897.
As the title itself announces, this is a collection of materials that can serve towards a study of monasteries, not such a study itself. The author repeats information as he has found it, without a critical examination. The bibliography he provides for each monastery, with brief annotations, is useful, but far from exhaustive. At times it seems to have been chosen at random—the author includes works that contain only a passing mention of a monastery and omits other basic ones.

INDEX

This index includes only names of monasteries and personal names. Abbreviations: abp = archbishop; bp = bishop; emp. = emperor, empress; ih. = ihumen, ihumenja; metr. = metropolitan; patr. = patriarch.

Adamovyč, Simeon, 144.
Adrian, patr., 21, 105.
Alexander, great prince, 37.
Alexandra, nun, 144.
Alexius, tsar, 39, 76, 77, 78, 79, 93, 94, 136, 140, 143, 162, 175.
Amvrosij (Ornackij), 9, 28, 51, 52, 198.
Anastasia, nun, 130.
Andrew Bogoljubskij, prince, 49.
Anfija, nun, 151.
Angelina, nun, 185.
Anna, emp., 113, 143.
Anyzyja, nun, 28.
Apostol, Daniel, 93.
Apraksina, Anna, 136.
Archinto, Alberico, 189.
Augustus II, king, 23, 32, 43, 117.
Augustus III, king, 116.
Avramovyč, Ivan, 96.

Balaban, Adam, 60.
Balaban, Dionisius, metr., 19, 102, 104-105.
Balaban, Maria, see Hulevyč, Maria.
Bantyš-Kamenskij, N., 17.
Baranovyč, Lazar, abp, 18, 64, 66, 167.
Baranovyč, Martha, nun, 18.
Barkalabava, 11-12, 58, 59, 67, 68, 74-75, 77-78, 79, 83-85, 86, 103, 104, 106, 114, 117, 118-119, 131, 139-140, 150, 152, 153, 156, 166, 168, 177, 191, 202, 211, 216, 217.
Basil, St, 105-109.
Baturyn, 12-13, 35, 36, 66, 93, 94, 96, 127, 154, 180, 211.
Beauplan, 139, 183, 186.

Benedict XIV, pope, 195.
Biala Podlaska, 13, 211, 216.
Bil'če, 13-14, 177, 211.
Biliński, Hypacy, 181.
Bibrka, 13, 168, 173, 211, 216.
Bilylivka, 14, 60, 211, 216.
Bočočka, Samuel, 79.
Bodnar, Paul, 13.
Boktevna, Helen, nun, 16.
Borec'ka, Evpraksija, 158.
Borec'kyj, Job, metr., 26, 64, 151, 158.
Borejky, 14, 43, 57, 211, 214, 216.
Borghese, Scipio, 16.
Borovs'ka, Christine, 60.
Borozdna, Evdokija (Helen), nun, 132.
Borozdna, Serafyma, nun, 133.
Borysovyč, Alexander, 164.
Borzanovs'ka, Anna, 16, 57.
Brahin, 14-15, 59, 118, 138, 202, 203, 211, 216, 217.
Braslav, 15, 75, 211.
Bratanovs'kyj, Anastasius, bp, 202.
Brjuxovec'kyj, Ivan, 93, 185.
Bryslavs'ka, Anna, 62.
Bučyna, 15, 211.
Bulhak, J., metr., 20.
Burlij, K., 19.
Bus'k, 15, 87, 197, 211, 214.
Bycen', 16, 60, 211, 214, 216.
Bystrycja, 16, 57, 151, 211, 214, 216.

Čarjeja, 50.
Čartorys'ka, Maria, 37.
Catherine II, emp., 55, 196-197.
Čemena, John, 112.

Čerčyci, 16-17, 174, 211, 216.
Čerkoviščy, 17, 211.
Černihiv, 18, 55, 93, 94, 96, 97, 113, 127,
    141, 166, 198-199, 211, 214.
Černjak, Ivan, 62.
Četvertnja, 18, 60, 66, 177, 211, 217.
Četvertyns'kyj, Gregory, 18, 60.
Četvertyns'kyj, Sylvester, bp, 103.
C'orox, S., 8, 9, 13, 15, 30, 41, 46, 50, 51,
    52, 53.
Čujkevyč, Anysija, 152.
Čyhyryn, 18-19, 140, 159, 165-166, 198, 211,
    214.

Daniel, ih., 47.
Daškova, princess, 37.
Denisov, L., 9, 11.
Derman', 50, 201.
Divyče, 50.
Bobrotvir, 19, 196, 211, 216.
Dobrynja, Silvester, 119, 148.
Dolgorukova, Natalija, 136.
Dorošenko, Michael, 133.
Dorošenko, Mytrodora Maria, ih., 123.
Dorošenko, Peter, 123.
Dorošenko, Serafyma, nun, 133.
Dorotej, 77.
Drohyčyn, 19, 102, 211.
Dubinski, Jan, 187.
Dubno, 10-20, 59, 89, 108-109, 117, 126-127,
    153, 155, 157, 178, 181, 201, 202, 203,
    211, 216, 217.
Dunin-Borokovs'kyj, Basil, 96.
Dusowce, 50.
Dyškevyč, Macrina (Margaret), 22, 104, 134,
    153, 157, 192.
Dzisna, 51.

Esman, Sophia Anne, 160.
Eugenia, ih., see Xlevyns'ka, Eugenia.
Euphrosine-Predyslava, nun, 38-39.
Evdokija, nun, 45.
Evpraksija, nun, 13.

Filaret (Gumilevskij), abp., 45.
Forošča, 20, 211.
Fylymynovyč, Methodius, bp, 143, 185.
Fylypovyč, Samuel, 79.
Fyrlijiv, 20, 211.

Galjatovs'kyj, Joanikij, 167.
Gasiorowska, Zuzanna, 64.

Gregory, monk, 178.
Golubinskij, 4., 7, 164.
Gosiewska, Madgalene, 83.

Hamalija, Athanasia, nun, 133.
Hamalija, Anton, 20, 61.
Hamalijivka, 20, 34, 61-62, 96-97, 113, 157,
    211, 217.
Hluxiv, 20-21, 62, 66, 94, 96, 97, 105, 119,
    133, 134, 146, 211, 214.
Holoskiv, 21, 142, 211, 214.
Holubec', M., 41.
Horain family, 18.
Horlenko, Anastasia, nun, 133.
Horlenko, Andrew, 61.
Horlenko, Joasaf, metr., 99, 151.
Horodyšče, 21, 211.
Horodyslava-Evdokija, nun, 39.
Hrebnyc'ka, nun, 130, 151.
Hrebenyc'kyj, Florijan, metr., 39, 46-47, 85,
    130, 189.
Hrodna, 21, 82, 86, 104, 108, 111, 120, 138,
    140, 147, 152, 153, 164, 202, 211, 214.
Hulevyč, Maria (Balaban), 18, 60.
Hul'kevyč family, 24, 58, 73.
Hul'kevyč, Ivan Bohuš, 24, 73.
Humenyc'ka, Agatha, ih., 73, 91, 132.
Hutorovyč, Michael, 79.

Ihnatovyč, Theophilus, bp, 145.
Ihumen, 51.
Ingegard-Irene, 23.
Ivan IV, tsar, 76.
Ivan Aleksievič, tsar, 94, 105.
Ivanovna, Helen, 143-144.
Ivanovyč, Alexandra, nun, 164.
Ivanovyč, Anna, nun, 163.

Janka, nun, 24.
Janovska, Dorothy, nun, 150.
Jarmolyns'ka, Serafyma, ih., 26, 151.
Jaroslav the Wise, 23.
Jaseniv, 22, 211.
Jasnohorod, 22, 59, 211.
Jasyns'kyj, Varlaam, metr., 105.
Javoriv, 22, 42, 88, 104, 106, 134, 137, 142,
    153, 155, 157, 178, 184, 192, 197, 211,
    214.
Javors'kyj, Stephen, 102-103.
Jelenska, Constance, nun, 80, 135.
John Casimir, king, 19, 30, 31, 87, 147.
John III Sobieski, king, 76, 184.

John Climacus, 167, 168.
Joseph II, emp., 55, 196.

Kamens'kyj Xutor, 22-23, 198, 211.
Kaminka Strumylova, 23, 172, 211.
Kapolje, Theodore, 27.
Karpovyč, Leontij, 107.
Kascjukovičy, 23, 211, 216.
Kiev
— Ascension, 15, 21, 24-25, 91, 92, 94,
95, 105, 119, 132, 133-134, 135, 139, 143,
144, 155, 156, 162, 170, 171, 175-176, 183,
185, 186, 212, 214.
— Jordan, 25, 144, 151, 158, 163, 166,
172, 181, 199, 212, 214.
— St Andrew, 24, 212.
— St Irene, 23, 212.
— St Lazarus, 24, 212.
— St Michael/St John, 25-26, 28, 64, 93,
133, 156, 158, 159, 169, 170, 172, 181,
198, 199, 212, 214.
— St Nicholas, 23, 212.
— Sts Florus and Laurus, 24, 25, 58, 73,
91-92, 93, 99, 106, 113, 114, 119, 125, 132,
134, 136, 140-141, 142, 143-144, 145, 156,
158, 172, 173, 183, 198, 212, 214.
Klynec', 26, 212.
Knjaže, 26, 212,
Kočubej, Basil, 62.
Kolenda, Gabriel, metr., 83.
Komar, Elizabeth, nun, 132.
Komarovs'kyj, Iraklij, 43-44, 57.
Kondratevyč, Herasym, 45.
Konsevycovna, Trofymija, ih., 13.
Konys'kyj, George, bp, 103, 200.
Kopyns'ka, Alexandra, ih., 29, 65, 118.
Kopyns'kyj, Isaiah, metr., 29, 65, 117-118,
139.
Korec', 26-27, 50, 60, 89, 151, 200-201, 212.
Korec'ka, Anna, see Xodkevyč, Anna.
Korec'ka, Serafyna, nun, 26.
Korec'kyj family, 118.
Korec'kyj, Bohdan (Bohuš), 26, 59.
Korec'kyj, Joachim, 60.
Kornelia, nun, 181.
Kornjakt, Constantine, 30.
Korobivka, 27, 65, 133, 171, 186, 199, 212,
214, 217.
Korop, 27, 61, 149, 212.
Korsak, Raphael, bp, 33.
Koscjuško, Christine, ih., 151.
Kosobucki, Peter, 187.

Kosov, Sylvester, metr., 66, 103.
Kossak, N., 9, 19, 20, 28, 30, 35, 36, 41, 51,
53, 181.
Kotlowna, Anastazya Tekla, ih., 106.
Kozelec', 27-28, 198, 199, 212, 214.
Kozinskyj, Varlaam, 169.
Kozlovyc'ka, Mytrodora, 152.
Krajsk, 51.
Krasnohora, 26, 28, 159, 199, 212, 217.
Krexiv, 51.
Krokovs'kyj, Joseph, metr., 101.
Kropyvnyc'kyj, Michael, 48, 58, 60, 89, 155,
157.
Krupec'kyj, Athanasius, bp, 43.
Krylos, 28, 212.
Kryns'kyj, Nicholas, 90.
Krypjakevyč, I., 9.
Ksenja, ih., 30.
Kulykiv, 28, 196, 212.
Kuncevyč, Josaphat, abp, 39, 74, 104,
138-139, 191.
Kupčyns'ka, Paraskeva, nun, 162.
Kurakin, F.F., 136.
Kurakin, Iroida, nun, 135-136.
Kutejno, 12, 29, 59, 67, 77, 78-79, 80, 85, 86,
102, 103, 106, 109, 117, 118, 120, 135-136,
139, 143, 147, 152, 153, 154, 155, 156,
160, 172, 174, 177-178, 182, 202, 212, 214.
Kvitka family, 99, 133, 151, 154.
Kvitka, Maria, ih., 99.
Kvitka, Teofanija, ih., 151.
Kymbar, Athanasia (Agatha Jefymovna,
Kymborovyč), nun, 20, 62, 66.
Kyrkor, Euphrosine, 147, 153.
Kyrkor, Fotynja, ih., 12, 78, 131, 153.
Kysil', Adam, 32, 40, 59, 89, 119, 131.
Kysil', Euphrosine, 40.
Kyška, Leo, metr., 14, 86, 107, 109, 110,
111, 148, 154, 164, 168, 189.

Ladislaus IV, king, 31, 63, 67, 76, 91, 119,
132.
Ladyn, 29, 59, 65, 118, 133, 135, 139, 141,
145, 155, 157, 167, 170, 172-173, 177, 181,
198, 199, 212, 214, 217.
Langyš, Candida, nun, 57.
Larska, Domentijana, nun, 192.
Łazarevs'kyj, A., 207.
Lazarevyč, Joseph, 127.
Lazarevyč, Maria, ih., 43.
Lebedyn, 29, 56, 124, 137, 198, 212.
Letynska, Elizabeth, 177.

Levanda, Ivan, 124.
Lisans'kyj, Heraklij, 188.
Lisovyči, 29, 212, 214.
Lubomirsky, Fr.X., 56.
Lukaševyč, Luke, 145.
Lukovs'kyj, Theodore (Lukowski, Lukom-
    ski), 46.
Lunkevyč, Alexandra, nun, 148.
Lupul, Basil, hospodar, 30, 80, 87.
Lupul, Maria (Radziwill), 80, 175.
Lviv, 30, 63, 87-88, 115, 116, 126, 134-135,
    142, 147, 183, 184, 188, 197, 212, 214.
Lypnyc'ka, Anfysa, nun, 149.

Macarius, patr., 168, 170, 171, 175.
Macarius of Egypt, 167, 168.
Macewiczowna, Bogumila, nun, 189.
Mahilev
    — Epiphany, 31, 32, 85, 103, 115, 131,
    141, 143, 144, 152, 157, 169-170, 181, 184,
    191, 202, 212, 215.
    — St Nicholas, 31-32, 63, 103, 154, 160,
    185, 212.
    — Savior, 30-31, 55, 136, 212.
Makošyn, 32, 59, 97, 113, 123, 192, 212,
    214, 217.
Maksymovyč, M., 186.
Manassija, nun, 65.
Maraščanka, 32, 212, 216.
Mariamna, ih., 127.
Marianna, nun, 13.
Markevyč, Adam, 25.
Markovna, Nastasja (Skoropads'ka), 20,
    61-62, 96, 119, 157.
Mazepa, Ivan, 13, 21, 22, 25, 27, 61, 67,
    92-93, 94, 95, 105, 127, 133.
Mazepa, Maria Magdalene, ih., 21, 25, 92,
    93, 95, 105, 119, 133, 183.
Mazyr, 32, 118, 212.
Melania, nun, 158.
Mena, 32, 212.
Methodius, ih., 177.
Mexeda, Evdokija, nun, 133.
Mexeda, Kyril, 133.
Minkiewicz, Barbara, nun, 163.
Minsk
    — Holy Spirit, 33, 64, 68, 77, 83, 107,
    108, 110, 111, 120, 129, 130, 138, 140,
    147, 148, 150, 154, 161, 168, 169, 188,
    193, 201, 212, 215.
    — Holy Trinity, 33, 82, 110, 111, 120,
    138, 140, 147, 150, 178, 180, 185, 202,

212, 214.
    — Sts Peter and Paul, 32-33, 60, 67, 80,
    81, 102, 105, 107, 108, 115-116, 119, 148,
    150, 155, 166, 175, 184, 192, 212.
Miracka, Angelina, nun, 135.
Mixajlov, Fedka, 78.
Mlodovs'kyj, Antony, bp, 65.
Mniszek, Stanislaus Boniface, 86, 178.
Mnohohrišnyj, Demjan, 66, 93, 94, 105.
Mohyla, Peter, metr., 31, 60, 104, 118, 128,
    137, 139, 151, 155, 156, 184.
Mohyljans'ka, Agrippina, 145.
Mohyljans'kyj, Arsenij, metr., 166.
Mokryc'kyj, Gregory, 140.
Monastyrs'ke, 51-52.
Moro, Jerome, 137, 161, 184.
Mozoliv, 33-34, 61, 68, 75, 102, 103, 118,
    143, 152, 156, 177, 188, 200, 202, 212.
Mutyn, 20, 33-34, 62, 113, 119, 212, 215.
Mužylovs'kyj, S., 19.
Mykolajiv, 34, 87, 212.
Mykulynci, 22, 34, 90-91, 132, 137, 141, 148,
    159, 173, 176, 180, 193, 196, 201, 212,
    215, 217.
Mymons'kyj, Peter, 178-179.
Mynodora, nun, 158.
Myslavs'kyj, Samuel, metr., 28.
Mytrodora, nun, 155.

Natalia, nun, 41.
Navahrudek, 9, 34, 60, 64, 82, 131, 138, 179,
    202, 212, 216.
Nečaj, Daniel, 183.
Nemyriv, 35, 202, 212.
Nemyrovyč, Alexandra (Nemyryna,
    Olexna), 37, 148.
Nemyrovyč-Sčyt, Christopher, 83.
Nikon, patr., 19.
Nižyn, 35, 62, 141, 186, 191, 198, 212, 215.
Nova Hreblja, 35, 212.
Novi Mlyny, 13, 35-36, 66, 93, 94, 95-96, 98,
    104, 125-126, 133, 136, 152, 166, 172, 182,
    183, 212, 215.

Oginska, Anna (Stetkevyč), 29, 59, 67.
Oles'ko, 36, 212.
Olgered, great prince, 46.
Ombyš, 36, 60, 212.
Orlovs'kyj, Myron, 43.
Orša, 29, 36, 64, 85, 86, 106, 131, 145, 174,
    179, 202, 212, 215.
Ostrejko, Antonina, nun, 193.

Ostrogožsk, 36-37, 98, 179, 199, 212.
Ostroz'kyj family, 59, 127, 128.
Ostroz'kyj, Constantine, 19, 59, 88-89, 108-109, 116, 157, 178.
Ovruč
— Birth of Mother of God, 37, 73, 148, 212.
— Sts Joachim and Anna, 37, 73, 212.

Pamfilija, nun, 21.
Pankratija, nun, 41.
Paraskeva-Zvenyslava, nun, 39.
Paraskevija, ih., 45.
Parfianovyč, Kondrat, 79.
Parfianovyč, Marusja, 79.
Paryziv, 52.
Paul of Aleppo, 132, 168, 175-176, 185, 186.
Pečenyky, 23, 27, 37, 61, 67, 95, 97, 133, 149, 159, 198, 212, 215, 216, 217.
Pelahija, nun, 162.
Peresopnycja, 37-38, 72, 212.
Peter I, tsar, 26, 62, 94, 97, 105, 112, 125, 133.
Petruševyč, A., 14, 15, 23, 30, 32, 41, 42, 48, 88, 172.
Pidhajci, 38, 212.
Pidluby, 38, 212.
Pikulice, 28, 212.
Pinsk, 16, 38, 55, 77, 130, 147, 202, 213.
Pletenec'kyj, Jelysej, 25.
Polock
— St Michael, 39-40, 129, 213.
— Savior, 38-39, 55, 73-74, 76, 83, 85, 104, 130, 135, 138-139, 161, 169, 191, 213, 215.
Polonne, 40, 141, 153, 201, 202, 213.
Poltava, 52.
Popivka, 40, 59, 89, 119, 131, 213, 216, 217.
Potij, Euphrosine (Catherine), nun, 131.
Potij, Joann, bp, 131.
Potocki, Vincent, 35.
Puškarivka, 40, 52, 56, 62, 198, 213, 215, 217.
Puškarka, 52.
Pustel'nyky, 40, 213.
Puzyna, Athanasius, bp, 17.
Pysarevščyna, 41, 62, 146, 198, 213, 215, 216, 217.

Radyvylovs'kyj, Antony, 167, 168.
Radziwill family, 148.
Radziwill Christopher, 75, 115.

Radziwill, Janusz, 80.
Radziwill, Maria, see, Lupul, Maria.
Rahoza, Michael, metr., 30, 63, 116.
Rakovyč, Joasaf, ih., 27.
Repnin, N.V., 140.
Ripjanka, 41, 181, 213.
Rohal'-Levyc'kyj, Basil, 137.
Rohatyn
— Ascension, 41, 142, 213, 215.
— Transfiguration, 42, 196, 213.
Roslavec', Elena, ih., 44, 64, 95.
Roslavec', Lukjan, 95.
Rovinska, Antonina, 150.
Rozhirče, 42, 57, 62, 137, 142, 213.
Rozumovs'ka, Agnes (Anna), nun, 134.
Rozumovs'ka, Elizabeth, nun, 134.
Rupniewski, Stephen, bp, 189.
Rusec', 42, 213, 215.
Rutskyj, Joseph Veljamyn, metr., 16, 21, 47, 60, 64, 66, 104, 107, 108, 209.
Ryllo, Maximilian, bp, 13, 52.
Rzepniecka, Magdalene, nun, 114.

Sadkovs'kyj, Victor, abp, 47, 143, 202.
Sakovyč, Cassian, 19, 117.
Samoilovyč, Ivan, 22, 61, 93, 95.
Samojlovyč, Maria, see Sulyma, Maria.
Samoilovyč, Semen, 37, 61.
Santini, Vincent, 190.
Sapieha family, 75, 129.
Sapieha, Benedict, 83.
Sapieha, Bohdan, 129.
Sapieha, Catherine (Evdoksija), ih., 33, 107, 129, 140, 153.
Sapieha, Euphrosine (Anna), nun, 129.
Sapieha, Ivan, 40.
Sapieha, Leo, 75.
Sapieha, Paul, 47, 75, 115, 129.
Sapieha, Regina (Tryzna), 16, 130.
Sapieha, Vasilissa (Barbara), ih., 15, 75, 129, 153.
Sasiv, 42, 196, 213.
Ščerbac'kyj, Timothy, metr., 84, 103, 145.
Ščerbyna, Jakiv, 27.
Šelexove, 42, 213.
Šembelev, Eugenia, nun, 32, 60, 67, 108, 155, 192.
Šeptyc'kyj, Athanasius, metr., 13, 42, 108, 111, 125, 140, 149, 150, 188-189.
Sigismund I, king, 148.
Sigismund III, king. 47, 115.
Sjeljava, Antony, metr., 33, 64, 74, 104,

130, 140, 145, 152, 161.
Sjemaško, Joseph, bp, 196, 200, 203.
Šklov, 42-43, 213.
Skoropads'ka, Anastasia, see Markovna, Nastasja.
Skoropads'kyj, Ivan, 20, 34, 61-62, 93, 95, 96.
Slovita, 19, 21, 28, 43, 50, 86-87, 88, 101, 125, 126, 134, 149, 152-153, 158, 161, 172, 177, 178, 179, 181, 189, 196, 197, 213, 215.
Sluck, 33, 43, 80, 103, 143, 148, 151, 154, 168, 173, 175, 202, 213.
Sluck family, 127, 148.
Smelič, Peter, abp, 114.
Smilnycja, 42, 43, 137, 142, 188, 197, 213, 215.
Smogorzewski, Jason, 150.
Smolkovna, Athanasia, nun, 139.
Sokal', 52.
Solomerecka, Helen, 12.
Sorokivna, Felicianna, ih., 107.
Sosnycja, 14, 43-44, 57, 213, 215, 216.
Srebnyc'kyj, Nikodym, bp, 97, 198.
Stanyslaviv, 44, 213.
Staryj Sambir, 44, 137, 213.
Stebnovs'kyj, Kesarij, abp, 145.
Stephen Batory, king, 39, 115.
Stetkevyč family, 12, 83-84, 117, 139, 209.
Stetkevyč, Anna, see Oginska, Anna.
Stetkevyč, Bohdan, 12, 58, 59, 67, 74.
Stetkevyč, John, 29, 59.
Sudnicka, Constance, nun, 163.
Sudova Vyšnja, 44, 213.
Sulyma, Maria (Semenova Samojlovyč), 27, 37, 61.
Sulžyns'kyj, Luke, 201.
Šumarovo, 44, 64, 95, 98, 192, 213, 215.
Šumljans'kyj, Joseph, bp, 101, 184.
Šumljans'kyj, Onufrij, bp, 42, 44.
Šums'ke, 45, 213.
Sumy, 45, 199, 213, 215, 216.
Suša, Jakiv, bp, 49, 65, 77, 120, 130, 138, 190.
Suxodolska, Marianna, 33, 60, 75, 156.
Svadkovskyj family, 14.
Švitrigaila, prince, 48.
Svjatoslav Vseslavyč, prince, 38.
Sylyč, Christopher, 66.
Sylyn, Joanikij, 93.
Syruciv, Fevronija, nun, 153.
Syruciv, Justyna, nun, 153.

Taita, nun, 155.
Tatarčenko, Ivan, 166.
Tatena, M.Ja., nun, 124.
Terebovlja, 45, 213.
Terlec'kyj, Cyril, bp, 16.
Ternovskij, F., 206.
Theodosius, St, 23.
Trucevyč, Joil, ih., 84, 117, 139, 209.
Tryzna, Anastasia, 76.
Tryzna, Anastasia (Zawisza), 75, 76.
Tryzna, Anne Elizabeth (Kersnowska), ih., 129.
Tryzna, Euphrosine, ih., 16, 60, 75, 77, 129, 130.
Tryzna, Gregory, 16, 60, 130.
Tryzna, Regina, see Sapieha, Regina.
Tuptalo, Demetrius (Rostovskij), 13, 25, 127, 180.
Tuptalo, Paraskeva, ih., 25, 151, 158, 163, 166-167, 181.
Turiv, 52.
Tyševyč, Pelahija, 144.

Uhlyc'kyj, Theodosius, abp, 149.
Uhnornyc'ka, Catherine, 36, 60.
Univ, 45, 213.
Utiškiv, 46, 213. 217.

Venatovyč, Varlaam, metr., 103, 104-105, 114.
Vasylevska, Scholastica, nun, 163.
Vasylevyč, Elizabeth, 131.
Vasylevyč, Theodosius, bp, 103, 131.
Važyns'ka, Joanna, nun, 130.
Vercynska, Suzanna, 45.
Vicebsk
— Birth of the Mother of God, 46, 127, 213.
— Holy Spirit, 46-47, 80, 82, 85, 86, 110, 111, 126, 131, 141, 142, 162, 166, 176, 186, 193, 202, 213, 215.
Vilna
— Holy Spirit, 47, 63, 76, 79, 80, 106, 107, 115, 131, 141, 148, 160, 175, 202, 213, 215.
— Holy Trinity, 9, 15, 16, 21, 33, 47, 63, 68, 75-76, 79, 80, 82, 104, 106, 110, 115, 120, 129-130, 135, 138, 140, 145, 152, 153, 154, 161, 162, 163-164, 165, 169, 176, 179, 184, 187, 193, 202, 213, 215.
Vinnycja, 48, 58, 60, 67, 89-90, 106, 109, 112, 132, 141, 155, 157, 174, 179, 186, 201-202, 213, 215.

Vlodava, 48, 213, 217.
Vojna-Orans'ka, Joanna, nun, 130.
Vojna-Orans'kyj, Pachomius, bp, 130.
Vojna-Orans'kyj, Silvester, 130.
Volčanskyj, Jerome, 148.
Volčaskyj, Silvester, 160.
Volja Arlamivs'ka, 48, 213.
Volodkovyč, Felician, metr., 17, 48, 65.
Volodymyr Volyns'kyj, 48, 65, 141, 180, 202, 203, 213, 215.
Volsvyn, 48, 213.
Volxovskij, Athanasius, bp, 31, 115, 141, 191, 202.
Vonljarska, Domentijana, nun, 200.
Vsevolod, prince, 24.
Vsevolod Ol'hovyč, prince, 128.
Vyhovs'kyj, Ivan, 18.
Vynnyc'kyj, Antony, metr., 188.
Vynnyc'kyj, George, metr., 101, 110, 111, 148, 149, 150, 190.
Vynnyc'kyj, Inokentij, bp, 148-149.
Vyšhorod, 49, 213.
Vyšnevec'ka, Alexandra, see Xodkevyč, Alexandra.
Vyšnevec'ka, Christine (Malyns'ka), 15.
Vyšnevec'ka, Eugenia Catherine, 76.
Vyšnevec'ka, Raina Korybut, 29, 65.
Vyšnevec'kyj family, 59, 65, 117-118.
Vyšnevec'kyj, Adam Korybut, 14, 59.
Vyšnevec'kyj, Michael, 29.
Vytovka, 52.

Wasiliewiczowna, Elisabeth, ih., 106.
Wiazowiczowa, 33, 178.

Wolyniak, 33.

Xlevnyc'ka, Euphrosine, nun, 153.
Xlevnyc'ka, Polyfronija, nun, 154.
Xlevnyc'ka, Teofila, nun, 153.
Xlevyns'ka, Eugenia, 12-13.
Xmel'nyc'kyj, Bohdan, 12, 19, 36, 45, 56, 93, 96, 208.
Xmel'nyc'kyj, George, 18, 93, 96.
Xodkevyč, Alezandra (Vyšnevec'ka), 14, 59.
Xodkevyč, Jan Karol, 59.
Xolm, 49, 65, 185, 213.
Xoroševe, 49, 98-99, 114, 119, 125, 126, 133, 151, 152, 154, 159, 170, 179-180, 181, 186, 191, 199, 213, 215, 217.

Zaborovs'kyj, Raphael, 113.
Zahvizdja, 49, 142, 213, 215.
Zankevyč, Demetrius, 110.
Zaturkevyč, Euphrosine, 127.
Zaturkevyč, George, 127.
Zavadz'kyj, Antony, 110, 150.
Zawisza, Anastasia, see Tryzna, Anastasia.
Zawisza, Jan, 75.
Zibolky, 53.
Zinkovs'ka, Serafyma, ih., 149.
Zolotarenko, Ivan, 78.
Žovkva, 49-50, 87, 134, 196, 213.
Žykovs'ka, Fevronija (Anastasia), nun, 126.
Zvenyslava-Evpraksija, nun, 39.
Zverinskij, V., 9, 11, 12, 15, 19, 30, 46, 51, 52, 64, 198.
Žydyčyn, 50, 57, 213.
Zynkovs'ka, Serafyna (Anastasia), nun, 152.